DISCARDED

Charter and Community Schools: A Director's Handbook

William Callison

A SCARECROWEDUCATION BOOK

The Scarecrow Press, Inc.
Lanham, Maryland, and Oxford
2003

A SCARECROWEDUCATION BOOK

Published in the United States of America
by Scarecrow Press, Inc.
A Member of the Rowman & Littlefield Publishing Group
4720 Boston Way, Lanham, Maryland 20706
www.scarecroweducation.com

PO Box 317
Oxford
OX2 9RU, UK

Copyright © 2003 by William Callison

All rights reserved. No part of this publication may be reproduced,
stored in a retrieval system, or transmitted in any form or by any
means, electronic, mechanical, photocopying, recording, or otherwise,
without the prior permission of the publisher.

British Library Cataloguing in Publication Information Available

Library of Congress Cataloging-in-Publication Data

Callison, William L.
   Charter and community schools: A director's handbook / William Callison.
       p. cm.
"A ScarecrowEducation book."
Includes bibliographical references and index.
   ISBN 0-8108-4602-0 (pbk. : alk. paper)
1. Community schools—United States. 2. Charter schools—United
States. 3. School management and organization—United States. I.
Title
   LB2806.36 .C354 2003
   371.01—dc21
                                                                    2002011393

⊗™ The paper used in this publication meets the minimum requirements of
American National Standard for Information Sciences—Permanence of
Paper for Printed Library Materials, ANSI/NISO Z39.48-1992.
Manufactured in the United States of America.

Contents

Foreword

The charter school movement initially launched during the past decade as a public school and legislative response to the perceived threat of vouchers and privatization can now count over 2,700 such schools nationally. The movement with its middle-ground position between "business as usual" public schools and the direct competition posed by private school vouchers fits nicely with the public's attitude (as reported in the thirty-fourth annual Phi Delta Kappa/Gallup Poll of the Public's Attitude Toward the Public Schools) favoring improving existing public schools (69 percent) as opposed to finding an alternative system (27 percent).

Much of the promise of charter schools as a reform mechanism is based on the credo coined by Max Abbott that "bureaucracy impedes innovation" creating hierarchical impediments to innovation in educational organizations.[1] Charter advocates propose that freeing educators from the constraints and strictures imposed by bureaucratic mandates and regulations will create an environment more conducive to educational change and improvement and thus more compatible with retaining high quality teachers and attracting those considering teaching as a career. Other characteristics of charter schools such as their generally smaller class/school enrollments and their stronger patterns of parent involvement are also consistent with current themes in school reform literature.

While greater organizational freedom and flexibility in charter schools can certainly result in creativity and positive change there may also be some downsides. In a study conducted for the Thomas B. Fordham Foundation, Michael Podgursky and Dale Ballou[2] report that their survey of 132 charter schools found that "charter schools are much more likely than traditional public schools to employ teachers who lack regular state certification." If, as much research suggests, the quality of teacher preparation is a crucial variable impacting student performance, then any substantial lack of preparation among charter school teachers may be a cause for concern.

Given the movement's relative infancy there has not been any definitive empirical study of the success (or failure) of charter schools vis-à-vis improved student performance. There are many anecdotal reports of successes from proponents but in terms of real evidence the jury is still out regarding whether or not the charter school movement will provide a model for the substantive improvement of public education.

NOTES

1. F. D. Carver and Thomas J. Sergiovanni, eds., *Organizations and Human Behavior: Focus on Schools* (New York: McGraw Hill, 1969).

2. Michael Podgursky and Dale Ballou, "Personnel Policy in Charter Schools," *Phi Delta Kappan* (September 2002).

Dennis Evans
Department of Education
University of California at Irvine

Preface

This book is written for school districts, community-based organizations, teachers, administrators, families, students, and other key stakeholders such as businesses. Charter schools are nonsectarian public schools of choice that operate with freedom from many of the regulations that apply to traditional public schools. The charter establishing each such school is a performance contract detailing the school's mission, program, goals, students served, methods of assessment, and ways to measure success. The length of time for which charters are granted varies, but most are granted for three to five years. At the end of the term, the entity granting the charter may renew the school's contract. Charter schools are accountable to their sponsors—usually state or local school boards—to produce positive academic results and adhere to the charter contract. The basic concept of charter schools is that they exercise increased autonomy in return for this accountability. They are accountable for both academic results and fiscal practices to several groups: the sponsor that grants them, the parents who choose them, and the public that funds them.

The intention of most charter school legislation is to:

- Increase opportunities for learning and access to quality education for all students;
- Create choices for parents and students within the public school system;
- Provide a system of accountability for results in public education;
- Encourage innovative teaching practices;
- Create new professional opportunities for teachers;
- Encourage community and parent involvement in public education;
- Improve public education broadly through leverage.

Charter schools are established for a variety of reasons. The founders generally fall into three groups: grassroots organizations of parents, teachers, and community members; entrepreneurs; and existing schools converting to charter status. Three reasons to create a charter school are as follows:

1. To realize an educational vision;
2. To gain autonomy;
3. To serve a special population.

Parents and teachers choose charter schools primarily for educational reasons—high academic standards, small class size, innovative approaches, or educational philosophies in line with their own. Some also have chosen charter schools for their small size and associated safety (charter schools serve an average of 250 students).

Charter schools that work do so for many reasons, as suggested in the information above. Maybe the most important reason they work is that parents are seriously involved in these schools. Extensive research indicates that parent involvement is a powerful force for improving student performance. In fact, it has replaced socioeconomic status as the key factor affecting student performance, other than instruction.

It is important that the administrator play up the success of change as it occurs. Constant feedback to all parties involved must be provided as to the status of the implementation of change. Be organized and provide the agenda for change to all parties. Let them know that they are playing an active part in implementing effective and sustainable change. Change is the law of life. As a school director, it is your challenge to keep all eyes on the future by providing activities that foster the need for change and improvement.

CHARTER SCHOOLS PERSPECTIVE ON CHANGE

Charter schools, reacting to pressures for initiating and responding to change, must develop strategies of change. For any school organization to succeed and to weather the changes that will occur, strategies for change must be developed and planned. Change is multifaceted, and the school organization must possess the mechanisms necessary to identify, categorize, and handle multiple sources of the impetus for change within the school environment.

To enable change to occur in a systematic process, strategies are needed to successfully react to, initiate, and respond to it. While there is no one correct way to bring about a desired change, the following aspects might be included:

- Dissemination of ideas and information pertinent to all aspects of a proposed change;
- Identification and handling of all possible constraints that might prevent the proposed change from occurring;
- Facilitation of influences that have a bearing on how the new plan might be received;
- Identification of potential opposition, conflict, or tensions, and advantageous resolution of them;
- Helping individuals to see and understand the need for change from their own perspectives;
- Implementation of the proposed change.

Acknowledgments

It is a great pleasure to have Dr. Brouillette write the first chapter of this book and to know that Yale Professor Seymour Sarason, in his foreword to Brouillette's book *Charter Schools: Lessons in School Reform,* says, "The reader who is unfamiliar with charter schools or their literature would do well to read this book as a basis for judging what else you decide to read." This from our nation's expert on the creation of new school organizations, which he calls "settings" in order to focus on the context in which the school operates. Dr. Brouillette has summarized the main points of her book to serve as the introduction to this one. I trust that you will find what she says valuable and want to read her book next.

I would also like to thank Jessica Banda, assistant director at the El Sol Science and Arts Academy in Santa Ana, California, for allowing me to interview her about this fine charter school.

Improving the Job Performance of Staff Members through Effective Evaluation and Documentation Procedures by Yolanda Finley, Lisa A. Hinshaw, and Janet Olsavsky is also a fine contribution to this subject.

Chapter One

Challenges Faced by Charter School Founders

LIANE BROUILLETTE, UNIVERSITY OF CALIFORNIA, IRVINE

Broadly speaking, charter schools represent the resurgence of a do-it-yourself attitude toward public education that had not been much in evidence in the United States through the middle decades of the twentieth century. The days when groups of local citizens would get together to organize a public school, find a building, and hire the teachers had all but faded from memory. Whenever significant educational reforms had been introduced, the changes tended to be in the direction of trying to make school districts more efficient. Most often, this meant reorganizing school districts so they could be run in the same top-down manner as corporations. Thus, the "principal teacher" of an earlier era became the school principal, no longer a leader among equals but an administrator whose job it is to organize and evaluate the work of others.

Key Concepts:
Challenges Facing New Schools
The Organization as a Work of Art
Before the Beginning: Confronting History
Challenges of the Initiation/Planning Period
The Cost of Ignoring Psychological Dynamics
Forging a Constitution
The Dangers of Just "Jumping In"
Research Methodology
Description of School Sites
Challenges Encountered by Charter Schools
Stark Differences in Organizational Dynamics

1

The Model School and the Opportunity Preparatory School
The Core Academy and Marblehead Community Charter Public School
Passages Charter School, Wesley Elementary, University of Houston
    Charter School
Taking a Broader Perspective

Most charter school supporters share a perception that, amid the current push for educational standardization, something of value has been lost. This chapter takes the reader inside the charter school movement, describing the experiences of charter school founders, along with the historical influences and policy issues that have shaped specific charter schools. At the core of the chapter are seven case studies: six charter schools and one district-sponsored alternative school. Schools profiled were chosen to represent the diversity—inner city and suburban, back-to-basics and child-centered—of the charter school movement, thus highlighting the variation that exists, both from school to school and from state to state. Elementary, middle, and high schools were included. Among those represented are teacher- and parent-initiated schools, as well as schools set up in partnership with outside institutions.

A case study of a noncharter alternative school (founded through a collaborative effort between an elite private university and a large urban school district) was included to provide an opportunity to explore similarities and contrasts between charters and an innovative school of a different sort, one that enjoyed many advantages most charter schools lack. For, of the schools in this study, the noncharter alternative school was by far the best financed, having benefited also from a three-and-a-half-year planning effort that brought in nationally recognized experts as consultants. In addition, this school serves as a useful reminder that school reform in the 1990s has not been limited to the charter school movement.

Among the charter schools examined here, some have received considerable help from their local school districts; others were created only after heated public debate and remain on uneasy terms with their local school districts. Two schools were parent initiated; three were initiated by groups of teachers; two had institutional sponsors. Moreover, each of the three states in which these schools were located handles charter schools differently. In Massachusetts, there is a central agency within the state's Department of Education that oversees charter schools; charter recipients are selected, by the state, through a request for proposal process. In contrast, Colorado makes the local school district the chartering agency (although groups applying for a charter can appeal to the Colorado Board of Education, which can direct a school board to approve a charter). Texas allows both school districts and the state to act as chartering agencies.

CHALLENGES FACING NEW SCHOOLS

Since charter schools are so often built from the ground up, they frequently face challenges—such as finding an adequate building or buying textbooks and furniture—that staff members in more traditional public schools do not usually have to deal with in such a hands-on way. But before looking at problems specific to charter schools, it is useful to consider the nature of the challenges faced by any new educational setting. For whenever people come together to pursue a common purpose, interpersonal issues tend to arise. This is true whether the setting is a medical clinic, a social service organization, or a school. To gain a better understanding the dilemmas faced by the teachers, administrators, and parents who initiate charter schools, I will refer to Seymour Sarason's work on the creation of settings.[1]

Sarason argues that all new settings face predictable hurdles. External problems center on the fact that a new setting exists within a larger social context, where competition for resources and prestige can render relations with existing settings extremely problematic. Internal challenges center on determining how lines of authority and communication will be established, the impact that new people entering the setting have on the original vision or idea. Sarason also outlines the stages that often can be observed in the growth of a new setting: initiation/planning, honeymoon, implementation, crisis, and aftermath. A more complete description of Sarason's framework is given below.

THE ORGANIZATION AS A WORK OF ART

Creating settings consistent with their purposes and sustaining them for more than brief periods of time is one of the great problems facing any society. Sarason notes that the first chapter of Jacob Burckhardt's (1965) classic *The Civilization of the Renaissance in Italy* was titled "The State as a Work of Art." Burckhardt described the appearance, in the early Renaissance, of a new political spirit that saw the state "as the outcome of reflection and calculation, the state as a work of art." There was a new awareness of the problem presented by "the deliberate adaptation of means to ends." A new self-consciousness became manifest in how records were kept, how changes were described, how discussions were recorded. The Florentine spirit, at once keenly critical and artistically creative, was incessantly transforming the social and political conditions of the state—and incessantly describing and judging the change. In a sense, this inquiry into the creation of charter schools is an extension of that same impulse.

Any new setting has a prehistory, local and national, that must be dealt with. Many different individuals and groups have a role in its birth. Resources are always limited (and usually overestimated, in part because of a sense of mission and boundless enthusiasm). Conflict within the setting (and between settings) is a fact of social life. Such conflicts are often exacerbated by conflicts between ideas. In the euphoria of creating something new, these causes of potential difficulty are too often ignored. Sarason argues that verbal agreement about values is no substitute for forging an organizational "constitution" that anticipates and helps deal with human differences—as well as future needs for change. Also, there is a need to build into the organization mechanisms for nourishing the morale and personal growth of participants once the initial burst of enthusiasm ebbs away. The danger is that, if the usual bureaucratic organization of the work environment is simply replicated—out of habit or because that is what people are used to—the weight of bureaucratic routine tends to extinguish curiosity and the sense of challenge, sapping away energy and causing the new setting to look more and more like those that have gone before.

What the leader of a new setting needs to possess—to literally feel that he or she "owns"—is a theory that lays out the variables to be dealt with. By "theory," Sarason means a set of ideas akin to what is in the head of a psychoanalyst approaching a patient. The psychoanalyst has a conception of what a human being is, how human beings develop, the obstacles humans encounter, the criteria for abnormality, and so forth. Theory, understood in this sense, is not only a conception about people in general (and patients in particular), but it is also a conception about therapists and how their actions must reflect an awareness of the human qualities they have in common with patients. Theory therefore functions both as a guide and as a form of control; it tells the therapist what to look for and provides a sensitivity to possible pitfalls.

BEFORE THE BEGINNING: CONFRONTING HISTORY

New settings are not viewed by their founders as mere duplications of what already exists, but as improvements. In one or another way, a new setting is expected to meet a need not now being met by existing settings. In the earliest phases, the creation of settings almost always (if not always) takes place in a context containing conflicting ideas and values, limited resources, a sense of mission and superiority on the part of some (and a need to preserve tradition on the part of others), and a need to protect the setting from outside influences. The social context of the new setting almost always includes or is seen as impinging on a large number of existing settings. Yet this matrix of factors is rarely described and discussed by the founders with the clarity required to anticipate how external forces are likely to affect the new setting's development and fate. Project directors routinely fail to ask these questions:

- What were the issues, problems, and conflicts that marked the prehistory of the new setting?
- What reactions might be anticipated as a result of the fact that the new setting will emerge from, and become part of, an existing organization of settings that had long-standing traditions and practices at variance with the new setting (which, if successful, would establish the superiority of its mission)?

There are characteristics of the new setting (such as claims to superiority of mission) and concerns on the part of existing settings (such as ideology and concern for resources) that all but ensure some conflict and competition. As Sarason points out, "Having to give up part of one's resources is a problem independent of personality, and to be unaware of this is asking for trouble." Inevitably, the new setting will need resources that, until then, had been expended elsewhere. Moreover, through the implication that the new setting has a superior mission, the new setting also competes with existing settings in the realm of ideas and values; that is, it disrupts an existing structure or pattern of relationships and causes new questions to be asked about the adequacy of the status quo. Such dynamics are independent of ideology. If the ideological positions of the new and existing settings were reversed, the reaction to the creation of the new setting would, in most cases, remain unchanged.

CHALLENGES OF THE INITIATION/PLANNING PERIOD

The leader of a new setting routinely thinks in terms of forming a core group to whom he or she delegates responsibilities. Choosing badly jeopardizes the future of the setting. But what does it mean to "choose" a member of this group? When asked, the most frequent answer given by the leader is that an individual has been chosen to do a certain job—to utilize specific knowledge, experience, and skills. That is to say, there is a match between what needs to be done and what this individual can do. This would be a reasonable answer, except that it ignores the fact that the individual and the leader will be in what is for them a new relationship, one that involves far more than is covered by the phrase "doing the job." Whether or not they can live together, whether or not their styles are congruent, whether or not their personal needs and goals clash—these are not questions contained in the answers that leaders give about why a person was hired.

The safest and most obvious prediction that can be made about the relationship between the leader and individuals in the core group is that there will be problems. When these problems will arise and what their specific character will be are not so predictable, but anticipating the exact nature of a problem is less important than understanding that there will be problems. Ground rules must be developed, not to eliminate problems, but to deal with them. When two people do not anticipate and discuss in advance how predictable issues affecting both will be handled, uncomfortable issues too often end up being faced and "resolved" in the worst of all situations: when feelings are strong and smoldering conflict and controversy are present. Sarason credits the common failure to anticipate predictable problems to four factors:

• The tendency to view the new setting as different from, and superior to, other settings generates an enthusiasm and sense of mission that color the future in a rosy way; superiority of ends is confused with superiority of means.
• For both the leader and the core group the attractiveness of the new setting inheres not only in what the new setting promises but in their disappointment in their previous settings.
• Participants do not view the creation of a new setting as a set of developmental problems that are fairly predictable—and about which one can formulate ground rules, so that when these problems arise, the element of surprise is diluted, and past discussions can serve as a basis for discussion in the present.
• Even when there is some awareness of probable developmental problems, discussion of possible problems at the point when the core group is formed is made difficult precisely because they are problematic, will arouse differences of opinion, and may require decisions and compromises that some may not wish to live with.

Such is the power of these factors that even when the leaders are veterans of other core groups in which their unhappiness with themselves, their work, and their colleagues reached a high level, they tend to create, not a mirror image of their previous setting, but a situation whose resemblance to that setting is unmistakable.

The usual way in which the leader organizes the core group—the arrangements made with each member, and the relationships of each with the others—usually reflects several assumptions held by the leader and each of the core group members:

• The appropriate kind and degree of motivation will overcome any and all obstacles, including those encountered by the leader and the core group in their previous settings.
• There is agreement on values and goals (perhaps the first assumption that, in point of time, is invalidated).

• There are sufficient resources, or the promise of them, to allow each of
the core group members to realize his or her goals.

From a purely internal standpoint, the major problems of creating a setting center on two related tasks: growth and differentiation on one hand,
and the forging of a constitution by which the setting will be governed on
the other. The ambiguities (only later recognized as such), inherent in the
usual way of selecting and organizing the core group, are a consequence
of the failure to view the creation of a setting as a constitutional problem.
Among the most important challenges in the creation of a setting are the
anticipation of problems and the ways they will be handled. Failure to
think in constitutional terms maximizes ambiguities, which usually leads
to informal, individual kinds of resolutions, such as heightened competitiveness and individual empires.

THE COST OF IGNORING PSYCHOLOGICAL DYNAMICS

Normally, during the formation and development of the core group, the
factor that is emphasized (indeed viewed as central) is the job that needs
to be done: to provide a service for others not part of the setting. The factor that is too often ignored or de-emphasized has two ingredients: the
professional and personal growth of the setting's members, and the ways
in which their mutuality can enhance growth. Usually, in the creation of a
setting, these personnel factors have been quite secondary to concern with
what is provided for others. Yet the greatest source of disillusionment and
disruption within a setting usually arises as a consequence of having ignored or de-emphasized these motivational factors. For, to the extent that
a setting becomes more and more focused on its relationships with the
outside world, its creators lose sight of what can (or must) be done for its
own members. Put in an alternative manner, it is of pivotal importance
that members of the core group remember a simple adage: We cannot do
for others, we cannot change others, until we learn how to do for and
change ourselves.

In its earliest phases, a new setting tends to be suffused with hope, enthusiasm, a sense of mission, and unity. The effect is to maximize selec-
tive perception. Another factor that inhibits a realistic assessment of what

is happening and why (and this is especially true of settings devoted to human service) is that they usually do help others. This result alone has tremendous reward value, particularly as such a result also serves as the basis for justifying the setting's existence. There is also a more subtle factor: In the early stages of the setting's existence, the process of helping others is usually accompanied by a personal sense of growth. The service is not experienced as a routine, without personal challenge and intellectual excitement.

Yet because the value of self-development is not viewed as equal to the value of helping others, over time the sense of challenge and change diminishes; routinization of thinking and action takes place. With the passage of time, members of the setting come to feel locked into their particular functions and increasingly experience a disruptive discrepancy between their desire to learn and change (the need for novelty and stimulation) and the perception that this need may not be satisfied. The exclusive focus on doing for others has been maintained at a very high personal price. Sarason notes that the widespread assumption that teachers can create and maintain conditions that make school stimulating for children, without those same conditions existing for teachers, has no warrant in the history of humankind.

FORGING A CONSTITUTION

The creation of a setting is a complicated process containing one booby trap after another. For example, there is a need for openness among participants. Yet this is not a mere matter of open talk or the expression of feeling as if these were virtues in themselves, not requiring the control and direction of organized conceptualizations. Telling the truth is not the same as being helpful (although it sometimes is), and being helpful is not a simple function of one's desire to help (although it sometimes is). In addition, the issue of openness is intimately related to another issue: How should decisions be made, by whom, and on what basis? Where can help be found when things get off track?

As the setting grows larger and becomes more differentiated, the amount of face-to-face contact between the leader and his or her core group noticeably lessens. The number of problems increases; the leader must make decisions and resolve issues and conflicts, usually not based on direct experience. The leader's knowledge of what is going on is increasingly obtained second- or thirdhand. There is usually one formal meeting each week between the leader and the core group that serves two purposes: (1) to bring important issues to the attention of the leader and (2) to provide an opportunity for the leader to state and clarify policy and direction, as well as to bring up problems. There are many more meetings between the leader and individual members of the core group. These individual meetings usually center on problems that either the leader or the core member does not feel comfortable raising and discussing in a group, or which he or she regards, on some basis, as not relevant to the larger group.

Sarason notes that he has seen new settings die at a very early age—and even more settings fail rather early in their stated purposes, even though as entities they survived. In every instance, a contributing factor was some form of strife between the leader and some core members that had never been allowed to surface in a way that could have led to resolution or compromise. The problems were not purely interpersonal, but the inevitable challenges encountered by the new setting had affected and transformed relationships, with effects that were dealt with only in self-defeating, indirect ways. The rate of change in a new setting (as in a newborn infant) is greater than it will ever be again, and this is mirrored in the transformation of relationships within the setting. If the consequences of this rate of change and transformation of relationships are not clearly recognized and dealt with (and they usually are not), substantive and interpersonal differences become fused and confused, rumor and gossip become major vehicles of communication, and the loneliness of everyone is heightened.

Leaders in general are a self-selected group, if only because they actively seek leadership. Leaders who create a new setting may be a somewhat different self-selected group, because they strive not only to lead but to create something "out there," the origins of which lie deep within themselves. Yet, regardless of his or her conception of leadership, the leader inevitably remains a private being like everyone else. The degree and content of a leader's privacy become a problem to the extent that she or he has not built into the new setting procedures that serve as external controls against all the errors to which purely private thought and feeling are subject. When a new setting's problems begin to be explained as due to "lack of communication," it is a clear sign that, at the very beginning, the issue of mutuality—or sharing of sentiments—was never squarely faced.

The process by which the leader attracts his or her core group almost never permits focusing on how to live with predictable problems and conflicts. On the contrary, the focus is on the marvelous opportunity the new setting presents for each individual to realize his or her ambitions within a context of shared values and team effort. Most leaders of new settings have no theory about the nature of the creative process in which they are engaged. How can they know, for example, that in the early stages the verbal commitment to openness is an easy gesture, but one that can effectively prevent anticipation of situations that will make openness difficult? That status differences work against openness? That competitiveness among those of similar status (such as members of the core group) also works against openness? That being a leader accelerates the pace of the processes of both self-discovery and self-deception? That absence of conflict may be symptomatic of trouble? This is not to say that leaders must become theoreticians. They are, after all, primarily people of action. They are practitioners. However this does not mean that they are incapable of understanding and being influenced by theory.

THE DANGERS OF JUST "JUMPING IN"

The pressure to get started (and to view anything before the beginning point as merely secondary steps to a primary goal) can have several consequences. First, it can result in a decision to bypass issues, individuals, and existing settings. Second, it can facilitate compromises (made willingly or otherwise) that will shape the future. Third, it can create or exacerbate conflict in the small group formed by the leader to create the new setting. Also, the existence of a fairly definite timetable tends to create a present dominated (and tyrannized) by a future that, when it arrives, is not the one that had been imagined. In most instances, problems arise because of specific factors: the basis and order of recruitment, the absence of problem-solving vehicles, the myth of unlimited resources and an untroubled future, specialization of function, competition among core members for resources, and influence on the leader.

Unconfronted conflicts in the realm of ideas and values can destroy a setting no less effectively than so-called personality clashes. Sarason notes that, in his experience, conflicts in ideas and values are more destructive; he also notes that, wherever he is given explanations in terms of personality, it seems obvious that these obscure conceptual differences. Yet, it is far easier to see personality differences than to hear conceptual ones. This is one of the reasons why Sarason urges the introduction of an outsider, an external critic, who can supply insights that allow members of the setting to confront and deal with problems before they reach a crisis point. To invite such an outsider in, not just for a day or a week, but as an ongoing source of insight and feedback, is a daunting prospect for the organizers of a new setting. The question that suggests itself is Why would they want to do that? The best answer might be that those who design settings, like those who design experiments, may not only want to prove something but to learn something. That is to say, they want to experience a sense of growth.

RESEARCH METHODOLOGY

Information for this study was gathered through interviews, on-site observations, and the systematic collection and analysis of archival data. At each school, structured interviews were held with teachers, parents, and administrators. Where opposition to the school had been intense, community members who were not members of the charter school community were also interviewed. Classroom visits were undertaken at all schools. The archival materials analyzed included individual school, school district, and state documents; newspaper accounts; and curriculum materials created by teachers.

DESCRIPTION OF SCHOOL SITES

Three of the settings described in this study were Colorado charter schools with contrasting curricular approaches. The first school, which served students in elementary and middle grades, had a highly structured curriculum based on E. D. Hirsch's core knowledge approach. A second school, which served students from kindergarten to twelfth grade, offered a highly individualized curriculum based on a successful "open school" in the same school district. The third, an alternative high school, focused on the special needs of at-risk students. In contrast, the noncharter Model School began as a collaborative venture between an elite private university and a large urban school district. This school was organized during the same time period as the charter schools in the study and thus provided an opportunity to compare the charter school experience to the creation of a break-the-mold school that remained under regular district control.

Wesley Elementary in Houston, Texas, had a rich prehistory as a regular neighborhood school, having been built during the era of segregation in the South. The school's first principal was a highly regarded African American educator. By the mid-1970s, however, both the neighborhood and the school environment had changed drastically. When Thaddeus Lott became the principal at Wesley in 1975, the building had deteriorated so badly that it was impossible for a teacher to put her purse on a cafeteria table without cockroaches running all over it. Sixth graders were reading at the second-grade level. By 1980, Lott (who had grown up in the neighborhood) had transformed the school. The standardized test scores of Wesley students ranked with those of affluent suburban schools. These days, Wesley Elementary has become a charter school, part of a special charter school district.

Whereas the curriculum at Wesley Elementary emphasized a direct instruction curriculum, the Human Development Charter School made use of a Piagetian approach. Created in cooperation with a large public university, this school was established with the goal of providing a living demonstration in constructivist education. Teacher–child interactions in the classroom were shaped by a strong focus on sociomoral influences. Located in an ethnically diverse neighborhood, this K–2 school admits children on a first-come, first-served basis, based on date of application and the need of individual classes to maintain a balance relating to sex, age, and ethnic distribution.

The final case study included in this chapter differs from the others in yet another way. My involvement with the school was not initially as a researcher but as an observer and informal consultant. Marblehead Community Charter Public School (MCCPS) was organized in my hometown of Marblehead, Massachusetts. When plans to hire a consultant to help with the charter application went awry, it seemed natural to help out. My role was never a decision-making one. The information about MCCPS was taken almost entirely from interviews, on-site observations, and archival materials. Yet, even long-range involvement inevitably has some impact upon one's perceptions. In the end, though, the value of providing something of an inside view of the organizational process was deemed of sufficient value to justify including MCCPS in this group of case studies.

CHALLENGES ENCOUNTERED BY CHARTER SCHOOLS

In an ideal world, the founders of charter schools would have a relatively simple task. Freed from bureaucratic restraints, charter schools would be able to pursue the educational vision their founders believed to be most effective for the children they served. All of each charter school's constituents would have actively chosen to be there (none would have signed up simply because they disliked the other options available to them). In an ideal world, all charter schools would have adequate start-up funds; all schools would be able to find facilities well suited to their purposes; staff members would not find their energies drained by ongoing political struggles outside the school. However, none of the schools described in this chapter existed in an ideal world.

This section focuses on patterns that emerged regarding the challenges faced by the seven schools. Some of the problems were all but ubiquitous. For example, the unified vision that the founders at most schools initially thought they shared tended to break down when decision making got down to specifics. Parents serving on governing boards had to learn to look beyond what they wanted for their own children; if the school was to be successful, board members had to realize that they must adopt policies that would enable all children at the school to thrive. Teachers found that taking over functions handled by administrators at their previous schools was, in the beginning, somewhat overwhelming. Almost everyone who had been involved in starting a charter school expressed surprise at how much work was involved, how many regulatory hurdles had to be jumped, and how many people felt entitled to have input into the process.

Creating a climate and culture that was consistent with the school's philosophy and vision was a challenge for all schools. There was a tendency to believe that because the founders had agreed that a particular goal was important, that goal would somehow take care of itself. But, in a situation where everything that the school did had to be created from scratch, there was also a tendency to fall back on what was familiar. Even though dissatisfaction with the "same old thing" had been an important part of the motivation for starting a charter school, at some point a feeling akin to "innovation fatigue" began to set in. As will be discussed later in this section, help from a friendly external critic often proved to be of great value in helping charter schools to regain their bearings, remove roadblocks, and move forward. Yet, despite the struggles, many stakeholders spoke of the opportunity to participate in the creation of a new school as a source of tremendous personal satisfaction and growth.

STARK DIFFERENCES IN ORGANIZATIONAL DYNAMICS

Overall, the problems encountered by charter school founders closely resembled those predicted by Sarason's theoretical framework. However, some challenges proved more problematic for one kind of school than for others. Grouping the schools according to type (parent-initiated, educator-founded, institution-sponsored) highlights the differences. For example, parent-initiated charter schools had somewhat different organizational dynamics than schools created by professional educators. Schools that had come into being through the sponsorship of existing public agencies (school districts or city governments) were strongly influenced by the institutional cultures of their sponsors.

THE MODEL SCHOOL AND THE
OPPORTUNITY PREPARATORY SCHOOL

When this research project began, the expectation was that the clearest contrast would be between the six charter schools and the K–8 Model School that had been set up as a collaborative venture between an elite private university and a large urban school district. The Model School, created during the same time period as the six charter schools, had been included to make possible a comparison between charter schools and a site-based, district-controlled reform effort. When the data were analyzed, however, it became clear that the bureaucratic restraints that had shaped the early history of the Model School were similar in their effect to the restraints that had shaped the early history of Opportunity Preparatory School, a charter high school for at-risk students that had been set up by a city council. Both schools were, essentially, subordinate units within politically run bureaucracies.

At both schools, teachers' efforts to build an independent school culture proved no match for organizational pressures originating outside the school itself. There had been critical periods during each setting's early history when a unique vision for that school might have been solidified. Teachers expressed a desire to actively address challenges involving curriculum and governance structure. However, the required leadership was lacking; teachers were left hanging by decision makers elsewhere. In the end, no action was taken because no one at the site had the required authority. Each school was initially headed by an established administrator who had expressed great enthusiasm for the program yet continued to have significant duties elsewhere. These duties made it impossible for either school's appointed leader to spend much time with teachers during the crucial planning period prior to opening the school.

In the case of the Model School, a well-respected district-level administrator was to have acted as the school's full-time principal, taking over several months before the opening of the school. However, a political crisis elsewhere in the school district called this administrator away during much of the summer prior to the Model School's opening. As a result, the teachers hired to staff the new school ended up spending much of this critical planning period marking time by attending canned staff development workshops provided by the school district. These summer workshops had very little to do with the challenges ahead. Yet, without the presence of the site administrator, no one had the authority to begin the important processes of (1) hammering out a constitution for the new school and (2) initiating discussion of pivotal curriculum implementation issues. Confidence and enthusiasm among the teachers wavered.

As opening day approached, there was great uncertainty about how the innovative programs described in the school's vision statement would be implemented. Many of the teachers had never taught in multiage classrooms before. They had signed on because they were willing to try; but there had been an assumption that they would receive extensive training in multiage grouping before the school opened. None of this happened. With the principal away, the decision-making role fell to school district administrators who had not been active in planning the school. They simply proceeded as they would have when opening any other school. Teachers had been promised a strong voice in governance; yet no structure for site-level governance had been set up. As an innovative site within a custodial system, the Model School found itself continually swimming upstream. As a result, whenever circumstances precluded staff members' putting maximum effort into fighting the current, they began to be swept downstream.

Over and over the same phenomenon could be observed. When teachers were not given adequate training in the innovative practices the school had been set up to implement, they fell back on teaching methods they had used at their former schools. This tendency was intensified by the controversies that marked the school's first year. Feeling besieged from the outside, teachers were hesitant to take risks. They retreated to doing what felt safe. One result was that the social justice concerns that had been much discussed during initial planning sessions received far less attention after the school opened. For example, after the school opened, the bilingual curriculum was never expanded beyond grades K–2, although the original vision statement called for a bilingual school that would allow the non-Hispanic majority of the student body to become fluent in Spanish.

What could not be set aside was the need to serve the diverse student population that had been recruited (through separate lotteries, ensuring that 50 percent of the students at the school would be drawn from across the district—with half of these students being African American and the other half Hispanic—while the remaining 50 percent of the Model School's student population would be drawn from the affluent neighborhood near the university). Originally the school was to have been a neighborhood elementary school serving the community near the university. Later, school district officials bowed to criticism that too much money was being spent in a few white enclaves within the district and decided to double the size of the Model School so that it would serve children from throughout the district, in grades K–8.

The major crisis of the school's first year took place at the middle school level. Teachers had been recruited from what were considered to be the best middle schools in the district. Accustomed to teaching affluent students from elementary schools that provided children with a strong academic foundation, the Model School's middle school teachers understood their role to be that of upholding high academic standards. However, many of the middle school students who attended as a result of the districtwide lottery were from low-performing elementary schools where academic expectations had been quite different. As a result, at the end of the first semester, many of the minority students who had been recruited from across this urban district were found to be failing subjects such as math.

The resulting controversy embroiled the Model School in charges of racism. Many minority students in grades seven and eight eventually decided to leave the school. Meanwhile, the school district focused its efforts on placating important constituent groups; the university distanced itself. Teachers at the Model School hunkered down and concentrated on bringing along the children in the lower grades so that, by the time these children would reach middle school they would be able to meet the school's academic standards. This had a profound effect on the culture at the school. Instead of developing an innovative model for teaching diverse populations that could be shared with other schools in the district, the Model School grew into a fairly traditional institution whose benefits were enjoyed primarily by those students who had "won the lottery" and gained entrance.

At Opportunity Preparatory School (OPS), the initial dream had been to create a college preparatory school for at-risk students. However, the nonavailability of the city employee, who had been the primary force behind opening the school, had crippled efforts to adapt the curriculum to the perceived needs of these students during the school's first year of operation. At this school, the titular principal was not just absent for a few months; he had many other duties and took the attitude that, having set out the blueprint for the school, he ought to be able to step back and let the teachers run it. But, lacking his participation, no one had the authority to flesh out the original vision, creating a school culture with well-understood rules and disciplinary procedures. There was an assumption that those whom the school was intended to benefit would recognize that they had been offered an important opportunity, and that they would respond—on their own—in the manner required for the school to succeed. Often this did not happen.

The problems faced by these two schools did not differ significantly from those faced by other charter schools studied. However, in the other schools there were no layers of administrative structure to insulate administrators from the conflicts and challenges that arose almost immediately. In contrast, at the Model School and (especially) at OPS, much of the decision-making power lay in the hands of persons who, at pivotal periods in their schools' history, had little day-to-day contact with events at the schools. As a result, both schools were deprived of one of the greatest advantages pointed to by stakeholders at the other charter schools: the ability to respond to emerging challenges in a timely manner, without having to bother with bureaucratic procedure.

OPS students divided their time between computer-aided instruction that helped them to catch up on basic academic skills and college-style seminars that encouraged creative thinking and were intended to prepare students for future university-level work. However, a majority of the OPS students had little interest in college. All that most of them wanted was to receive their high school diplomas; they had little interest in preparing for, or participating in, the seminars. Yet the founder of the school, who had little contact with the students, held firmly to his original dream of a college preparatory program for at-risk students. As a result, teachers found themselves foundering in a vacuum, unable either to change the mandated curriculum or to make it work for the students who were actually attending the school. Morale withered and dissension grew.

At the Model School, the problems were not so readily apparent. Nationally recognized experts had been brought in as consultants during a three-and-a-half-year planning period. On the surface, it would seem that this was a carefully designed school. However, the planning activities had been financed by grant funds raised through the university. Proceeding according to its own institutional culture, the university had used this funding to hold a series of stimulating seminars, to which all those involved in planning the Model School were invited. Visits by renowned educators excited a great deal of interest; committees of stakeholders were formed to explore various possibilities. Yet, there was no mechanism in place to coordinate the efforts of these committees or to decide which of the disparate innovations discussed by a committee would become part of the curriculum.

As the planning period drew to a close, the stakeholder committees delivered suggestions on subjects ranging from curriculum to school governance. These suggestions were sewn together into an expansive vision statement that included something for everyone. No attempt was made to decide which of the many innovations listed should be given the highest priority. Moreover, the teachers for the school were not hired until the spring before the school opened (after the planning process was completed). Therefore, many of the teachers never saw the planning document. Some never knew that it existed. Nor had the school district ever actually committed to following up on the suggestions that came out of the planning process.

Both the university president and the school district superintendent who had set the planning process in motion had, since that time, accepted positions elsewhere. With their original sponsors out of the picture, no one connected with the Model School project wanted to make waves. All of the problems that Sarason has described in connection with the honeymoon period were, therefore, present in especially acute form. No one wanted to disturb the good feelings that had been aroused by the discussion of intriguing new ideas by asking hard questions about what would happen when the school actually opened. So the project went forward virtually on autopilot, with backers worried that any attempt to address predictable problems might cause tensions that would result in the project being shelved. Had those charged with the creation of this school actively made use of a theoretical framework of the sort suggested by Sarason, many problems might have been avoided. The benefit of theory, in this case, would have been in giving decision makers a ready rationale for bringing up issues that they might otherwise have been reluctant to mention.

At the Model School, volatile emotions were aroused when preadolescent children from inner-city schools were brought into a school where half the students came from upper-middle-class homes. In addition, a keen sense of resentment was expressed by some school district employees at other schools as they watched extra resources, procured through university contacts, being poured into this school. If advance planning had made it possible to lay the necessary groundwork for coping with these challenges, their impact may not have been so traumatic. Without such preparation, natural self-protective instincts kicked in. Many aspects of the school's innovative vision were abandoned as the staff sought safety by sticking to practices that were safe, familiar, and noncontroversial.

Of the seven schools studied, the Model School and the OPS ended up furthest from their initial visions. This is not to say that these programs were failures. By most standards, the Model School offers an excellent educational program. Yet the dream of creating an educational program whose influence would extend beyond the school's immediate stakeholders—making it a model for other urban schools—has been all but abandoned. Similarly, OPS has come to resemble many other last-chance programs for at-risk students. Both schools are now under the direction of new leaders. Both have adapted in ways that were largely dictated by the requirements of the school district and the city council that had administrative authority over these two schools.

THE CORE ACADEMY AND THE MARBLEHEAD COMMUNITY CHARTER PUBLIC SCHOOL

The two parent-initiated charter schools—the Core Academy, located in Vista, Colorado, and Marblehead Community Charter Public School in Marblehead, Massachusetts—encountered strikingly similar challenges. In both cases, the founding coalition was made up of parents brought together primarily by a shared discontent with the educational options currently available to their children. Both schools were located in affluent suburban areas where the neighborhood schools would be considered good, in comparison with the national average. However, as the charter school parents were quick to point out, the U.S. national average does not compare well with achievement levels in other industrialized nations.

An article in the March 30, 2000, issue of a British newsmagazine, *The Economist*, summarizes statistics similar to those that had set off alarm bells for many charter school parents:

> At fourth grade (ten years old), American children score better in reading and science than most pupils in 20 other rich countries, and are about average in mathematics. At eighth grade, they are still slightly better than average in maths and science but fall behind in reading. By 12th grade, they are behind 95% of the children in other countries. The longer children stay in American schools, the worse they seem to get.[2]

The same article points out that the growing educational disparity cannot be traced to differences in spending. The United States spends almost 6 percent of its national income on primary and secondary education, more than any other Organization for Economic Cooperation and Development (OECD) country except Denmark and Canada. Some inner-city schools get less money than suburban ones—but others get more. While providing sufficient funding is important, the crisis lies in the delivery system:

> Almost three-quarters of ten-year-olds in the poorest public schools have not yet begun to read or write; the illiteracy rate among 17-year-olds is one in seven. Poor education lies behind the looming problem of inequality, between the new economy's winners and losers.

The charter school parents were determined to procure for their children an education that would enable them to compete with students anywhere. The problem they faced was that significant disagreement existed among the founders as to exactly what the educational excellence they collectively sought would look like in practice. This lack of consensus led to a very turbulent shakeout period. Most noticeable were problems related to creating an effective working relationship between the original core group (which consisted of parents) and the teachers who were hired to make the parents' vision for the school a reality.

Many of the parents had never before served on the board of a nonprofit organization, nor had they supervised employees. They also lacked firsthand knowledge of what it takes to guide a class of twenty through a rigorous academic curriculum (while also supporting the children's emotional growth and social development). However, the parents had invested an enormous amount of time and energy in getting the school started; they very much wanted the school to come into being just as they had envisioned it.

Sarason notes that, whenever he asks people to choose between becoming the leader of an existing setting or creating a new one, the choice invariably seems to be the latter. People feel that creating a setting allows one to mold it to one's purposes, unhindered by any existing tradition or practice. Yet, although this answer always refers to socially acceptable, impersonal practices, underpinning this answer is a vision of the leader in the role of the artist, someone who chooses the material, fashions and re-fashions it, and ends up with the concrete embodiment of his or her ideas and efforts. Moreover, when people explain their preference for creating a new setting, they seem unaware that they are describing the relationship between the leader and the setting as analogous to that between the artist and his or her materials; the setting is passive, malleable, at the service of the leader.

As Sarason points out, there is, at this point, nothing inherently wrong in the leader's way of thinking. There is no setting; the leader is alone with his or her thoughts. What is fateful for the leader and the projected setting is how the leader's attitude changes as the setting is created and the leader must confront real people, along with the need to accept some compromises between what the leader wants and what others want. The fact that what others will want for themselves will always be somewhat different (and may frequently be quite different) from the leader's own vision presents some deeply personal issues. The leader does not question the obligation to be consistent with his or her values and goals. But to what extent, if any, should the leader accept limits in order to help others in the realization of their goals?

At each of the parent-initiated schools, one or more very enthusiastic parents had spearheaded the organizing effort. These enthusiastic parents had communicated their vision of the school to other parents in such a way that setting up a charter school had seemed merely a matter of selecting teachers, imparting to them the vision for the school, and watching as everything and everyone fell into place—precisely according to plan. Moreover, in their eagerness to win support, these enthusiastic parents had emphasized somewhat different aspects of the planned school when they were speaking to different groups of potential supporters. In addition, two sources of all-but-inevitable disappointment had been present from the beginning: (1) lack of recognition that the teachers hired would have a powerful impact on the character of the school and (2) lack of a mutually understood way of deciding which educational innovations introduced at the school should be given highest priority.

Such challenges were made more explosive by the fact that some members of these parent-led boards had become so identified with the new setting that each obstacle was viewed, not as a problem requiring compromise, but as a moral battle in which good was pitted against the forces of

disillusionment and evil. These board members had created an imagina-
tive vista in which the happiness of everyone involved with the setting
would stem from willingly—and completely—identifying with their vision for the school. As Sarason has noted, this way of thinking is psycho-
logically quite similar to the way parents tend to fantasize the future of a
firstborn child, as an independent and unique individual possessing striv-
ings and characteristics that are completely in accord with what is in the
minds of the parents.

The teachers, for their part, saw things from quite a different perspective. During the hiring process, the charter school's prospects had been
described in glowing terms. The opportunities for professional growth
had been emphasized, along with a sense of how much the school staff
would contribute to making the school a reality. Those who did the hiring were aware that there was more turbulence behind the scenes than
they were letting on. However, they felt that such difficulties would
somehow be surmounted. In addition, they were convinced that, if tal-
ented teachers could be attracted to the setting, the difficulties would be
minimized. Thus, a situation evolved in which, because of the desire of
those doing the hiring to attract good teachers (and the teachers' desire to
be attracted in ways fulfilling to their own ambitions), an understanding
was arrived at that did not include any explicit discussion of personal or
professional ambitions.

All through the hiring process a kind of dance took place in which the
discussion did not explicitly and directly deal with possible conflicts of
ambition. The new setting was, for the parents who founded it, a deeply
personal affair. Arguably, a number of influential board members were
motivated by a fantasy of the new setting that was populated by only one
set of real people—the founding coalition. Sarason points out that often
the leaders of new settings will use novel language in talking about the
hiring process, subtly communicating the expectation that if others choose
to come aboard it is because there is a captain who decides directions.
What the leader is not aware of is that such attitudes tend to produce a
ubiquitous organizational problem: faulty communication.

In contrast to the Model School and the OPS, where organizational
pressures external to the setting became the greatest obstacle to the attainment of the setting's original goals, at the two parent-led schools the
greatest obstacles turned out to be internal: (1) growth and differentiation,

and (2) the development of a constitution. Again, among the most important challenges in the creation of any setting is anticipating problems and deciding how to handle them. At both these schools, the failure to think in constitutional terms maximized ambiguities, leading over time to informal, individual kinds of resolutions, among them attempts by individual board members to actively intervene in the day-to-day running of the school.

At both sites, the stabilization of the school as a viable setting was directly connected with solving the governance problems that had bedeviled these schools from their early days. Both settings could have benefited from access to a theoretical framework that warned of the common pitfalls in the process of creating a setting. Such a theoretical framework might have provided an early warning system that (1) alerted the parents who founded these schools to dangers of which they would not otherwise have been aware and (2) suggested how problems that had presented themselves might be effectively dealt with, as well as what interpersonal dynamics might have given rise to the problems that occurred. Had they been able to think of the challenges they faced in constitutional terms, participants might have been able to avoid personalizing predictable problems. This, in turn, might have enabled them to avoid destructive interpersonal tensions as they struggled to deal with conflicts and misunderstandings.

The experiences of the stakeholders at these two schools would seem to be congruent with Sarason's argument that the creation of a setting is a set of internal and external problems that are fairly predictable. Among these predictable challenges are the following:

- History is always a variable.
- People represent different values, interests, and ambitions.
- The uses and allocation of power are best not left solely to the ambiguities of motivation.
- The individual and general welfare are not always perceived as synonymous; conflict is neither bad nor avoidable, but ignoring it is calamitous.
- Checks and balances are necessities, not luxuries.
- Growth is a double-edged sword—the problem is how to manage it consistently with first principles.

Facing these predictable needs, problems, and issues may take some of the joy out of the honeymoon period. Yet they are the realities around which the constitution of a new setting has to be forged. If they are addressed effectively through hammering out a mutually agreeable constitution for the setting, steps taken to cope with these early problems can increase the likelihood that a viable setting will eventually be created.

PASSAGES CHARTER SCHOOL, WESLEY ELEMENTARY, UNIVERSITY OF HOUSTON CHARTER SCHOOL

The last three charter schools studied in this book were initiated by educators and were based on successful existing programs. Passages Charter School in Big Plain, Colorado, serves students from kindergarten to twelfth grade, offering a highly individualized curriculum based on that of a successful open school in the same school district. In the 1990s, Wesley Elementary became a charter school, part of a special charter school district organized under the leadership of Dr. Thaddeus Lott. The University of Houston (UH) Charter School of Technology was created in cooperation with a large public university and was established to provide a living demonstration of constructivist education.

The programs offered by these schools could not have been more different. Whereas Wesley Elementary used a highly structured direct instruction curriculum, the UH charter school emphasized spontaneous teacher-child interactions in the classroom. Passages Charter School used a highly individualized, experiential approach built on the philosophical principals associated with progressive education; each student had a personal learning plan created by the student, advisor, and parent. There were also sharp differences in the demographic characteristics of the schools. Passages was located in a middle-class suburban area, in sharp contrast to the central city neighborhoods where Wesley and the UH charter school were located. Yet, similar organizational challenges played a significant part in the development of each of these schools.

The demands on staff members at each school were high. As one teacher at Passages commented, explaining her decision to resign: "This school has dealt with too many stressors. The stress of the first year, the stress of an inadequate facility. . . . It's just not worth it anymore." Staff members were being asked to throw a tremendous amount of effort into starting the new school. How long they could sustain this level of effort was open to question. At Wesley, whose twenty-year history as a high-achieving school makes it possible to study the results of such energy demands over time, only a small cadre of teacher-leaders had remained at the school year after year, while large numbers of young teachers had stayed only two or three years. After a stint at Wesley where they honed their teaching skills, many opted to "throttle back," moving to an easier school.

As Sarason has observed, during the planning of a new setting, the factor that is emphasized (indeed viewed as central) is the job that needs to be done. Attention is focused on providing an important service. The professional and personal growth of the setting's members and the ways in which their mutuality can enhance that growth are often ignored. Usually, in the creation of a setting, these factors get little attention. Yet the greatest source of disillusionment and disruption within a setting, later on, tends to arise as a consequence of having de-emphasized these motivational factors. When a setting becomes so focused on its relationship to the outside world that it loses sight of what it can (or must) do for its own members, staff burnout becomes an immediate threat. Unfortunately, the culture of public education affords little opportunity to recognize and avoid this problem.

All of these schools performed functions that others needed and valued. In the beginning, this alone had tremendous reward value, particularly since it also served as the basis for justifying the charter schools' existence. A more subtle factor was also at work: In the early stages of each teacher's involvement, the process of helping others tended to be accompanied by a personal sense of growth. Teaching at these innovative schools was not experienced as a routine, without personal challenge or intellectual excitement. However, over time, the sense of challenge and change diminished; teachers' work became more routinized. Teachers were still working very hard, but they were getting less in the way of stimulation, excitement, a sense of personal growth.

Here we touch upon a deep-seated problem, endemic within public schools in the United States. Education is not just the learning of useful skills and facts, but also the chance to escape the narrow boundaries of one place or time, the opportunity to draw from the collective cultural inheritance passed down to us from earlier generations as well as to learn from our contemporaries in every part of the world. There is much in what educators do that could be the source of excitement and inspiration. However, the way public schooling has been structured all too often cancels out these aspects of the profession, emphasizing rules, routines, and paper work.

If we are to experience a renaissance in the field of public education, a way will have to be found to make more room for the life of the mind. In this area, despite the difficulties they have faced, charter schools offer considerable promise. These are schools that were born out of enthusiasm and hope, founded by people who believe that the future need not be a repeat of the past. What is lacking at many of these schools is someone with the experience to help staff members recognize problems before they begin to undermine the effectiveness of the school.

TAKING A BROADER PERSPECTIVE

Given the differences in viewpoint and opinion that exist within many charter schools, how could such schools be expected to diagnose their own problems in time to avoid trouble? Sarason suggests the appointment of an external critic who would accept the task of understanding and responding to the purposes and values of the setting, the consistency between words and actions, and the sources of actual and potential problems. This external critic would be an independent outsider, but an outsider knowledgeable about—and sympathetic to—the purposes of the setting. The external critic has no responsibility except to observe, study, and report. The critic does not wait for problems to be brought to him or her, but seeks them out.

The use of mediators to settle trade disputes might provide a model for how this could work. To be effective, a mediator must be acceptable to all involved. Similarly, the external critic who advises a charter school must be trusted and respected by stakeholders at the school. Charter school participants in this study often spoke of the important role that outside advisors—some paid for by the state—had played in their schools' success. As the charter school movement expands, one way state government could help to promote the healthy development of these schools would be to invite each charter school to identify an external critic (who is also acceptable to the state), who would visit the school regularly, providing advice and assistance. A list of previously approved candidates (representing a range of curricular specialties and political viewpoints) could be provided, with schools also given the option of nominating an external critic who was not on the list but whose expertise was deemed especially useful to that school.

We have long framed the debate over charter schools in terms of whether or not such schools ought to be given "freedom from" certain restraints. Providing funding for an external critic would help give schools the "freedom to" succeed. Most charter schools are institutions whose stakeholders are strongly motivated to learn from mistakes, to change, to grow, to provide an example for others. Yet the very intensity of stakeholder involvement often makes it difficult for those at the site to stand back and objectively assess both what is happening and what needs to be done if the school is to remain true to the vision of the founders. This is where an external critic could provide an invaluable service.

NOTES

1. Seymour Sarason, *The Creation of Settings and the Future Societies*, 2d ed. (Cambridge, Mass.: Brookline Books, 1998 [1972]).

2. *The Economist*, "America's Education Choice," accessed on April 1, 2000, from economist.com/displaystory.cmf?story_id331761.

Chapter Two

Parent Involvement Strengthens Academic Performance of Students

A critical dimension of effective schooling is parent involvement. The term parent refers to any caregiver who assumes responsibility for nurturing and caring for children, including parents, grandparents, aunts, uncles, foster parents, and stepparents. Many schools are now using the term family involvement. Research has shown conclusively that parent involvement at home in their children's education improves student achievement, including test scores. Furthermore, when parents are involved at school, their children go further in school and they go to better schools. Substantial parent involvement may be the key reason for charter schools' academic success.

Key Concepts:
The Big Picture
What Is Parent Involvement?
What a Policy Should Include
Parent Involvement Research
What Parents Can Do to Help Their Children

The Center for Education Reform (CER) recently released additional data documenting the positive effects of charter schools on students, parents, and communities. The data show conclusively that charter schools have made an indelible mark on education. Findings continue to reinforce the facts: charter schools are working, parents are happy with them, traditional school districts have been propelled to make improvements, and children are thriving in a charter school setting. These findings and reports are so definitive they leave little room for those who say charter schools hurt public education. Of sixty-five studies, sixty-one show positive effects of charter schools. Of particular note are two U.S. Department of Education studies confirming the ripple effect charter schools have on local districts by driving these schools to implement new educational programs, make systemic changes, or create similar programs within the traditional public schools.

There is increasing evidence that parent involvement increases test scores.[1] This means that teachers and administrators, who are under pressure to increase scores and may receive rewards if they do, are interested in parents contacting them and asking how they can help their children progress.

Educators have an excellent opportunity to make changes based on the experiences of schools already dealing with the need to set high standards and institute programs that will be successful.

I prefer the approach of raising standards where high levels of assistance are provided to staff, not the testing approach where students may be retained a grade because of a single test score. I will show methods that were used to get parents involved in a meaningful way in the programs geared toward helping students improve their performance in a variety of assessments. I will also explain some of the real world complexity that leads to successful programs and give examples of language that communicates clearly to parents.

THE BIG PICTURE

Ronald Brownstein, writing in the *Los Angeles Times*, sees four goals for improving schools:

1. Parents need to commit to helping their child's education through reading for fun every day; watching television less; discussing homework; and making reading materials available.
2. Title I, the federal program to assist low-achieving students, needs competition. It may spend too much on poorly qualified teacher aides and not enough on after-school programs, for example.

3. The states need a benchmark for judging student progress, since some states reduce their expectations to fit their student test results. Brownstein suggests that schools use the National Assessment of Educational Progress (NAEP) to keep our state officials in line.
4. We need federal programs that are large enough in scale to make a difference. With many millions of students underachieving, programs to get better-trained teachers into hard-to-serve schools need to be more on the scale Al Gore proposed (850,000 per year) rather than the one George W. Bush proposed (11,000 per year).[2]

WHAT IS PARENT INVOLVEMENT?

The National Coalition for Parent Involvement in Education (NCPIE) is dedicated to the development and strengthening of family/school partnerships. Based on the broad experience of NCPIE members, here are some specific ways teachers, parents, administrators, and community leaders can work together to strengthen relationships between schools and parents.

By exchanging information, sharing in decision-making, helping at school, and collaborating in children's learning, parents can become partners in the educational process. When parents/families are involved in their children's education, children do better in school. Schools improve as well.[3]

Policy makers at all levels are increasingly aware of the pivotal role that families and the community play in the education of our children. This is apparent in the Title I, Special Education, Head Start, and other federal programs that mandate consultation and collaboration with families. Many state and district policies also stipulate programs and practices to involve all families, not only those with children who receive special services.

With the momentum ongoing, organized family participation at the school and district levels increases, and so does the demand for family involvement program information. What follows are some general policy suggestions, keys to successful programs, and specific program ideas.

WHAT A POLICY SHOULD INCLUDE

The process of developing policies should include community-based organizations (CBOs), teachers, administrators, businesses, families, students, and other key stakeholders. Here is a checklist of important policy inclusions:

- Opportunities for all parents/families to become involved in deciding how the family involvement programs will be designed, implemented, assessed, and strengthened;
- Outreach to encourage participation of families who might have low-level literacy skills and/or for whom English is not their primary language;
- Regular information for families about the objectives of educational programs and on their children's participation and progress in those programs;
- Professional development for teachers and staff to enhance their effectiveness with families;
- Links with special service agencies and community groups to address key family and community issues;
- Involvement of families of children at all ages and grade levels;
- Opportunities for families to share in decision making regarding school policies and procedures affecting their children;
- Recognition of diverse family structures, circumstances, and responsibilities, including differences that might impede parent participation. The person(s) responsible for a child many not be the child's biological parent(s), and policies and programs should include participation by all persons interested in the child's educational progress.

This is a checklist for increasing parent involvement:

- Assess family's needs and interests about ways of working with the schools;
- Set clear and measurable objectives based on parent and community input, to help foster a sense of cooperation and communication between families, communities, and schools;
- Hire and train a parent/family liaison to contact parents directly and coordinate family activities. The liaison should be bilingual as needed and sensitive to the needs of the family and the community, including the non-English speaking community;

- Develop multiple outreach mechanisms to inform families, businesses, and the community about family involvement policies and programs through newsletters, slide shows, videotapes, and local newspapers;
- Recognize the importance of a community's historic, ethnic, linguistic, or cultural resources in generating interest in family involvement;
- Use creative forms of communication between educators and families that are personal, goal oriented, and make optimal use of new communication technologies;
- Mobilize parents/families as volunteers in the school assisting with instructional tasks, meal service, and administrative office functions. Family members might also act as invited classroom speakers and volunteer tutors;
- Provide staff development for teachers and administrators to enable them to work effectively with families and with one another as partners in the educational process;
- Ensure access to information about nutrition, healthcare, services for individuals with disabilities, and support provided by schools or community agencies;
- Schedule programs and activities flexibly to reach diverse family groups;
- Evaluate the effectiveness of family involvement programs and activities on a regular basis.

PARENT INVOLVEMENT RESEARCH

Schools that undertake and support strong, comprehensive parent involvement efforts are more likely to produce students who perform better than identical schools that do not involve parents.[4] Schools that have strong links with and respond to the needs of the communities they serve have students that perform better than schools that don't. Children who have parents who help them at home and stay in touch with the school do better academically than children of similar aptitude and family background whose parents are not involved. The inescapable fact is that consistent high levels of student success are more likely to occur with long-term comprehensive parent involvement in schools.

Parents and school staff should help parents develop parenting skills to meet the basic obligations of family life and foster conditions at home that emphasize the importance of education and learning. They should also promote two-way (school-to-home and home-to-school) communication about school programs and students' progress. Find ways to involve parents, with appropriate training, in instructional and support roles at the school and in other locations that help the school and students reach stated goals, objectives, and standards. Also provide parents with strategies and techniques for assisting their children at home with learning activities that support and extend the school's instructional program. Find ways to prepare parents to actively participate in school decision making and develop their leadership skills in governance and advocacy and provide parents with skills to access community and support services that strengthen school programs, family practices, and student learning and development. These six areas of parent involvement roles require a coordinated schoolwide effort that has the support of parents, teachers, students, and administrators at each school site. Furthermore, research indicates that home–school collaboration is most likely to occur if schools take the initiative to encourage, guide, and genuinely welcome parents into the partnership. Professional development for teachers and administrators on how to build such a partnership is essential.

The issue of parent involvement in the education of their children is much larger than improving student achievement. It is central to our democracy that parents and citizens participate in the governing of public institutions, and parent involvement is fundamental to a healthy system of public education.

WHAT PARENTS CAN DO TO HELP THEIR CHILDREN

This book is directed toward charter and community school staff and parents, regardless of parent income. Parents whose background is most like that of the teachers in a school may find it easier to relate to the teachers and other school staff and, consequently, to work with them.

At the national level the Parent Teacher Association (PTA) has worked to create a list of standards that can also help a group of parents as they prepare to have meaningful involvement in schools. There is an extensive overlap between the California State Department of Education and the national PTA, for example, which includes the following five areas:

1. Develop parenting skills;
2. Use two-way communication between home and school;
3. Involve parents in student learning;
4. Assist in school decision making; and
5. Work with the community.[5]

It is important that these objectives be seen in the context of programs that provide staff development and other kinds of support to teachers as they seek to improve student learning and raise school test scores. Worded differently, parents should be careful to learn whether their child is attending a school where one test score can prevent their child from being promoted to the next grade, or one where there are several assessments. Education is high on the national political agenda, and this is true for most states as well. Consequently, there is a temptation for governors and legislators to want a "quick fix" for school improvement. The quickest way to improve scores is to focus entirely on test scores and not on the broader issue of improvement of instruction across the board. As in so many aspects of life, a quick fix will not be long lasting.

The narrow focus is often called test preparation or "prepping." This name is associated with so-called prep or independent schools where many students come from affluent families. These schools tend to focus on excellent instruction and use a variety of assessments to judge student performance. The "prepping" is done primarily after school or in other noninstructional time. Consequently, parents who are not familiar with prep schools are led to believe that if their school focuses on narrow test preparation they are like "prep" schools. This could hardly be further from the truth, and our common sense tells us that it is unlikely that well-educated, affluent parents would pay large fees for "quick fix" education that does not focus on problem solving, critical thinking, and other instructional approaches that are found in a broad and powerful curriculum.

Another issue for parents to discuss with school staff is the use of tests in the school. Standardized tests, those that states often require, are designed for comparisons of large groups of students. Some schools use the scores from these well-known tests to evaluate teachers and schools. For example, a realtor might suggest a parent would want to purchase a home in School A's attendance area, where the score on a statewide test is higher than in School B's, not taking into account the background of the students.

Another common mistake would be for a parent to ask that her child be moved from Miss Brown's room to Miss Black's room because she had seen that the reading, math, and language scores are higher in Miss Black's room. These required scores might hide the difference in the student backgrounds in the two rooms. Miss Brown may have many more students who do not speak English very well, for instance.

We hope these ideas will give parents some useful guidelines about what to emphasize in a parent involvement effort.

NOTES

1. Jeanne Allen, "What the Research Reveals About Charter Schools," http://www.edreform.com (accessed January 18, 2002).

2. Anne T. Henderson and Nancy Berla, "A New Generation of Evidence: The Family Is Critical to Student Achievement," Washington, D.C.: Center for Law and Education, June 1994.

3. Ronald Brownstein, "2 Gloomy Education Reports Should Serve as Guideposts for Reform Effort," *Los Angeles Times,* April 16, 2001.

4. —— "A New Generation of Evidence," *Los Angeles Times,* April 16, 2001.

5. California Department of Education, http://www.cde.ca.gov/fc/family/board.html (accessed April 18, 2002).

Chapter Three

Leadership and Charter Schools: Providing Purpose and Direction

Some purposes a charter school director should focus on include efforts to: (1) improve pupil learning; (2) increase learning opportunities for all pupils, with special emphasis on expanded learning experiences for pupils identified as academically low achieving; (3) encourage the use of different and innovative teaching methods; (4) create new professional opportunities for teachers, including the opportunity to be responsible for the learning program at the school site; (5) provide parents and students with expanded educational opportunities within the public school system without the constraints of traditional rules and structure; and (6) provide schools a way to shift from a rule-based to a performance-based system of accountability.

Key Concepts:
El Sol Santa Ana Science and Arts Academy
Dimensions of Leadership
Formal and Informal Types of Leadership
Setting Priorities and Goals
Three Components of Leadership
Conclusion

When I interviewed the person responsible for charter schools in my county he indicated the key area of leadership was understanding how charter schools are funded and how the monies they receive actually move through the administrative system. He also said that in his experience the best charter schools have a leader who gets help in fund-raising from the private sector. He calls these schools public/private schools.

Following is an example of a public charter school that raises additional funds beyond those generated by average daily attendance. Its key strategy is to use a 501(c) (3) tax exempt or nonprofit organization status called the Charter Development Alliance. The executive director is a skilled fund-raiser and leader. She raises funds from both the public and private sectors.

EL SOL SANTA ANA SCIENCE AND ARTS ACADEMY

El Sol is the first K–8 public school of its kind in Orange County, California; as a charter school, it demonstrates high levels of educational performance and accountability and provides school choice to parents and students. Emphasizing a mix of arts and sciences and two-way Spanish and English immersion, students are encouraged to gain hands-on experience and develop their interests through specialized courses, field trips, and community service. Its mission is "To provide a rigorous academic environment that prepares students for entrance into a college preparatory track at the high school of their choice and to create a culture of kindness, creativity, courage, and honesty that will permit our graduates to assume leadership roles in the 21st century."

A Recipe for Learning

El Sol believes that education, community, and diversity are integral parts of a child's character development. The educational structure is based on values and ethics, integrity, social responsibility, and positive identity. Through community collaboration, corporate involvement, and extended learning programs, El Sol embraces the multicultural heritage of its community and provides students with the opportunity to excel in the fields of art, science, and technology.

Education

The educational focus of El Sol is to offer a curriculum that is intellectually rich and focused on problem solving. Students enter high school with well-developed skills in reading, writing, mathematics, science, and a refined artistic ability. The dual immersion program, promoting bilingualism and biliteracy in English and Spanish, prepares students to excel in the global marketplace.

Community and Diversity

Located in downtown Santa Ana, California, El Sol celebrates the ethnic diversity of the population it serves and is committed to racial integration. Students learn the primary components of service, pride, respect, and tolerance, which are necessary for global citizenship. With an emphasis on community outreach and parental involvement, students have a strong support structure available at all times.

Faculty Planning

Fully credentialed teachers, who have demonstrated subject matter specialization and team teaching abilities, comprise El Sol's teaching staff. To keep the educational curriculum and methodology up-to-date with current trends and new technology, El Sol provides instructors with ongoing professional development opportunities.

DIMENSIONS OF LEADERSHIP

Implementing the twelve dimensions of leadership described below requires flexibility and insight on the part of the leader because at the same time one needs to take into account the expectations of the followers. Leadership is a process that begins where followers are and moves them toward more participative forms of leadership behaviors. In this sense, it follows good pedagogy in that learning begins where the learners are and leadership begins where the followers are, not where the leader would like them to be. The twelve dimensions of leadership are:

1. Instructional Leadership and Supervision—The leader must understand the instructional process and is well versed in a variety of instructional techniques; evaluates classroom instruction relative to teacher objectives and student performance.

2. Human Relations—Leader perceives the needs, concerns, and personal problems of others; recognizes conflicts; deals tactfully with persons from varying backgrounds.

3. Judgment—The leader reaches logical conclusions and makes quality decisions based on available and acquired information; exercises skills in identifying educational needs and setting priorities.

4. Organizational Ability—The leader organizes prior to an event and plans and schedules the work of others using resources optimally as well as considering societal and governmental constraints.

5. Educational Values—The leader possesses a well-reasoned educational philosophy; places high priority on needs and the welfare of students; is receptive to new ideas and change, but understands the need for stability.

6. Oral Communication—The leader clearly presents facts and ideas orally to individuals and groups using language that is precise and appropriate for the audience.

7. Written Communication—The leader expresses ideas concisely and precisely in writing.

8. Problem Analysis—The leader seeks and analyzes relevant information to determine important elements of a problem using information to distinguish problem significance.

9. Creativity—The leader generates and recognizes innovative solutions in work-related situations and exhibits an openness to new ideas demonstrating originality in developing policies and procedures.

10. Decisiveness—The leader recognizes the need for a decision and is willing to act quickly, to make decisions, render judgment, take action, and accept responsibility for consequences.

11. Group Leadership—The leader possesses and projects a sense of vision, exhibits confidence in self, involves others in accomplishing goals and solving problems, and recognizes when a group requires direction.

12. Resourcefulness—The leader actively attempts to influence events to achieve goals and considers work important to personal satisfaction. The leader also evaluates his or her own work, initiates activities, and takes action beyond the minimal requirements.[1]

Now contrast these generic dimensions of leadership with the following performance standards.[2] The director is able to: articulate a vision for the school; gain insight into the school members' hopes; apply understanding of important new trends; align reward systems with enduring values; facilitate direction setting; see the school as part of larger systems including the district and the community; foster innovation; and build on the specific strengths of staff.

Theoretically, leaders should be those who can do things best for a group or school. But in many schools today, the authorities are assigned to leadership roles even when there are others who have greater skills and insights about certain difficulties or problems. Researchers have identified six leadership styles of school administrators.

1. Teller—The leader shares what has been decided.
2. Seller—The leader shares the decision the leader made.
3. Tester—The leader shares a tentative decision to see the reaction.
4. Consulter—The leader seeks input prior to the decision.
5. Joint Efforter—The leader gets equal participation from members.
6. Abdicator—The leader delegates the decision to others.

School leaders today move between any of these styles in as many minutes with every action of the leader influenced by the relations between the leader and the staff, students, and parents. Every member of the staff has conscious and unconscious attitudes that tend to distort how they see and understand the messages of the director. It is important to look at oneself critically and upon self-reflection determine how much of the time you use a variety of these styles. Or do you tend to favor only one or two? How much of the time do you vary your style? Are any of these styles difficult for you to use? Ask fellow leaders to assess your styles and help you assess which styles work well and those that need work. Just becoming aware of and learning these different styles will help leaders work more effectively and successfully with their staff.

FORMAL AND INFORMAL TYPES OF LEADERSHIP

Leadership types fall into two categories: formal and informal. Both operate within the same organization. A director may successfully use both types depending on the situation or interaction. The school director has been designated by the state as the legal-rational authority in the school building. In this setting leadership is a formal type. But leadership is not just limited to the director and can be appropriately demonstrated in an informal style when assigned to those who can best serve the needs of people at particular times and places. In the classroom or teacher's lounge, many staff who are followers in faculty meetings become informal leaders, creating positive or negative feelings in other staff members. This ability of individuals to shift from the role of follower to that of leader is often observed in schools and corporate structures. Because of this, research into small group life has shown the leadership role as a shared function, rather than a quality assigned to a particular individual.

Nobody can be the "cool and competent" person all the time, yet this is often the front that leaders are asked to present in their everyday dealings with people. Some situations demand personal knowledge about students; others require skills and insights that are most developed by staff or counselors. Attention given to the social interaction and feelings evoked from teachers, parents, and students is a key responsibility for a leader to build trust and psychological security.

SETTING PRIORITIES AND GOALS

Your personal vision may well include high standards that are reachable. Standards that are too high or too low are ignored by school staff operationally, even though they may give lip service support to survive politically. Since your primary objective is often the widest possible success by your teachers, you may find the 10 Percent Discrepancy Model helpful.

Let us say you are working on the standard for reading at grade two. The test your district uses reports percentiles where 99 is the best possible. The mean score for grade two last year was 83. You subtract 83 from 99 and get a discrepancy of 16. You then take 10 percent of 16 and get 1.6 rounded to 2.0. You then add 83 and 2 for a new target of 85 for the coming year.

The advantage of this model is that it provides a realistic target. If your scores are low, the expected increase is large, and in fact larger gains are realistic in this situation. If you are a high scoring school, the gains expected are small, and, as you no doubt know, they are hard to reach. But all of these goal-setting strategies get you nowhere if you are not communicating well.

When engaged in conversation, consider these following questions:

- Do I like the person I am talking to? If I do, how well am I listening to what is being said?
- What am I saying on a nonverbal level, and how is this person responding? Is his or her body language and presence indicating that he or she trusts our conversation and me?
- Are either one of us acting as though we were not paying complete attention to each other? Are either one of us distracted by other concerns?
- If there are distractions, what am I doing to deal with these problems now?

THREE COMPONENTS OF LEADERSHIP

As we seek to understand the behavior of school staff and students, it is helpful to stand back and see if there are more general human behaviors that we can study in order to gain insight into what happens in schools. For administrators, power, authority, and evaluation are key concepts in this search for clarification. Power can be defined as a person's ability to get another person to do what one wants him or her to do. Authority, by contrast, is legitimized power. Power can be made legitimate by a member of the school, say a teacher, getting approval of a proposed action from one or more of three sources of legitimization. These approvals can come from one's superior, a majority of one's equals, or a majority of one's subordinates.

Evaluation is the use of one's authority, say as a director, to control staff behavior in an attempt to focus staff energy on priority goals and objectives. Effective schools are characterized by administrators who use their authority to carry out evaluations that help teachers to prioritize their goals and objectives and implement them successfully. You will read more about these concepts in chapter 15.

CONCLUSION

Some conclusions can be drawn about successful leadership. First, it begins with the identification of the needs and concerns of people and then proceeds, over time, to include levels of trust, involvement, and understanding. It is flexible and varies from situation to situation.

No one director has the skills, knowledge, insight, or information to provide effective leadership in every situation. Some situations call for specific knowledge and skills in specialized areas. Leadership often requires some aspects of counseling as well as teaching. When dangerous situations occur and members are confused and troubled, teachers and students may respond to school leaders without thinking much about it. If such leadership persists beyond these moments of crisis, an overly directive leadership style may develop. So we may say that the identification, authority, and functions of leaders are determined by the organizational structures of schools and the ongoing social processes that occur between teachers, parents, and students in their everyday work together. An analysis of effective school leadership shows that it is a shared rather than an individual effort, with all stakeholders sharing in the tasks at hand and working together to bring about the cohesiveness of the group.

NOTES

1. National Association of Elementary School Principals, *Streamlined Seminar* (Alexandria, Va.: National Association of Elementary School Principals, 1993).
2. Scott D. Thomson, ed., *Principals for Our Changing Schools* (Fairfax, Va.: National Policy Board for Educational Administration, 1993).

Chapter Four

Instructional Strategies for Community and Charter Schools

Activities that offer extrinsic rewards to students include strategies such as creation of an active and thoughtful learning setting, various types of visible recognition, creation of curricula that interest these students, setting clear goals, using positive reinforcement, cooperative learning, inducing a readiness to learn, encouraging student responses in class, teacher efficacy, self-concept development, tutorial services, flexible scheduling, and alternative schooling options. Two key instructional approaches that provide practical means for helping students who have not been succeeding in school are also introduced. Howard Gardner offers a focus on Multiple Intelligences, seen as appendix A, and Mel Levine directs our attention to the All Kinds of Minds or learning styles of students, discussed in appendix B.

Key Concepts:
Characteristics of Small Schools
Create an Active Learning Setting
Visible Recognition
Building an Interesting Curriculum
Set Clear Goals
Use Positive Reinforcement
Cooperative Learning
Induce Readiness to Learn
Encourage Student Responses
Teacher Efficacy
Alternative Instructional Strategies

CHARACTERISTICS OF SMALL SCHOOLS

In our experience, schools that are outstanding in delivering instruction to students often have the following characteristics:

- The teachers emphasize communication between teacher and students and between students and other students.
- Classrooms are organized to use heterogeneous groups rather than homogenous groups.
- Teachers use integrated curriculum where reading and science and social studies might be blended together, as art and mathematics can be.
- Instruction is given to small groups most often, and rarely to the whole class.
- Heterogeneous groups are constantly reformed into new ones.
- Teachers working with at-risk students begin instruction by asking lower order questions such as, "What color is this?" and later move to higher order questions.
- Classes seem like families, teachers treat students like sons and daughters.
- Writing goes on constantly with prompts such as "How did you feel?" and "What did you think?"
- In the early grades in schools with students who speak Spanish as their primary language, all writing is in Spanish; in the third and fourth grades there is a transition to English.
- Teachers are advocates for students and demanding of students.
- Teachers work autonomously and are clear about why they do everything; they argue strenuously with the principals to get to do what they want.
- Schools have good parent involvement.
- Teachers rarely refer students to remedial classes or special education; problems are handled in class, often with the help of other students.

CREATE AN ACTIVE LEARNING SETTING

Students need to be challenged by active learning opportunities and many different instructional strategies. Some students are easily bored, which makes them difficult to teach. It is therefore worth extra effort on the part of the teacher to set up an active learning environment. J. Kierstead suggests teachers focus on sharing responsibility with students for creating an active learning setting.[1]

While allowing students to operate independently through planning the use of their own time and by making decisions regarding pace, sequence, and content of the projects, the teacher never fully relinquishes control. Instead, the teacher establishes a set of rules, routines, and consequences that make it possible to monitor and guide what students are doing. For example, students are taught to follow a procedure that looks like the following:

1. Gather materials and equipment: They begin by gathering what they need to carry out their work. These resources are usually kept in a preestablished location, within easy reach of the students, so that they do not waste time searching for them or waiting for them to be handed out.
2. Carry out the task: Students know what is expected of them as they work. They understand the rules for general behavior such as where they may sit, how much talking and walking about is acceptable, and whether they may work with other students. Standards for the quality, quantity, and complexity of work have been established. They know where and how to get help. Peer tutors or a student "buddy system" encourage them to share information and ideas with fellow students.
3. Have work checked and signed off: Students are responsible for asking the teacher to check and sign off on their work upon completion of all or a predetermined portion of a project. At this point, they receive specific feedback and may be required to make a correction or expand the work and then return for another check before the teacher completely signs off on it.
4. Record that work is complete: Once the teacher has made the final check, the student indicates by a visual signal (usually by checking off on a class chart) that his or her task is complete. This allows the teacher to see, at a glance, how far each student has progressed during the project period.

5. Turn in completed work: Students usually place completed work in a central location so the teacher can look through it outside class time. This allows the teacher to assess student work and plan which students should receive special attention during the next project period.
6. Return materials and equipment: Students know how to care for and return materials and equipment to storage areas so that they remain in good condition.
7. Begin another activity: The student knows what to do once the first portion of a project is complete.

In addition to creation of an active learning environment, teachers should consider questioning strategies that encourage a "thoughtful classroom." This is especially important for students with poor self-images who have not been "quick" enough to play an active role in most classes in the past.

When teachers rely on questions with short, correct answers and call on students with their hands raised, they are encouraging recall in some students and ignoring others entirely. In contrast, teachers should ask questions that have a range of appropriate responses, all of which require some explanation of the student's thinking; wait five to ten seconds for all students to think; and then call on students without anyone raising hands. By doing this, several important purposes are accomplished: All students know they are expected to think; they are given the time and silence to think; and all students must be ready to communicate their thoughts.

VISIBLE RECOGNITION

The following ideas offer extrinsic rewards to the potential dropout who may place little or no intrinsic value on education. These activities could have a positive effect by encouraging students to attend school.

- Award the most improved attenders a certificate of recognition.
- Provide special field trips for improved attenders.
- Reward improved attenders with paperback books.
- Hold a drawing for special prizes donated from local businesses open to students with the greatest improvement in attendance. Ask businesses to

provide reduced price coupons for products and services that students like.

- Send letters of commendation home to parents of students with excellent improvement in attendance.
- Provide special lunchtime and end-of-school parties for students with improved attendance.
- Allow students with the greatest improvement in attendance to opt out of some examinations; base grades on work in class.
- Publicize attendance awards such as the above in your local newspaper; seek television coverage for attractive attendance-oriented events. Reward and publicize schools/classrooms with the greatest improvement in attendance and related issues like reduction in tardiness.
- Schedule special assemblies and other attractive events on Mondays and Fridays when students are often absent.

Getting students to come to school and to stay in school are critical steps in improving attendance and instruction. Many schools are using computerized attendance programs that help administrators routinize parent contact by automating the personalized letters that are mailed to students' homes. Some programs offer period-by-period attendance record keeping as well. Making student records easy to access and use takes time and money, but improved attendance can result from these efforts.

BUILDING AN INTERESTING CURRICULUM

Students are motivated in school when their studies relate to topics that have real interest to them. Here are some ideas to help establish an interesting curriculum program:

- Use questionnaires to identify general and specific interests of students.
- Observe what students do in their free time to guide you to their real interests. Plan surprise activities and events. Use instructional games, especially those involving the computer.
- Consider how student interests can be integrated into the curriculum as starting points of lessons, examples of concepts, and applications of skills they have learned.

- Individualize by providing choices, so students have more opportunities to select assignments, activities, or projects that are interesting to them.

SET CLEAR GOALS

Students will move toward goals when they know what the goals are. The goals need to be specific, challenging, and communicated as expectations for the results of learning. Listed are some ideas to implement this in a school setting:

- Involve students in some of the goal setting for the class and for themselves individually.
- State objectives in behavioral terms so you can measure students' progress and find out which of your approaches work best.
- Communicate your goals and objectives to students before each lesson, orally or in writing.
- Design new lessons that take advantage of your approaches that prove to be most effective.

USE POSITIVE REINFORCEMENT

Positive reinforcement can be used as a powerful extrinsic motivator. Effective employment of reinforcement strategies requires careful reading of the models, skill, and understanding in establishing them, and patience and practice to finally refine them so they work for you. Here are some ideas to give students that reinforcement:

- List the specific things students do that you want to reinforce so you can work consistently and systematically toward rewarding them for the appropriate behaviors.
- Use verbal and nonverbal reinforcers immediately after movement toward your target behaviors on the part of your students.
- Remind students of specific academic objectives or social behaviors that you will be looking for, and then acknowledge them and show your appreciation for the examples you see.

• Give specific praise for what you can find that is correct and successful in students' work.

COOPERATIVE LEARNING

Motivation can be enhanced by actively teaching students how to cooperate in achieving academic goals. Cooperation can build supportive relationships and group morale as well as increasing student motivation. Here are some ideas:

• Assign learning tasks to students in heterogeneous pairs, triads, or small groups. Group as well as individual grades and recognition may be given.
• Develop a "skill bank" of student experts where, to the extent possible, every student is expert at something and is asked to help other students.
• Teach small group skills directly. Let effective groups discuss how they work so they can serve as models to the other groups.
• Have students evaluate their own group processes and effectiveness; discuss these results in class when it is appropriate.

INDUCE READINESS TO LEARN

Effective teacher-motivators plan specific instructional activities that create interest in a topic about to be taught. Inducing readiness to learn requires planning and imagination. Try to build on the natural power of student anticipation. Here are some methods to try:

• Ask thought-provoking questions that can only be answered in an activity that follows.
• Start with an event in school or community life and work back to the topic of the lesson.
• Use cartoons, pictures, newspaper headlines, taped excerpts from television programs, records, computer activities, and other strategies to liven up class and get students' attention.
• Design specific activities to introduce lessons and then check to see if student progress is greater than it is for lessons where you have not done this.

ENCOURAGE STUDENT RESPONSES

Students need to be encouraged to respond to questions and to interact with one another during most lessons. Dropout-prone students are often quiet and special effort needs to be made to draw them out in class. If you as a teacher do not feel you are effective with these students, work with the administrators to put fewer of them in your classes until you have improved your skills (see the next section on "Teacher Efficacy") in working with them. Here are some ideas to build your skills:

- Ask students questions to find out what they know and do not know. Avoid questions that tend to trap, trick, or punish students. Allow students to demonstrate what they know, believe, and value.
- Give more "wait time" (time the teacher waits for slower students to react) to questions you ask. You may be pleased at the responses of students who never get recognized if you don't consciously wait for them.
- Ask questions that you do not know how to answer. About one in four dropout-prone students is gifted (and very bored) and this gives students an opportunity to explain things they know about to you and the class.
- Suspend judgment when students respond to queries. Instead of saying "right" or "not quite," move on and gather several responses before commenting.

These principles of motivation, when used by a competent teacher, can help turn routine instruction into exciting teaching. The thrill of catching the interest of a formerly apathetic student is a sweet memory for years to come.

TEACHER EFFICACY

High-efficacy teachers create a more positive classroom climate than do low-efficacy teachers. They are less likely to punish students or scold them, and at the same time, more likely to accept their feelings and ideas than is true for low-efficacy peers. High-efficacy teachers also are more likely to include all students in their class in instruction and seatwork activities than is true for their counterparts. Administrators might seek to schedule, to the extent possible, dropout-prone students into the classes of high-efficacy teachers. In order to be fair to the high-efficacy teachers who are receiving the difficult students to teach, the low-efficacy teachers could be asked to participate in training activities that help them improve classroom climate, strengthen human relations skills, increase their interest in motivating weak students, and strengthen their instructional skills through clinical supervision and similar strategies.

Administrators could improve the organization of schools and teacher effectiveness by encouraging collaborative planning between teachers who instruct the same dropout-prone students, by involving these teachers in key decisions that affect their problem students, and by seeking special funding that allows the teachers release time and needed resources to meet the special needs of students they have identified in their collaborative planning.

ALTERNATIVE INSTRUCTIONAL STRATEGIES

Some students are not successful in a regular classroom setting but they can work effectively in less formal environments. They often need to be involved in a program to improve their self-awareness and self-esteem in order to develop a positive attitude about pursuing their education. Emphasis may be given to building a feeling of self-worth through the arts, for example, or wherever a sympathetic teacher is willing to give this effort their special attention. Tutorial strategies can use other students to help those likely to drop out. Similarly, peer counseling efforts have been organized in scores of districts to help students learn how to work with substance-abusing students. Use of retired persons as volunteers in classrooms and as tutors has been a successful strategy in some districts, and college students who are not as active socially as they would like to be make excellent candidates for cross-age tutoring of secondary students. Retired teachers are another fine group to approach when a school is looking for tutors for students with special needs.

Student tutors can be recommended by their teachers on the basis of responsibility, conscientiousness, and reliability. During training sessions, tutors learn their responsibilities, positive tutor behavior, and the content of their "skill-based" reading and math tutoring units in a successful program of matching tutors and tutees on a one-to-one basis for the entire year. Tutoring sessions range from thirty minutes twice a week to thirty or forty minutes five times a week. Tutors meet once per month to share insights and problems. At least twice per month, the trainer meets individually with each tutor to discuss the progress of the tutee. A network of referrals among tutor, teacher, and trainer keep everyone working together. Thorough written evaluations take place at the end of the year. The program changes, grows, and improves each year.

Successful teachers often involve students with issues they see as vital; spend time discussing human differences; teach major concepts and general principles; involve students in planning what they will be doing; apply ideals such as fairness, equity, and justice; and involve students in real-life experiences.

Alternative schooling of many types appears attractive to some students. Some of the options include work experience, independent study of various designs, opportunity classes aimed at special interests, and a variety of nontraditional experiences that allow teachers and students to operate in a casual environment. Teachers need to be interested in the personal lives of these students and their families and be willing to be involved in the myriad personal problems that fill them in order to move toward success in their academic efforts.

NOTE

1. J. Kierstead, "How Teachers Manage Individual and Small Group Work in Active Classrooms," *Educational Leadership* 44 (October 1986).

Chapter Five

Understanding and Managing Conflict in Small, Highly Democratic Schools

Almost by definition the parents, students, and staff of a small school, seeking to be more personal and democratic than a standard public school, are going to care intensely about many issues. For example, they will want to discuss how the school is to be governed, not once but many times. They will be very interested in what the rules are and how and by whom they will be enforced. The curriculum may be a topic of continuing debate, long after it is "approved." Sarason identifies two areas that generate conflict in newly established schools. These are the impact of new people as they express their ideas and concerns, and how the school will be governed.[1] Other topics that will generate strong emotional reactions include: funding for key projects; trouble attracting and keeping students; difficulty in finding staff suited to the school's program; disagreements over what the curriculum should be; and difficulty in obtaining an appropriate school site. The director plays a key role in establishing an understanding of the rules for managing the conflict that is part of life for those who care deeply about these issues.

Key Concepts:
Developing a Positive Work Climate
Hiring of New Staff
Using a Range of Incentives
The Confrontation Process
What to Expect
General Behavioral Guidelines for Staff

One strategy found to be helpful in setting the rules for debate and discussion is to introduce the idea of conceptual levels for a topic. For instance, students may expect the director and teachers to offer more "second chances" when rules are broken than would be true in a large public school. Probation and expulsion are words that can lead to violent reactions. When a topic that elicits fiery reactions is perceived, the director may explain that looking at the issue from a higher or more abstract level can make it easier to discuss. Probation, expulsion, and rules in general can be looked at as part of the authority structure of an organization. That is, what means have been established to see that everyone is treated fairly and in an objective manner? This requires that certain people be appointed to guide the work of the school and to see that the instruction that takes place is successful.

The director might lead speakers to focus on an imaginary school, for instance, rather than letting individuals confront each other on a personal basis. Once the value of other people's experience in other settings is established, understandings from research can be used as a guide.

DEVELOPING A POSITIVE WORK CLIMATE

The job of a principal as an effective manager of human relations includes several aspects that range from identifying the need for personnel, defining the job to be done, interviewing and hiring, supervising, evaluating, and providing professional growth opportunities. Managing all of these while keeping a vision and focus on the established mission is extremely important in developing a positive work climate.

What characteristics can be seen in a positive work climate? First and foremost is a feeling that all who come to your school know they are welcome and that it is truly a place where all who attend can and do learn. There is also a feeling of caring, safety, and security in your school. It is not enough just for students' needs to be met for a school to be successful, but also for those who constantly work and give of themselves to feel valued and appreciated. For students, staff, and parents to be comfortable at school, the climate must breathe success and be welcoming.

The site administrator must at all times understand the feeling tone of the staff, students, and parents and support them. Support is given by carefully managing all of the resources at the school. This means ensuring ample supplies and materials, as well as having a campus facility that is well maintained, clean, and safe. Support is also demonstrated in having a thorough understanding of scheduling of students and staff to meet all needs. These are essential elements important to the establishment of a positive feeling tone and demonstration of support.

HIRING OF NEW STAFF

As director another major responsibility is the effective hiring of new staff who share beliefs and attitudes toward education and student success similar to the staff presently at the school. Being visible in the classrooms on a regular basis, attending all school functions, and being actively involved on campus models are critical. Many administrators say they have an open door policy. If that is so, the significant question is, Just how accessible are you? Do you "walk your talk"? The key is to be "authentic" in your dealings with the entire school community. You must invest more than just a passing interest with staff by knowing their goals and striving at all costs to nurture and support them. For a positive working relationship, the feeling tone must exist that any job you would ask someone else to do you would be willing to do yourself. This applies to all job classifications and descriptions, not just for the teachers, but for classified staff, parents, and students. The modeled message must be that you are willing, and you will roll up your sleeves to work together in all areas and for all causes. You understand this, you believe it, and you invest your time and resources wherever the need occurs to see it will happen. This might even be arranging for an after-school program, which, while you don't totally agree with it, you don't find it in opposition with any identified school goals, so you do it.

You work to develop congruence between individual needs and the organizational roles and expectations. You view your teachers as valuable resources who must be nurtured and developed. By being such, you expect them to meet the objectives outlined in your school plan, striving always to do what is best for the students.

We all recognize the effectiveness of rewards and punishment in the workplace. Just as in the classroom setting, rules are determined with appropriate rewards and consequences, incentives for adults works well too. Teachers need incentives just as much as auto salespeople do. The use of positive reinforcement is bound to reap a good harvest down the road via teacher support and also will allow for staff to become more motivated in the classroom.

USING A RANGE OF INCENTIVES

A range of incentives to use with employees as well as various types of sanctioning approaches can be successfully used in schools. The first type of reward incentive would be where every teacher is rewarded equally regardless of performance. This often occurs purely for the sake of building positive morale and for rewarding the works of the "whole." Sometimes it can be used because an administrator is not comfortable in making differential rewards either because he or she lacks understanding and knowledge of the staff and their needs or feels all staff must be treated equally to be fair and to show no partiality. If the same reward is used for all, it should be for a specific purpose or event. For example, to welcome staff back to school at the beginning of the year or for Teacher Appreciation Day. But the "generic" type of rewarding should be avoided when it is not meaningful or warranted, for that type of rewarding can be perceived as being equal to not being recognized at all.

A second type of approach is when teachers are rewarded randomly in a casual manner, often based on feedback from other staff members or from the director's own observations. This is effective when a staff member has gone above and beyond in organizing a grade-level performance or come to the rescue of a colleague at a special time. But again, the display of public recognition should be something that supports the hard work and appreciation for a job well done. Rewards repeatedly to certain individuals gives a sense of favoritism that only certain ones are members of the "distinguished club." That will destroy morale in a very short time. School staff are perceptive about who should get what and when.

Teachers need to be given praise for a job well done. If they feel their work is not appreciated, their performance will diminish as they may feel that they are not adequately recognized. Each teacher brings to the position and classroom unique styles, talents, and methods, and each needs to be appreciated individually. How you recognize these individuals should depend on their job performance as well as what makes them feel comfortable or motivated to improve. A director must be aware that individual staff members have differing value orientations and may also respond differently to the various positive sanctions of organizational life. For one staff member, public praise at a staff meeting might be the best incentive, while for another, that might embarrass them to no end and a private or personal note of thanks might be most effective. You need to be sensitive to each individual and how he or she views him- or herself in relation to his or her job on campus.

It is a good idea to vary the reward system. Recognizing the staff with a weekly drawing can become routine and lose its excitement. For one staff meeting bring in some ice cream sundaes or even cancel the meeting during an extra busy week. When all staff are treated as professionals with respect and confidence and the belief that they are knowledgeable about the tasks for which they are responsible, that in and of itself can do a tremendous job in building a positive work climate. Likewise, support with resources and opportunities to grow professionally will help create a positive climate. Just setting a relaxed tone where people can flourish can often be reward enough. Moreover, remember to recognize all staff. Keeping the custodian happy tends to keep everyone happy!

Through a positive environment you can provide more readiness for growth and potential for change. The atmosphere will be more conducive to helping staff reach their established goals as well as open up discussion at planning conferences and lesson observations. It is meaningful to show you are concerned with individual staff members' sense of belonging and security within faculty groups.

Creating a balance between classified staff, certified staff, and parents is extremely important in keeping a welcome feeling tone. Establishment of an environment where staff members do not feel they are outside the network of teachers is crucial. This can be done by encouraging social participation in outside events and by creating activities where teachers interact with other staff members. Try to be available for counsel and advice as well.

THE CONFRONTATION PROCESS

One of the most difficult tasks of a teacher is that of confronting problematic behavior. In fact, confronting students can be so difficult at times that teachers are often tempted to ignore the problem, hoping it will go away. Unfortunately, the opposite is true. Especially if the problem is that of substance abuse.

Teachers who fail to confront their students can logically expect one or more of the following to occur:

- The problem will become worse.
- There will be a drop in class morale.
- The student will lose respect for the teacher.
- The class will probably develop an informal leader.
- There will be a drop in overall class performance.
- The teacher's job will become more difficult.

Inappropriately addressing behaviors can have a negative impact on both the student and class in general. The following guidelines should be met to help ensure a successful exchange:

- Meet with the student as soon as possible after the incident or behavior has been observed. However, never confront a student while still angry (timing).
- Develop a plan or outline to ensure that you cover everything you want to discuss.
- Choose a private, neutral location for your talk.
- Hold all calls. Keep interruptions to a minimum.
- Prepare yourself for the worst.
- Explain the reason for your meeting (be tactful, but direct).
- Demonstrate your concern for both the student and his or her behavior.

WHAT TO EXPECT

There are four stages of crisis management: (1) anger; (2) denial; (3) defensive attitude; (4) personal problems. There are many ways you can react, as listed here:

- Actively listen to your student.
- Remain calm.
- Return to the reason for the confrontation (behavior or incident).
- Reiterate your concerns.
- Offer your or another's assistance if appropriate.
- Make your expectations of the student's future behavior clear.
- End the meeting on a positive note. "I have faith in you, I know you can do this," etc.
- Follow through!

Remember that the three most important traits or qualities a teacher can possess when dealing with problem behavior are: concern, consistency, and follow-through.

GENERAL BEHAVIORAL GUIDELINES FOR STAFF

Here are a number of guidelines for general behavior of staff members:

- Do maintain full supervision over every student in your charge at all times.
- Do make your presence known by your interested alertness and initiative and by taking action when needed.
- Do remain objective, fair, and consistent in dealing with your students.
- Do call for help or ask instructions for handling an explosive situation before it gets out of control.
- Do watch your language, dress, and deportment. The students are watching and modeling after you.
- Do assume your share of responsibility for the behavior of the entire school population.

Here are a number of behaviors you will want to avoid:

- Do not leave any student or group of students unsupervised at any time, anywhere.
- Do not forget that slackening supervision means surrendering control.

- Do not attempt to handle alone any emergency that is beyond your resources.
- Do not be a poor model for students by your dress, language, or behavior.
- Do not limit your supervision to those in your immediate care. You are a staff member representing the entire school.

NOTE

1. S. Sarason, *The Creation of Settings and the Future Societies* (Cambridge, Mass.: Brookline Books, 1988).

Chapter Six

Introducing Change within the School

An important part of organizational change is effectively identifying student needs. To help people move toward understanding and bring an organization to effective change one needs to place a great deal of emphasis on two key factors: personal interactions and communication skills. The director needs to become familiar with a number of conceptual planning models in order to help solve problems where planning can make the difference within the school organization.

Organizations reacting to pressures for initiating and responding to change must develop strategies of change. Several recent studies and information from educators and researchers are shared in this chapter, as well as ideas for implementing and sustaining change in schools to transform them into successful learning organizations.

Key Concepts:
Change Is Continuous
Change Starts with a Decision to Move toward a New Objective
The Identifiable Mechanisms for Making Change
The ABCs for Creating the Environment for Change

CHANGE IS CONTINUOUS

Change must be looked at as constant and something that must be dealt with in a proactive and productive manner. Discontent is the mother of progress. Change in education, especially over the past thirty years, has been as consistent and predictable as the coming of each new month. From an historical perspective, with the emergence of *Sputnik* came the space race of the 1960s. The effect of the space race on education was support for increased funding for the development of curriculum and individualized instruction to enable the United States to be "first" and "competitive" in the fields of math and science. The 1970s brought the realization that the changes of the 1960s were not bringing the successful results that had been hoped for. By the end of the 1970s the effective schools movement began to report that while there were effective schools that did make a positive difference, a number of reports such as *A Nation at Risk*, the *Paideia Proposal*, as well as the works of John Goodlad and Ted Sizer all intensified the movement for harder content, stricter course requirements, and a longer school year. This push for educational excellence was labeled the first wave of reform.

Restructuring, the term of the late 1980s, has been called the second wave of school reform. Rather than focusing on easily quantifiable changes such as increased enrollments in advanced classes, the second wave sought to change the organizational structure of decision making in public schools. The restructuring movement and the "effective schools approach" both borrow concepts from a similar movement in business management that focuses on participative management and Japanese business practices. The second wave stresses teacher empowerment and bottom-up communication and reform. For most theorists who support restructuring, this means reforms that increase the responsibilities of teachers, giving them greater voice in decision making. The movement has been criticized by some as giving teachers more power than they were able to gain at the bargaining table or the picket line. Another focus of this approach has been on site-based decision making rather than centralized decisions made at the school district office.

In addition to these two waves another reform movement has broken on the educational scene; school-linked social services for students and their families. Some theorists have labeled this a third wave. This reform is an effort to provide to children and their families social services that they may need in an integrated and collaborative fashion. Parent involvement helps increase student performance, and low-income parents ask for social services when given the opportunity. It requires the school to work cooperatively with a variety of public and private agencies to treat the child and family holistically. This third wave is the result of numerous factors including divorce, blended families, low incomes, inadequate housing, lack of basic needs, chemical abuse problems, unemployment, emotional instability, grandparents raising their grandchildren, spousal incarceration, lack of a support system, putting career first and children second, trying to live through kids, and the list goes on. Students in our schools today represent a multitude of diversities and have multiple factors affecting their achievement. This effort to reach into the community has increased the public's willingness to support new "community-based" schools, such as charter schools and voucher schools. These represent changes that must be addressed and responded to.

CHANGE STARTS WITH A DECISION TO MOVE TOWARD A NEW OBJECTIVE

Once a decision for change has been made, a better ability to go on may be created. Change and related improvement involve two key components, and both must be addressed for a successful result to occur. First, skills must be acquired, and second, participants must come to believe improvement is possible. Both are required for change to be initiated and sustained. It doesn't necessarily matter which occurs first, but usually if the belief is there, the skills are easier to acquire. If the skills are learned, but the belief is lacking, change will not happen. Improvement activities must be supported by community, district, and state efforts to be sustained. A site director cannot bring about change unless it involves all who will be involved with the change. At present, more emphasis is currently being given to the need for collaboration and allowing sufficient time for the change to occur and be sustained.

Adequate time must be allowed for people to get in touch with their visions and values and to see how they fit in and relate to the proposed change. Successful change needs to be viewed as an incremental process. Where this is not true, a paradigm shift must be made to meet the challenges and needs of tomorrow. This happens by creating a new mind-set for change. The instructors will need to realize that change is constant and that administrators do not have all the answers. It is important to create a school with a learning environment that is thinking and action oriented, continually evolving, growing, and changing! The school learning organization needs to seek out collaboration, accountability, planning, and decision-making strategies. The phrase "the only constant is change" holds true especially for effective schools of today and the role of the director. One of the positive aspects of being a site administrator is that every day can be different with new adventures and challenges, each requiring decisions to be made. The variables that affect managing a school and delivering quality education to students are many. Because of the vast variety of factors to consider, change presents itself differently. There are those times where decisions need to be made immediately and change is a priority. There are also times when change is a planned process that will take longer to implement. It is important that the administrator be a leader who can effectively react and respond to the pressures that accompany change. It is the responsibility of the director to develop a variety of strategies that can be initiated to enable the learning organization to respond to situations and bring about necessary change.

Some education theorists have suggested that for effective and meaningful education to take place in the United States, not only must schools change, but, so too, must our perceptions of school. When most parents visit schools, they are looking at the past, not the future.

To those on the outside, each school year may seem to be the same. Students come and students go, but teaching is the same! To those within the school setting there are numerous factors that make each year very different. At the beginning of the year, there are staff changes, changes in the student population, changes in curriculum, changes in grade levels, changes in programs. Loss of funds and loss of programs are added responsibilities with which school personnel must deal. There may also be changes at the district level that impact the school, or even changes within the parent organization requiring time to educate and orient. But the changes do not just occur at the beginning of the year. They continue throughout the year.

There are also changes in the physical plant, such as the addition of portable classrooms because enrollment has increased. Projections in enrollment and projections for staffing are just projections. Real numbers are not known until the students show up. Creating classroom lists and new teacher position assignments are just a few of the "known" and "to be expected" changes with which an administrator must deal. One move of one faculty member can create a domino effect that brings change to numerous people and students. If the premise is true that children and their education is the first and top priority, all decisions made must be based on what is best for these students. That alone creates difficulties in the change process, as so many factors are dependent on each small decision.

In instruction, teachers constantly try to present conceptual models to help students learn and achieve. Isn't it also then appropriate that a model be suggested for teachers to help bring about change in behaviors and ideas of the staff? The model of change examined here is based on the assumption that individuals can change their behavior in a systematic fashion if there is strong motivation and support from what we call our "significant other." A significant other in this case is any person a teacher can turn to for advice and sympathy when there are problems or important decisions to be made, either in the work setting or at home. It might be your spouse or the teacher down the hall.

THE IDENTIFIABLE MECHANISMS
FOR MAKING CHANGE

There are three stages for making change. The first is unfreezing or creating the motivation for change. The second is changing when one develops new responses based on new information received, and the third is refreezing. This is when the change is internalized or stabilized and becomes integrated in one's thinking processes. Each stage is a result of the individual's response to certain activities that serve as the conduits to produce change.

When unfreezing occurs, a person has an emotional or attitudinal shift that moves him or her to a new point of readiness for change. This can occur through a lack of confirmation of one's previously operating self-image. An example of unfreezing would be if a teacher had been uncomfortable teaching science, but now a new science framework has been implemented and a new curriculum in science is on the horizon. This teacher might become ready to make a change through the feelings of inadequacy or failure seen in her- or himself. Unfreezing may also occur through the removal of self-imposed barriers that have prevented change.

Two types of attitudes, both cognitive and emotional, can be at play during this time of readiness to accept change. Cognitive attitudes are not deeply ingrained and are susceptible to being altered by new information. Emotional attitudes connect perceptions to values and therefore are not as easily changed. For example, if you have an "antitechnology" value, you probably would not read a book on computer applications. On the other hand, you may not be a technologist, but you may be willing to read the arguments for using handheld computers if you see the value of using computers as tools to access and acquire information. Therefore, the new information you obtain may change your behavior and your attitudes. Change occurs when a person locates information from a source deemed credible and that enables that person to redefine the situation in new terms that are sensible, enabling the person to alter his or her behavior.

The following exercise will help you determine your own stage of unfreezing and readiness to change.

THE ABC'S FOR CREATING
THE ENVIRONMENT FOR CHANGE

For each of the ABCs listed below, record the steps you need to create the process of change you desire. In order to create a readiness for change I will:

- Analyze my behavior and see if I find some inadequacy in the area of concern;
- Broaden my frame of reference;
- Change my criteria for making a judgment;
- Do my best to remove a barrier that is preventing change;
- Examine what other teachers I respect are doing in order to see new possibilities;
- Follow through on using new definitions of terms;
- Guide conversation with significant others to discussion of the need to change;
- Help identify questionable assumptions and beliefs;
- Identify alternatives that make sense for me;
- Jot down an alternative made by the decision to change.

To assist in integrating these new behaviors it is important to (1) work to see that the new behavior and attitudes are integrated in a thoughtful way with your general behavior and attitudes; (2) ask your friends to help you see if your new behavior and attitudes are on target and are taking you where you want to go; (3) consider the "unfrozen" feelings of new behaviors and attitudes so you can start over and do a better job integrating the new behaviors and attitudes with the old. You will find as you consider the new thoughts that "refreezing" has occurred as you begin to integrate these new responses and information into your personality and into significant personal relationships. You will find that with this process, after change has occurred, you become comfortable with your new approach to a situation.

Chapter Seven

Establishing a Plan to Promote Change and Agreement within the School Organization

Establishing agreement within the school is a task easier said than done in a highly participative environment. Some staff may feel that in a small school, little planning is needed. This is far from the truth. It is difficult to build trust where each staff member wants to have input into many issues, unlike a large school where most staff take interest in just a few issues. The key to building agreement and trust may be the use of long-range planning. There are few surprises to lower trust levels if real effort is used to implement planning strategies. These efforts can help with both routine and not-so-routine changes that affect schools.

Key Concepts:
Continuous Organizational Renewal
Types of School Plans

CONTINUOUS ORGANIZATIONAL RENEWAL

Establishing a school plan creates the opportunity for continuous organizational renewal at a school site. Through the process of self-study and continual assessment, renewal and improvement can occur, which will bring about successful and permanent change. The planning process is as continuous as is change itself. Both planning and change work in tandem, for with an effective planning process, one with objectives clearly outlined and defined, the process of change can be much easier to facilitate.

Problem-solving planning, especially when teams of school staff are involved to develop ownership, is an effective tool in school management. There are three steps in the process. First, analyze the problem, second, develop and select appropriate strategies to use, and third, implement the proposed solution or solutions. The analytic step of problem solving is most complex because it can be very difficult at times to identify the actual problem and not a surface manifestation of it. For example, in studying poor attendance one is tempted to suggest an attendance software program that is easy to obtain and implement, rather than probing deeper to find that the curriculum has no "career connection" to motivate students who are interested in preparing for jobs.

Planning for change within a school can be most successful if research that has been conducted on the subject is implemented. Current research indicates there are eight techniques characteristic of successful interventions: (1) involving key members; (2) clarifying goals, theories, and technology used to bring about the change; (3) moving from structured activities such as training a whole group on a topic to the application of new techniques, perhaps individualizing training and skill development depending on the needs of individuals; (4) moving from shared information to action planning; (5) rotating subgroup membership so everyone sees the whole picture. This is especially effective in a school setting where quite often teachers work in intragrade-level groups rather than in intergrade-level groups; (6) treating all ranks equally. This means giving as much of a voice to the classified staff as to the certificated. On many campuses classified staff do not attend staff meetings. However, to bring about change that involves all stakeholders of a school, they must all be included in providing a voice to the decisions made and to the discussions held; (7) trying new organizational structures as needed, such as assigning roles and responsibilities to a variety of stakeholders. Quite often the same people volunteer, and because it is easier, a director allows that to occur. Provide opportunities for traditional roles to change and rotate among the staff; (8) planning to continue your efforts into the future.

As with all successful organizations, establishment of a workable ongoing plan is essential to bringing about the continued changes that need to occur at all schools. The planning process and resulting actual school plan become the road map for enabling a school to achieve the established goals and to reach the tenets addressed in the school mission statement.

TYPES OF SCHOOL PLANS

In developing a school plan, there are basically three types of plans that can be distinguished by the amount of time in the future for which you are focusing. The first is a plan to solve a problem that has been identified and is short in duration, perhaps only one month. This type of planning is the shortest in terms of planning and implementation. It might be to resolve a scheduling conflict or staff development in-service.

The second type is the creation of an operational plan, which is the primary school plan that takes all staff, students, and parents through the school year. This second plan, often referred to as a "plan of action," has many dimensions to it including the planning of school activities and events for the next school year, as well as a staff development plan, a calendar for the year, and attendance and reporting periods. This plan is revised and rewritten annually.

The third type is that of a long-range or strategic plan, which would be for a period of many years, perhaps three to four. Many schools involved in a formal school improvement process revise the yearly planning process every three or four years in conjunction with developing the strategic plan.

Strategic plans are longer in duration, which while tending to be the most costly in staff time, have the greatest potential benefits. In effective planning, it is important to understand the difference between long-range planning and strategic planning. Long-range planning is based on the notion that things in the future will be just as they are now—a static theory. Strategic planning is based on the idea that we must try to predict how the future will be based on such factors as shifts in enrollment and changes in state and local funding levels. Hence, strategic planning usually involves the use of a spreadsheet on a computer so time can be spent estimating the impact of budget adjustments both up and down in increments from 1 percent to 10 percent. A spreadsheet provides the opportunity to look at numeric forecasts. Strategic planning provides economic forecasting with attention to numerical data and percentage increases projected over the next few years. Problem-solving planning was defined above.

One can understand schools more readily by learning to use metaphors for characteristics comprising the organizational structure. For example, if one thinks of the school organization as a machine with interlocking parts, where when all the precision parts interlock and work smoothly—very much like the division of tasks—the performance can be optimal.

A key task of a site administrator in preparing a school to respond to needed changes is to perfect the approach needed to articulate major goals and priorities to staff and community. To be effective, expectations must be consistent with those of the significant stakeholders. If they are not, it is essential to bring the stakeholders up to the administration's knowledge level. Or even better yet, to ask the question, "Why aren't the stakeholders up to the same level and apprised of the same information?" By having knowledge of the key people and how they react, what they believe, and how they approach tasks to be accomplished, effective plans can be more easily established.

Chapter Eight

Parent Involvement Using Shared Decision Making

Comprehensive parent involvement treats parents as stakeholders. Parents are involved in key decisions and attend staff meetings. This leads school staff to think of parents as equals and parents to feel supported by the staff and administration. This leads quite naturally to sharing key decisions with parents, which makes sense since their support leads to improved student achievement.

Key Concepts:
What Is Shared Decision Making?
Steps in the Decision Process
Decision-Making Model
Other Decision-Making Processes
Who Makes the Decision?
Ways to Facilitate Decision Making
Site-Based Decision Making
Clear, Frequent, and Concise Communication

WHAT IS SHARED DECISION MAKING?

Shared decision making is a process that includes the input of parents, teachers, administrators, community members, and often, students in decisions about how a school operates. Charter schools typically use this practice. School-based management allows those who are most aware of the educational needs of the school to help direct it. In a school-based management system, shared decision making shifts the power from a central authority, such as one individual or a school board, to a broader representation, such as a council or "team." School management becomes a shared responsibility, although the school or governing board is still legally responsible for the decisions made. Many educators believe that parent representation in key decisions in their child's school is preferable to offering them vouchers and is more likely to lead to an excellent education.

Some areas of parent involvement in decision making would include: after-school activities; budget issues; class size; curriculum/textbook selection; disciplinary procedures; length of school day/year; long-range planning; school lunch programs; special programs (gifted, remedial, dropout); staff evaluation/retention student assessment; training for staff, parents, and community members; and transportation. Parents need to know not only what areas of school life they can be usefully involved in, but how decisions are made in a school that seeks to welcome parent input.

STEPS IN THE DECISION PROCESS

Initial aspects of effective decision making including the choice of a useful decision model that fits the problem at hand, stating the problem accurately, and understanding the assumptions behind the problem statement.

Numerous decisions are made daily within the classroom and throughout the school. Decision making can be defined as a process wherein an awareness of a problem, influenced by information, values, and beliefs, is reduced to competing alternatives. From these alternatives, a choice is made. The initial aspects of effective decision making include first, identifying and stating a problem or situation accurately. Second, understanding the assumptions behind the problem, and third, choosing a useful decision model to resolve the problem or situation.

Decision making may be defined in a variety of ways. It can be seen as a problematic state that is reduced to competing alternatives, among which a choice is made, based upon an estimated outcome. Values affect all decisions that are made. And individuals, depending on their own style, reach decisions in different ways. Moralists, for example, tend to strive for reaching the "right" decision in the "right" way. Expedients tend to want to reach a decision in the method that is the easiest. And then of course there are those who take both seriously and want the right decision reached as quickly as possible. However, regardless of when a decision is reached, it may or may not be successfully implemented. Implementation of the decision must be carried out through a plan of action developed with sequential steps to ensure ownership and participation of as many players as possible.

Individuals tend to fall into four distinct groups when implementing decisions. And every school site has staff members who make up these four groups. First are those members who are always willing and able. They never hesitate to volunteer and become involved. They don't ask if they can handle one more job or task, they just do it. They are usually the campus "cheerleaders" and a pretty energized group of individuals. The second group are those individuals who are willing but not able. These are the ones who need extra help in implementing the decision. The third group are those individuals who are not willing but able. These are the ones who say it doesn't concern me, I don't need to do it, or else they need an extra incentive to ensure buy-in. They will, typically, ask if they will be paid for their after-school hours. Fourth are those individuals who are not willing and not able. With these, it is difficult to bring about the shared decision as they take extra time and instruction by the director to ensure that the decision will be carried out.

DECISION-MAKING MODEL

Decision making takes place in different frameworks or environments, and these influence the choice of an appropriate decision model. Information that the administration obtains provides the basis for decision making, and special attention may be given to the amount, form, and flow of information obtained. A useful decision-making model to facilitate agreed-upon decisions contains the following seven basic steps.

First, clearly state the problem. This step sometimes can take the longest, as a deep understanding is paramount to effectively implement a decision-making model. Perhaps the most complex aspect of decision making pertains to the way a problem is stated. Sometimes it is appropriate to be very specific and at other times it is necessary to be abstract and general. In this step, the problem is stated more specifically. It is important that the decision problem be stated in words that are clear to the listener/reader so that accurate assumptions about the problem can be made by all with the information at hand and the way the problem is stated. A parent may have a very specific idea about how she or he feels the decision should be resolved. Therefore, it is extremely important to state the problem that needs a decision, based on group reaction. Shared decision making helps to ensure that the decision will be carried out.

The second step is to list the assumptions. Everyone involved with the problem has certain preconceived notions, values, and beliefs. It is important to list all the assumptions shared by the stakeholders, for without all of the information laid out in advance, the agreed-upon decision may not be implemented because so many people disagreed on assumptions and had no actual realization of the problem. If you doubt this, list a decision your group has made and then ask each member to write down one or two assumptions behind it. Typically, there will be almost no agreement.

Third is deciding on the framework. Decision making takes place in different frameworks or environments. Thus you have more wiggle room on a decision that affects one grade level than you do when it affects all grade levels. The framework influences the choice of an appropriate decision model. Again the information obtained by the administration will be crucial. In essence, this step is establishing the ground rules to which the group will adhere.

The fourth step is to list the information sources. Information must be timely to be useful. It must also be at the right level of detail and presented at the right time. The quality of your decision rests in part on the quality of the information available to help make the decision. Reference needs to be given to (1) deciding on who should collect the information; (2) deciding how the information should be gathered; (3) collecting the information; (4) consolidating the information to form a proposal; and (5) presenting the proposal using an agreed-upon format or process. The KISS approach works well, "Keep It Short and Simple." Keep to the pertinent and salient facts only.

The fifth step is to decide on values. By this time in the process, a decision is close to being made. However, before the final decision can be made, recognition of values must be addressed, for decision making is influenced by the values of those providing data as well as the decision maker's values. In this step, each person involved has very different perceptions of the same event. The group needs to be able to recognize the impact value systems have on decision making. For example, a school where most parents are very competitive about the type of college their children will attend may not value full inclusion of special education students as much as a group of parents who are not so focused upon college.

The sixth step is to list the alternatives. Decision making is strengthened by having several good alternatives from which to choose in moving to a specific decision choice. To facilitate the process of using alternatives in decision making, it is helpful to state the criteria one uses to judge alternatives and to be aware of the "probability for success" judgments in selecting one alternative over another. The director needs to be able to recognize the value of stating alternatives in the decision-making process. Better decisions are the result of better alternatives.

The seventh step is to make the decision! A consensus or near-consensus decision-making structure that ensures that all stakeholders have been allowed to speak and express their opinion is important to making a final decision.

Another popular approach to making a decision that is used when all factors have equal bearing is a force field analysis. With this strategy all alternatives and choices toward the final decision are listed. The facilitator then ranks all of the alternatives according to how feasible they will be to solve the problem. Through a forced ranking process oftentimes the consensus reached can lead to a successful decision.

This seven-step process is effective when dealing with problems that require input from the major stakeholders. However, be aware that there are times when telling is most effective. Not all decisions can nor should be accomplished through a shared process. Only each particular group can determine which decisions should be shared. Past knowledge of the decision-making processes used will help to determine what steps to take and when to use the steps listed in this process.

OTHER DECISION-MAKING PROCESSES

What is the best type of decision-making process? The seven steps given above provide a generic type of model, but all decision making should start where the staff members or stakeholders are in their development and in each situation. If a school staff is used to being told what to do, for example, in a previous school, a new leader might be tempted to take the easy way and just try telling them what needs to be done. With these individuals the democratic approach might be resisted, for, previously, ideas and input had not been solicited and the stakeholder may feel unsure about how to follow through without being told how to do something specifically. Of course in situations where stakeholders are more used to a participative or democratic style, this style should be continued as much as possible. Decisions that are made democratically do take the most time, but they usually gather greater support from the staff. And this support helps teachers to be more successful than they would be otherwise. While authoritarian decisions are easier to make, they can often have unintended consequences. Teachers and parents may repress their feelings and feel discounted. Tasks will still get done, but the interpersonal problems created may make for new difficulties later on.

The group process of reaching decisions is only useful when a large group consensus is needed. There are three types of situations when telling is most effective. The first is when a decision needs to be made that does not require committed action by the whole group. The second is when a simple decision does not require coordinated effort of many of the group. The third is when the outcome that will result from the decision doesn't have an impact on staff members.

WHO MAKES THE DECISION?

When it comes to reaching a decision, it is important to know who has the authority to make the decision and who has the responsibility to do so. For while reaching a decision is important, defining who has the responsibility to make that decision or who has the authority to see it through can have a great impact on how or if a decision is reached. Sometimes one may have the authority, but not the responsibility, or just the opposite. A guideline about the chain of command in terms of who can make a final decision may be helpful. In school and district office administration the smoothest operations are a result of knowing who is in charge of what and when. The roles of the school/governing board, superintendent, district administration, and school site director need to be well defined and have clarity on two issues: Whose responsibility is it and who has the authority? To assist in defining the chain of command, you may use the following checklist:

B = Decisions made by the board.
S = Decisions made by the superintendent or immediate staff.
D = Decisions made by the school-site director.
T = Decisions made by teacher or group of stakeholders.
A = Decision made by another staff member.
C = Decision made by collective bargaining agreement.
U = Unclear—clarification is needed before decision is made.

Consider your situation and try using the symbols above to answer these questions:

1. Whose decision is it to call off school because of inclement weather?
2. Whose decision is it to change the bus stop from one corner to another?
3. Whose decision is it to change a teacher's grade-level assignment?
4. Whose decision is it to release news to press about honor students?
5. Whose decision is it to determine which textbooks are to be used?
6. Whose decision is it to give teachers a "free period"?

As you consider who should make a decision, keep in mind that the decision process, democratic as it may be, may not improve student achievement, as indicated in a recent article on the National School Boards Association Web page.[1]

WAYS TO FACILITATE DECISION MAKING

To expand empowerment of school staff and parents a school can involve as many as possible in different stages of the decision-making process.

Possible committees include director's advisory committee, a leadership committee, a school improvement/leadership committee, and the school site council. They are also selected to have one individual school-wide responsibility. This can range from facilitating weekly staff meetings to handling student leadership activities. This process of shared decision making lets participants know that what they think and how they would like to see something accomplished is important. They are responsible for supporting the essential agreements that are made in that once a decision has been made, whether or not they are for or against it, they agree not to sabotage the decision and will support it and follow through.

The director's job is to provide different techniques and processes to enable consensus to be reached and to support the staff in decision-making processes. It is also her or his responsibility to bring to staff members those things that matter and try to focus on those things that support school goals. It is also the administrator's responsibility to interfere when necessary to allow teachers and staff to successfully accomplish what they need to get done and not have time taken away from their job of educating students when their decisions aren't necessary.

SITE-BASED DECISION MAKING

Site-based decision making is a strategy occurring in schools throughout the country. To help build a community of professionals sharing unified goals along with individual goals (i.e., teaming, shared decision making, and shared curriculum ideas), a school-based advisory committee or director's advisory council is helpful. This group of individuals is valuable in providing feedback about how staff members generally feel and what they need in terms of resources and support. It also serves to allow staff members to communicate across grade-level lines. While grade-level meetings allow for the potential of consistency, an advisory committee in an open forum format helps articulation, the sharing of ideas, and the fostering of effective dialogue and communication.

Another reason why shared leadership and site-based decision making is so effective is that creativity and decision-making abilities are widely distributed in the population and not necessarily determined by the position a person holds. A director's advisory council can help to provide for the effective use of all of these abilities within the formal organization. While it is the responsibility of a director to establish broad parameters of appropriate behavior, consistent with general school policies and good educational practice, it is also a director's obligation to seek input from individual staff members or identified groups of parents. Allowing wide latitude for problem resolution and final decision making and supporting staff as they share their opinions demonstrates that the administration recognizes that both the private goals of organizational members as well as the agreed-upon school goals affect the achievement of their school.

The attainment of a positive feeling tone comes to a school in many ways, but the crucial foundation for student growth are the twin pillars of parent and school staff support. It is no surprise that the students with the best overall performance come from loving and responsible homes where what the student learns at school is reinforced. Parents who receive consistent communication from the school, including notes from the teacher and the director, demonstrate greater feelings of trust and contentment. Effective organizations are characterized by a variety of communications media and a free flow of information laterally and vertically throughout the organization. Importance must be placed on a variety of communications, including face-to-face and nonverbal cues.

The phrase "A picture is worth a thousand words" applies to schools as well as books. A monthly newsletter sharing what has been happening as well as what lies ahead is important, but these newsy items must be shared in person to ensure that what is being said is being understood. Seek first to be understood, then to understand. This is particularly applicable to schools where educators are comfortable using jargon in conversation.

If important information such as a proposed change in curriculum or scheduling will be occurring, then a formal meeting must be scheduled in addition to any written form of communication sent home. Parents knowledgeable about the school's vision are more likely to become involved when they are connected with the school. They are also more likely to be strongly supportive and help spread positive public relations about their school and, hopefully, public schools in general.

Some schools send home a lively newsletter at the beginning of each month. This serves to communicate what is happening and what to anticipate during the coming month. They may also use a monthly column in the

PTA newsletter perhaps called the "Director Thoughts." This can be more philosophical or educationally based. In this article one can share educational tips with parents as well as parenting advice. One can also try to share research or address any of the concerns they have heard from parents and then link it to the school culture. Some directors also write a weekly article in the local newspaper sharing one event from school for that week. Teachers also send home notes attached to weekly or daily homework assignment sheets in addition to a monthly classroom newsletter.

Through experience I have found that parents need to hear things two or three times to be able to truly make sense of what is happening and to understand. This is even more true when changes or new concepts are being introduced. As use of the Internet increases in our homes and schools, having a school home page can be a wonderfully effective way to keep communication ongoing. Likewise, through the use of e-mail, two-way communication can be encouraged and parents can be kept truly informed. This helps to build the positive climate and feeling tone desired for a school. Do your parents have your e-mail address? With the technology available today, there is little excuse for a lack of communication.

CLEAR, FREQUENT, AND CONCISE COMMUNICATION

Lack of communication or inconsistent implementation of policies are the two key factors that will destroy a positive school climate for staff and parents. Consistency and rationale for why things are occurring as they do are key in building and keeping trust. While clear, frequent, and concise communication is important with parents, it is crucial with staff. The director needs to seek open communication with staff at all times. Workings within a school setting will occur on two levels: formal and informal. The formal dimensions occur during classroom observations, staff evaluations, staff meetings, and in-services. The informal dimension has great influence on individual behavior and provides its own system of rewards. It occurs in the teacher's lounge at lunch, and while it may or may not exhibit goals congruent with the formal organization, it gives a sense of community to small groups within the school setting. As a manger of human relations, you must be aware of these informal groups and realize that they are often determined by grade-level groupings or lunchtimes. Teachers often find security in these groups in order to vent frustrations and to band against an unpopular decision. Of their own nature, they aren't negative, but you must be aware that they often can take the form of a clique and be productive as well as destructive forces. To help lessen their impact you can do a few things.

At lunchtimes, vary the groups with which you sit and the times you take for lunch. Make it a priority to become familiar and chat informally with all staff. Observe them and ask your secretary to share observations she or he has that you need to be apprised of but may not have the opportunity to know on your own. Frequently at a school, because of the part-time hours of classified staff, months can go by in between opportunities for formal communication. Schedule meeting times for all staff to allow time to encourage communication and interaction. Frequently question staff, parents, and students as to how well things are going. Clarify with them issues that have been communicated in memos or discussed at meetings.

A positive work climate is one where staff look forward to coming to work each day and where they truly believe their school is the best! In a positive workplace, teachers feel the rewards of coming to work just by the interactions and feedback they receive from their colleagues, parents, and students. Their belief that their school is the best is based on accurate gathered information and data. It's the place where they will want to work and spend their time!

NOTE

1. National School Board Association, "Reinventing School-Based Management: A School Board Guide to School-Based Improvement," (accessed January 10, 2002), www.nsba.org/na/achievement/reinvent_execsum.htm.

Chapter Nine

Parent Involvement Improves Academic Performance

There is considerable research on the importance of parents talking, explaining, asking questions, and providing (positive) feedback to their children. The case study provided here of the Riley Charter School details its efforts to improve student performance and bring it up to the district average, even though Riley has a greater proportion of disadvantaged students than the district does overall. The focus at Riley is on reading and language arts improvement. The support teacher program and implementation of whole language are likely reasons for the improvement. The Riley staff also focused much of their energy upon parent involvement, resulting in a remarkable improvement in student performance.

Key Concepts:
Parent Involvement Research
Sunshine District Improves Reading
Riley Charter School

PARENT INVOLVEMENT RESEARCH

An article by Paul Chance in the March 1997 *Phi Delta Kappan* discusses an intensive longitudinal study of the effects of parents' behavior on the intellectual development of children. Researchers indicate there are wide differences in the experiences parents provide their children. Surprisingly, the biggest difference is in the amount of talking to their infants that parents did.

The better educated a mother was, the more she spoke to her child. Welfare parents addressed an average of about 600 words per hour to their children, working-class parents directed about 1,200 words per hour to their children, and professional parents addressed more than 2,000 words per hour to their children. These differences were stable across time and were not attributable to the child's gender, the number of siblings, whether both parents worked, or the number of people present during observations.

The differences were qualitative as well as quantitative. Parents who talked more also did more explaining, asked more questions, and provided more feedback, especially positive feedback. Professional parents, for example, commented positively on their children's behavior ("That's right," "Good," and so on) an average of thirty times an hour. This was twice the rate of working-class parents and more than five times the rate of welfare parents. When low-income parents did comment on a child's behavior, they were far more likely to criticize than to praise. All the families were loving and showed sincere interest in the welfare of their children. They simply interacted with them differently.

The differences in parental behavior were associated with differences in the infants' achievement. Those children whose parents talked frequently, providing lots of positive feedback, lengthy explanations, and so on scored higher on an IQ test and on measures of vocabulary development at age three. When twenty-nine of the children in the study were followed up in the third grade, the pattern of early parental behavior continued to predict performance on language and IQ tests.

Neither socioeconomic level nor race could account for the differences in intellectual accomplishments. In fact, the correlation between socioeconomic level and test performance declined from age three to grade three, while the association between parental behavior and test performance remained strong. What matters, it seems, is not whether the parents are African American or white, rich or poor, educated or uneducated; what matters is what they do. If the decision makers in Riley's Sunshine District reading project (described below) had known about this research they certainly would have found a way to get parents to increase talking, explaining, asking questions, and providing (positive) feedback to their children. As you will see, they worked successfully on many related parent-child interaction tasks.

SUNSHINE DISTRICT IMPROVES READING

Sunshine District City Unified School District is a large school district in California. The student population is continuing to grow. The ethnic makeup of the district is Hispanics, Caucasians, African Americans, and Asians, as well as other ethnicities.

The purpose of the district's Master Plan for Categorical Programs was to provide a framework for making maximum use of categorical funds in order to have a significant, positive effect on the achievement of educationally disadvantaged youth, especially in the area of reading.

The Master Plan for Categorical Programs was developed by a forty-two-member task force. The task force members were divided into five committees that were asked to address program, instruction, parent involvement, change, and evaluation issues.

The subcommittee for Parent/Community Involvement was asked to look at and define types and amounts of parent involvement needed to positively impact student achievement and to define specific strategies for achieving parent involvement.

Parent Involvement Policy

The board of education adopted the following policy relating to parent involvement:

- establishing and maintaining a PTA program;
- establishing and maintaining a school site and/or school advisory council where appropriate;
- including parent participation in the program and curriculum development;
- helping parents develop parenting skills;
- providing parents with the knowledge of techniques designed to assist their children in learning at home;
- promoting clear two-way communication between school and family about school programs and student's progress;
- involving parents, with appropriate training, in instructional support roles at the school;
- supporting parents as decision makers, and helping them develop their leadership in governance, advisory, and advocacy roles;

- establishing a parent center with materials and books for parent use;
- developing a family support team to assist parents with resolution of those home problems that interfere with student learning;
- developing a home–school agreement delineating home, school, and student responsibilities.

Riley's primary focus is to improve reading. They want all students to become independent readers who have a love and joy of all literature-based reading. The full implementation of all materials provided by the Houghton Mifflin literature series, including listening, speaking, reading, and writing skills in conjunction with the language arts portfolios for each student, was very beneficial.

In addition, Chapter I and school-based coordinated money was used to provide a Slavin model reading program in grades one through three, and it helped accomplish the school reading goals. Staff development was an integral part of the program.

RILEY CHARTER SCHOOL

Riley Charter School was a pilot school for categorical programs in the Sunshine District City Unified School District. Many innovative programs have been implemented including a very comprehensive parent education program. The purpose of the Sunshine District City Unified School District's Master Plan is to provide a framework for making maximum use of categorical funds in order to have significant, positive effect on the achievement of educationally disadvantaged youth.

The principle underlying the parent educative component in the Master Plan is that parents and community play an essential role in the success of students, and the goal of the plan is to actively involve parents and the community in the education of students.

The innovative projects allowance is intended to promote program improvement as well as to give more local flexibility in providing Chapter I services. Part of the innovation funds are used to encourage innovative approaches to parent involvement or rewards to, or expansive use of, an exemplary parental involvement program.

Riley School Parent Involvement Program

Riley School began to implement the district Master Plan for Categorical Program two years ago. Here are some of the programs instituted for parent involvement.

- First-Grade Parent Club Meetings: These monthly meetings are conducted by the reading support teachers and are designed to instruct parents in language arts strategies they can use with their children at home.
- Home–School Agreements: As part of the Master Plan, home–school agreements were designed to involve parents in taking an active role in their children's education and to take responsibility in ensuring their child's attendance and homework responsibilities.
- Parent Library: With some of the Chapter I Innovation Funds, library books were purchased for check-out to parents of first and second grade students. These books are checked out on a weekly basis.
- School Advisory Council, School Site Council, and Bilingual Advisory Councils: These councils are in place and are very well attended. Also, they have representatives who attend the district advisory council on a monthly basis.
- Parent Volunteers: Historically, Riley School has had a fair number of volunteers who give time within the classroom. The number of volunteers, although lower than ten years ago, is still relatively high and volunteers are a viable part of the instructional program.

Last year the parent education program expanded to include:

- Take-Home Computers: The take-home computer program targets second grade students who have been involved in the reading support program. Parents and students are trained together in the use of the computer as well as the software that is provided. The computers are taken home during the student's off-track time. Older, inexpensive computers are utilized.
- Family Reading Style Classes: These classes are held in the fall and spring and are targeted for all parents and students. Parents are taught different ways of reading to their students as well as providing an environment conducive to reading.

- Literacy/ESL Class: Many of Riley parents are semiliterate or illiterate. To compensate for this need, literacy classes are held for our parents every Thursday from 10 A.M. to noon at the library. Ann Freeworth, director of the literacy program, conducts these classes. Also, ESL classes are held at the library on a weekly basis for parents who are limited English proficient.
- CASA: The Community and School Alliance (CASA) program is a joint effort between the community and the schools to generate grants for teachers for specific school projects. Riley has a CASA grant for kindergarten students. It is a listen and learn story tape project. Story tapes and books are sent home with students and are checked out on a weekly basis.
- The Family Support Worker: The Family Support Worker is the liaison between community and school. The Family Support Worker makes home visits and phone calls to families in "at-risk" environments.
- The Family Support Team: This team consists of the program facilitator, assistant director, Family Support Worker, counselor, Chapter I nurse, health aide, and sociological services worker. The Family Support Team looks very closely at students in kindergarten and first and second grades who are referred by their classroom teacher because of absences, homework, tardies, clothing, glasses, or behavior issues. The team provides a variety of family support assistance.
- P.R.I.C.E: This is a parent education workshop to help parents build self-esteem within their children and to give parents strategies in working with their children in the areas of discipline and self-esteem.

Monitoring Performance Results

The current year of the pilot program encompassed program evaluation, taking an in-depth look at the implementation of the reading support program and the whole language program; refinement such as how to "fine-tune" existing programs, and dissemination-expansion of programs throughout the grade levels as well as bringing these programs into other schools.

Progress toward Meeting Three-Year Objectives

The Continuous-Reading program is a set of materials published by Houghton Mifflin that allows the school to implement its whole language curriculum. Continuous-Reading is the reading portion of the program. There were 269 continuous students at Riley with pretest scores on the Individual Tests of Academic Skills (ITAS). ITAS is a standardized test given to assess achievement in reading, language, and mathematics. Their average pretest score in reading was 36.0. The average posttest score was 38.1, a gain of 2.1.

At all grade levels (except third) Riley students showed significantly greater gains (or less loss) than the district as a whole. The support teacher program and implementation of whole language are likely reasons for the improvement. At grade one continuous students averaged 43.3 in total reading, which was up from the previous year's 41 normal curve equivalent (NCE) average and only 6.2 NCEs below the district average.

When one considers that Riley School's population is one of the most economically depressed populations in all of Southern California and that the large majority of students begin here with little or no exposure to books, these scores are remarkable. Further, these students did not have the highly successful whole language experience in kindergarten that this year's kindergarten had. Riley staff expect even better results next year because of the kindergarten program.

When the program began not many people thought Riley students could make this kind of progress because of the "at-risk" environment in the Riley area. The doubters included many teachers. There are no longer doubters at Riley School. Extensive parent involvement will be continued at Riley and at other schools in the district.

Chapter Ten

Seeking Funding for Your School

Having a need for service can be very frustrating when there is no money to meet those needs. Working in a high need situation over time can lead to staff burnout, as good ideas stop and energy is used instead to distance and protect oneself from feeling overwhelmed by the needs for which there are no resources to meet.

Unfortunately, there are no automatic answers to funding programs and maintaining good morale in charter schools. However, there is often a high correlation between well-funded and implemented programs and a high sense of efficacy among staff as well as program participants.

Key Concepts:
Writing Proposals for Outside Funding
Need/Target Population

There are several successful techniques that have been used to achieve stable or increased funding, and it all starts with a caring, energetic staff with good ideas. A plan to stabilize funding over time should include a number of strategies. It's a lot like the mutual fund concept in that you don't want to be overly dependent on any one income source. In addition to writing proposals for increased funding, which are described here in detail, program planners may want to try other strategies as well, including:

1. Review who benefits from your service, either directly or indirectly. Have you asked them to contribute in some way? Contribution could be through matching funds, in-kind services, or as volunteers, perhaps.

If you can't find some support at this level, perhaps your service is not valued as it exists and needs to be restructured or your service population needs education regarding the benefits of the service.

2. As a workgroup, develop or review your mission statement, purpose, or goal statement. Are your program activities related to it? Time management is easier and programs are better implemented and funded when you focus time on tasks relating to the mission. A mission helps you see the big picture as well as the current needs you are striving to meet.

3. Think creatively about how you do what you do. This is often done best in a brainstorming group session. Is there another way? What resources, human, technical, or communication-based do you think would make it work better? How do you know it works? Can you find out?

4. Maintain an attitude that experimentation (willingness to change) is positive, and look for new things to try, while maintaining what works and discarding or revising what doesn't work (even if it was your idea!). The habit of focusing on positive outcomes, with the belief that good ideas will appear, goes a long way toward maintaining good morale.

5. Can you expand your vision in a way that is complementary to the mission and brings in resources, such as training or providing materials to others? Related to this is the need to let others know about what works in your program. Sharing information through newspaper articles, publications, presentations, and networking can start new income sources you hadn't even thought about.

6. Focus some energy on getting resources to try out your ideas. You can often do this quickly on a small scale or pilot program by convincing key supporters how it will benefit them or something they care about. Persuading key supporters to operate differently or to contribute manpower or financial support usually involves writing a case statement. A case statement details why an institution merits support, with considerable documentation of its services, resources, needs, and potential for greater services and future plans. A case statement should focus on a positive outcome (i.e., helping youth become productive citizens, not stopping delinquency) as well as address the information needs of the target audience, not internal reviewers.

7. Identify resources that are interested in funding your ideas and write proposals to them. Since many innovations get started through governmental or private competitive funding of proposals, this is described in greater detail.

WRITING PROPOSALS FOR OUTSIDE FUNDING

Certainly one of the more enjoyable ways to develop identification and intervention services for students is to apply for and receive additional funds from government or private sources. Although grant writing is labor intensive and not guaranteed, receiving a grant, like childbirth, makes up for a lot of pain. The key to successful grant writing is to first clearly think though the idea, get excited about it, and then describe it clearly in writing.

The second important key to grant writing is to carefully follow the directions given by the funding agency (e.g., clearly respond to each grant section). Typical grant headings include an assessment of need and identification of the target group, identification of project aims, background and significance of the new effort, description of objectives and activities for the project, project design and methods, formative and summative evaluation, plan of operation, budget and cost effectiveness, and commitment and capacity.

Below are some brief "starter" sentences from proposals to illustrate the various sections. These sections would typically be reordered and renamed to fit the suggestions of the request for proposal from the funding agency. The type of detail seen in a typical proposal is given.

NEED/TARGET POPULATION

A winning proposal typically includes a strong presentation of need for the activities that are listed in the proposed project. Take time to gather information from staff and other research sources about the special need for your new effort. This is often a good place to define the target population with lots of descriptive words and numbers to present the need. Try to show how some promising things have been accomplished, but that more resources will really make all the difference in building the new approach. Here is an excerpt from our proposal: "The magnitude of alcohol and other drug abuse problems has caused increasing nationwide concern among educators, policy makers, and the community at large. Although the rates of drug use have declined recently (NIDA, 1988), smoking and drinking are still very prevalent teenage activities. In fact, high school students in the U.S. are more involved with illicit drugs than youth in any other industrialized nation (Johnson et al., 1989). A recent survey of drug use and dropouts in California and Irvine found . . ."

Project Aims

Present the purpose of the project clearly, demonstrating an understanding of what research indicates is effective. For example: "The aims of the District At-Risk Management Project are to develop a computer management system that will: (a) identify potential substance abusers and potential dropouts; and (b) use an expert system to connect identified students-at-risk with appropriate interventions which will reduce student risk levels."

Background and Significance

Describe background steps logically leading to current proposal. For example: "Project activities were developed during the past eight years from needs assessments with staff and students and a review of the current literature on high-risk and substance-abusing students. Components respond to the research findings, particularly the research on high-risk factors for adolescents."

Objectives and Activities of Project

Present a plan for accomplishing the aim of the project, describing the objectives to be accomplished and the activities that will lead to the completion of these objectives. For example: "The proposed program offers a comprehensive holistic approach for preventing alcohol and other drug use by 500 high-risk middle school students. The project addresses the needs of the student, his family, the school, and community, in a comprehensive approach to prevention, through the following:

- Student Objective: Decrease the use of alcohol and other drugs in participating students at a .05 level of significance.
- Student Activity: Provide individual and small group counseling to identified students. Assign and monitor progress of identified students in interventions.
- School Objective: Increase knowledge and skill levels of educators to implement interventions to reduce risk factors, as measured by pre/post assessment."

Project Design and Methods

Describe the process of program services as part of the overall design and describe individual program components more completely if necessary. For example: "A data gathering system involving students, parents, school personnel, and community resources to identify students who need help is being developed.

1. A database of all students in the district identifying the lower quadrant based on academics, low test scores, and students exhibiting at-risk behaviors is being developed.
2. A referral form for teachers who have identified a problem with a student and a procedure for handling referrals and tracking disposition of each referral is being developed.
3. An information system to let referring teachers know the disposition of the referral is being developed.
4. A plan for sharing information with parents of students will be developed."

Formative and Summative Evaluation

Describe your evaluation plan, linking it to the measurement of objectives you described. Try to think of an accurate and easily gathered measure of your success in each area. The evaluation ought to focus upon two areas: process (Are the steps to achieve outcomes conducive to program success?), and product (How well is the program accomplishing its specified objectives?). For example: "Teacher knowledge and skills in implementing the computer management system will be measured by locally developed pre/post tests and observation checklists. Outcome evaluation will be based on significant changes (improvement at the .05 level) in baseline data gathered from participant surveys on drug use against which future drug-use and parenting practices of high-risk students' parents will be compared."

Plan of Operation/Budget and Cost Effectiveness

List general information describing your organization, including the line of authority and role definitions for project staff. Generally describe and support the budget requested. For example: "The Board of Education is responsible for the project and management operations. The project director will coordinate all program activities and supervise project staff. The budget is adequate to complete project activities and is cost effective in that . . ."

Accomplishments/Capacity and Commitment

List any related accomplishments of your program and how they relate to the present effort. Show commitment to continue activities beyond the funding period. For example: "The district has a history of commitment to addressing the needs of at-risk students and has developed a number of innovative prevention programs (e.g., the STAGES Program, which assists at-risk students in being successful in school despite stressful changes in their lives). This proposal develops an at-risk management system, which complements these existing prevention and identification strategies now in place. This at-risk management system will make a significant impact on reducing student drug use by creating a computerized delivery system for drug abuse prevention and intervention that utilizes the latest research to predict potential abusers and dropouts with an identification system that, in turn, links to some of the most effective interventions in the country. The identification and intervention services will continue after initial funding through . . ."

An example of a charter school proposal is seen as appendix C.

Chapter Eleven

Planning and Supervision of Curriculum

This chapter focuses on curriculum design, interpreting district curricula, carrying out curriculum needs assessments, planning curriculum changes within your school, aligning curricula with outcomes, and required test and planning styles for curriculum adoptions.

Key concepts:
Curriculum Design
Knowledge of Content Trends
Formal, Informal, and Hidden Curricula
Mapping the Taught Curriculum
Curricular Alignment
Selecting Assessment Instruments
Needs Assessments
How Do Students Learn ?
Cultural and Socioeconomic Diversity
Knowledge of Evaluation

Directors need to thoroughly understand one or more content areas in order to plan for improvement across the curriculum. Curriculum materials are usually written to accomplish a general objective, such as emphasizing cultural diversity or teaching basic skills. Good materials also are written to use a variety of modes of instruction so they will appeal to a variety of learners.

CURRICULUM DESIGN

The first concern in curriculum design is to find out how well the present curriculum in a content area is working. To do this the director should carry out a needs assessment addressing each of the content areas he or she is seeking to improve. The next concern is the format the curriculum is set in and the assumptions behind the format. For example, I recently had an opportunity to talk to a sixth grader who was failing in his work. He seemed alert in general conversation so I was surprised to find him failing. The teachers in his school have little knowledge of the world of work so they had constructed a curriculum based on the implicit assumption that all of their students were preparing for college. To say it another way, the teachers and the director had never considered what the content of the sixth-grade curriculum might be like if they seriously attempted to relate it to the interests and needs of the majority of their students. In fact, about one-third of those students from that local high school continue on to college. An advisory committee with several local businesspeople as members would be a logical way to start the process of building curricula that meet the needs of a diverse student group, most of whom will not attend college.

KNOWLEDGE OF CONTENT TRENDS

An effective director is aware of content trends in the standard content areas, as well as the practical and fine arts. This becomes especially important as teachers become interested in combining several content perspectives, such as language and social studies, as they create curriculum. They may need help in seeing patterns that facilitate cross-curricular efforts, for instance, such as using some of the multiple intelligences materials based on Howard Gardner's developmental work over the past twenty years. The director, if he or she is a member of the Association for Supervision and Curriculum Development, might have received *Multiple Intelligences in the Classroom*[1] by Armstrong, which provides many excellent suggestions for building on student strengths in areas other than language and mathematics utilizing the Gardner research. Appendix A, the Multiple Intelligence Instructional Activities Manual, is used to conduct workshops for instruction on preparing curriculum.

FORMAL, INFORMAL, AND HIDDEN CURRICULA

Every school has three forms of curricula. The informal curricula are the norms, mores, and practices that affect students even though they are not planned as elements of the formal curricula are. For example, some school staff "know" that girls typically are not good at math and so they are informally guided away from science and technology interests. Hidden curricula are unspoken assumptions, like school staff who offer "college prep only" activities in classes where many students are mainly interested in preparing for jobs. These assumptions may have devastating effects on student self-image as the work-oriented student gets Ds and Fs for several years and then begins to smoke, drink, use marijuana, and eventually move into gang life. In this example, the hidden curricula is so powerful for some students that it overpowers the formal curricula. The director needs to recognize each part of the triad and use them in a constructive manner.

In some schools students are actively learning about many "noncollege prep" occupations, for example, and learning to write simple resumes that include skills they have learned such as beginning carpentry, plumbing, and landscaping. Visits from people who work in a variety of occupations may have an effect on teachers as well as students, as teachers begin to actually learn what skills are needed in various types of work and to include classroom activities and examples that refer to these skills.

MAPPING THE TAUGHT CURRICULUM

The skilled director understands how to gather information about the taught curriculum using mapping techniques such as content, time, and sequence data, which can then be used to make revisions and to improve curricular focus. To continue our occupational example, content data could be gathered about the number of occupations presented, the amount of class time devoted to each, and the sequence in which they were offered. For example, one might want to begin with occupations in the local area where many jobs are available and work toward those that are at some distance and that employ fewer local people.

CURRICULAR ALIGNMENT

The curriculum needs to be aligned with tests and textbooks to give the greatest benefits. This is especially important in areas where test results have a powerful effect on community support for schools and may be published in the newspaper. There may be one or two content areas where test results are lower and in these areas very careful work needs to be done to align the curriculum, or possibly to change it to make it effective.

There will always be parents and others who accuse the staff of "teaching to the test," and it takes considerable public relations skills to explain the subtle difference between teaching to the test and aligning the curriculum in an effective way.

Technical understanding of how tests are developed and textbooks adopted may become survival skills requiring immediate in-service support from district staff if testing becomes a media issue.

SELECTING ASSESSMENT INSTRUMENTS

One of the most common errors a director can make is to choose a test that does not test what is being taught. This is not a simple matter, since teachers often provide inaccurate information about what they are teaching. In one district the scenario was even more complicated. A new superintendent found that math scores were lower than other scores a year after he came on the job and went right to work on the problem. He purchased new tests (at great expense) that went with the texts that were being used and math scores went up. At this point math scores became a statewide issue and the superintendent of public instruction at the state level selected a blue ribbon committee that recommended a statewide test that worked for some districts and their chosen texts and not for others. The superintendent was right back where he had been, for the new test did not test what the texts in his district covered. These issues become political, and the superintendent felt he could not use the state test. His dissidents were alert and immediately initiated a recall campaign, which forced him to then change and use the inappropriate statewide test. For reasons like this no one is ever surprised to learn that superintendents last an average of 2.7 years in their jobs.

The directors were of course right in the middle of this fiasco, some on one side and some on the other. Gradually they began an expensive double testing program that allowed them to test what was taught using their (excellent) texts and test using the statewide test. When the media representatives called they gave them both results, and life returned to normal, except for the $100,000 wasted in the double testing program.

NEEDS ASSESSMENTS

There are several distinctions that are important in planning a needs assessment. The first has to do with the scale and the related costs. If a school has a large-scale concern, like all math at K–6, a survey could be used that can be scored by machine and all the expense that this entails. If the problem is math at grade two in one school, a simple questionnaire prepared by a knowledgeable person can do the job.

The second concern is whether staff and the community perceive the problem accurately and that the related concern may be picked up by the media and become a job threat.

I was involved in an assessment of reading at grade two in a New England community some years ago. In terms of scale, this was large scale, district-wide, and I was able to get federal funding for the project by adding an unusual feature to the project. Few districts test qualitative as well as quantitative aspects of student growth. I proposed to adapt a qualitative instrument and to use it as well as the usual quantitative test, so the school was funded and carried out the project to improve reading scores and student attitude toward reading.

The perception problem came when I reported the results of the project at the end of the grant. Many parents and staff were mainly interested in the quantitative results, as expected. When I reported the qualitative findings, which were positive, a parent became upset because it appeared the school was imposing values on the community and a reporter jumped right in, seeing the possibility of several weeks of conflict and stories under her byline. The school was saved by a practice many administrators ignore—always use a published model, if possible, to guide a new project. In this case I had adapted for elementary use an instrument developed for the secondary level by the Educational Testing Service (ETS) and the reporter lost interest in the story. She accurately predicted that the community perceived ETS as a legitimate organization that would not try to impose values on a school community.

HOW DO STUDENTS LEARN?

A critical consideration in planning curriculum is the director's understanding that students learn in many different ways. For instance, some students learn best by behavior reinforcement such as seen in programmed learning in computer software. This is connected to the learning theory of B. F. Skinner. Another student may learn effectively when materials are presented in a "chain of learning" sequence that begins with the main concept and moves to subpoints as articulated by Robert Gagne. Sometimes the learning theory is explicit, as in the examples above. More commonly, the theory is implicit. For example, materials that stress problem solving may be influenced by the work of Jerome Bruner (Mr. Discovery Learning).

A good curriculum specialist seeks to help teachers identify materials that reflect the values and attitudes of the community. That is why administrators should be aware of community values as they hire staff.

CULTURAL AND SOCIOECONOMIC DIVERSITY

One of the primary areas of focus in charter school curriculum at present is the cultural and socioeconomic diversity of the schooling situation and the ways teachers can be more effective in the learning situation. But these encounters between teachers and students and between teachers and administrators do not take place in a vacuum. The history and social functions of schooling need to be understood. They form the social context within which schooling pursues its primary purposes of socialization, inculcation, and social stratification. They provide a background that can help new leaders understand why racism and socioeconomic factors have loomed so large in the academic success or failure of certain groups in U.S. society. Many classrooms today have students from a variety of ethnic groups.

A child learns his or her language and worldview from his or her parents. This teaches the child who he or she is and what his or her cultural background has been; it helps the child to differentiate him- or herself from other persons and groups in that child's environment.

School leaders need to understand what it means to be a minority person, a woman, or a racially different person in U.S. society. They need to analyze the different groups that form in their schools and the ways these groups interact within themselves and with other groups in the school. Cultural and linguistic factors must be considered by leaders if they are to understand the experiences certain individuals are having in schools. And common threads uniting all peoples can only be developed when the differences are acknowledged and validated by educational authorities.

KNOWLEDGE OF EVALUATION

Evaluation uses the same or similar models as research, but evaluation and research can have different purposes. Both fields tend to use strategies that we connect to scientific method, where one conducts studies using experimental and control groups. The purpose of evaluation is to provide information for decision makers, while the intent of research is to create new knowledge.

Some of the important things for a director to know about evaluation of curriculum are listed here with examples:

* How to Focus an Evaluation: Student needs and student expectations—If each person were to write down his or her expectations for this book and I would write down what I think your needs are, reconciling these expectations would be a key issue.
* Types of Evaluation: Quantitative such as reading scores and qualitative where the question is asked, "Can we improve teacher attitude toward full inclusion of mildly handicapped students?"
* Goals and Objectives Oriented: Formative evaluation studies procedures and processes week by week. It is often called feedback evaluation and is teacher oriented to guide students as the project develops. Every project should allocate some resources to formative study.

Summative evaluation presents end-of-the-year results, often required, and mainly for administrative use.

• Decision-Budget Oriented: Shall we continue the McGraw Hill Reading Series for grade two? Often timing is critical in this type of evaluation since the decision makers must have the recommendation during the planning of the coming year's budget in February and March.

• User Oriented: Who are the powerful people? Is this for the use of the superintendent's cabinet or for directors as well? What do they want to know about? Are test scores the only issue or do parent perceptions need to be included?

• Issue Responsive: Why do vocational education staff feel second class? What can be done to improve the situation?

Without clear goals and objectives, the director will not be able to know whether he or she is succeeding. Evaluation is the key to curricular improvement.

NOTE

1. Thomas Armstrong, *Multiple Intelligences in the Classroom* (Alexandria, Va.: Association for Supervision and Curriculum Development, 1994).

Chapter Twelve

Planning and Supervision of Instruction and the Learning Environment

Effective directors provide instructional leadership by acquiring an instructional knowledge base and collaborating with staff to plan, implement, and evaluate instructional programs. They utilize competencies that have been tested in many classrooms in order to plan effective instruction and learning strategies with their staff. When teachers are hired, especially teachers new to the profession, adequate time must be spent to bring them up to the same knowledge base as their grade-level colleagues. The site administrator can work to instill effective instructional leadership skills within teachers including collaboration, empowerment, and ownership.

Key Concepts:
Support for Instruction and Learning
Concept: Develops School Unit Goals and Objectives
Concept: Allocates Staff
Concept: Allocation of Time and Space
Concept: Utilizes Material, Equipment, and Facilities
Concept: Coordinates Supporting Noninstructional Services
Concept: Develops Positive School-Community Relations
Concept: Develops Appropriate In-Service Training
Concept: Assesses the Needs of the School

SUPPORT FOR INSTRUCTION AND LEARNING

Administering and improving the instructional program is an important domain of responsibility for school directors. The statement that competency in support for instruction and learning is of prime importance does not imply that the typical school director is especially effective in this role nor that teachers typically consider their directors to be valuable sources of assistance in instruction. It is likely that teachers would be more receptive to their directors in the role of improvement of instruction if the directors performed this role more competently. In any event, according to J. Culbertson, "there can be no doubt that superintendents, and Directors themselves, are convinced that Directors should be 'instructional leaders.'"[1] The following concepts and performance statements have been adapted from Culbertson.

CONCEPT: DEVELOPS SCHOOL
UNIT GOALS AND OBJECTIVES

The director (seen to be a leader in the discharge of responsibilities listed here, and not a lone wolf) develops school unit goals and objectives to guide instruction.

Task 1: The director relates needs of students to school system goals and legal requirements.

Measurable Indicator of Task 1: The administrator has at his or her disposal resource materials and consultants outlining specific district instructional goals and legal requirements to augment personal knowledge and experience.

Task 2: The director must be able to work effectively to provide essential input as well as coordinate the efforts of others to combine their knowledge and resources into an effective instructional program.

Measurable Indicators of Task 2: Appropriate contact people are identified at the district level for instructional program guidance. The director considers pupil test scores, teacher input, his or her own scholarly experience, and changing attitudes of the community toward learning outcomes when relating student needs to system goals.

Task 3: The director defines goals and objectives that are appropriate to the needs of the school unit.

Measurable Indicator of Task 3: The director meets with teaching staff to outline appropriate instructional programs for the new year.

Example: Reading/Language Arts—Houghton Mifflin/Integration of Reading and Language Arts: Children will be able to read literature in an anthology; groups of stories are organized around an important literary theme. Children will also read several paperback novels. Daily writing activities are stressed: responses to the literary selections; selected topics of interest; poetry forms; personal experiences in "news" journals.

Task 4: The director guides the development of instructional units to implement goals and objectives.

Measurable Indicators of Task 4: The director meets with team leaders of each grade level to assess current program unit status, needs, and concerns. The director and staff (re)define current unit goals and objectives to operate within school logistical limitations (available teachers, rooms, materials).

Task 5: The director articulates goals and objectives for subunits within the school.

Measurable Indicator of Task 5: The director meets with the various subject coordinators (i.e., science coordinator) to identify the unit materials and equipment necessary for unit presentation under the established goals and objectives.

CONCEPT: ALLOCATES STAFF

The director allocates staff personnel to accomplish instructional goals.

Task 1: The director defines job requirements for each position in terms of instructional processes and/or products.

Measurable Indicators of Task 1: The director determines the operating budget for each position, assesses available equipment necessary for unit, assesses time/space allocations, determines class size, necessary materials.

Task 2: In assisting in the recruitment and selection of personnel for instructional responsibilities, the director seeks evidence that candidates meet the stated criteria for instructional performance.

Measurable Indicator of Task 2: Interacts with personnel office staff to screen potential candidates, interviews potential candidates/reviews resumés.

Task 3: The director assigns or reassigns instructional staff to optimize conditions for learning.

Measurable Indicators of Task 3: The director is aware of staff backgrounds, experience, and capabilities when considering teacher reassignment. The director considers current class needs and characteristics when considering placement of a new teacher. The director is aware of district rules/regulations regarding reassignment procedures (i.e., union requirements, seniority, returning from leaves, furloughed employees). The director is aware of intra- and interdistrict openings to fit the best qualified people into the most appropriate programs.

Task 4: The director recommends staff members for reemployment, promotion, or dismissal based upon evidence of instructional performance.

Measurable Indicators of Task 4: The director is aware of individual staff capabilities by: (1) frequent contact through staff meetings to share current status of teachers' progress in their classrooms; (2) frequent (weekly) classroom visitations to monitor classroom learning environment; (3) periodic teacher observation/evaluation and feedback throughout the year; (4) feedback from mentor teachers, colleagues, students, and parents; (5) feedback from peer review of mentor teachers of first year and other teachers who need special coaching in order to be more effective.

CONCEPT: ALLOCATION OF TIME AND SPACE

The director makes appropriate allocation of time and space for the accomplishment of instructional goals.

Task 1: The director inventories the changing needs for time and space for various instructional purposes.

Measurable Indicators of Task 1: The director must remain aware, through district communication, of changing state-mandated minimum program requirement times; communicate with teaching staff regarding space/programs needs. The director must know supply requisitioning procedures.

Task 2: The director optimizes time and space allocations to meet instructional purposes.

Measurable Indicators of Task 2: The director constantly oversees program dynamics and makes appropriate adjustments and changes when necessary.

Example: An assembly requires the multipurpose room, thus requiring the music program to move to an alternate location.

Task 3: The director assigns students to appropriate spaces and time units for instruction.

Measurable Indicator of Task 3: The director is available and willing to constantly interact with teachers, parents, and administration to monitor students who may need relocation to an improved learning environment, due to discipline problems or other inhibiting factors.

CONCEPT: UTILIZES MATERIAL, EQUIPMENT, AND FACILITIES

The director develops and utilizes material, equipment, and facilities to accomplish instructional goals.

Task 1: The director inventories the changing needs for materials, equipment, and facilities to accomplish instructional goals.

Measurable Indicators of Task 1: The director must maintain regular contact with instructional administrators at the district level to remain apprised of current state and/or district adopted policies regarding programs of instruction. The director relies on communication (meetings, memos, word-of-mouth) from site staff to become aware of their changing needs/requirements for additional equipment, space.

Task 2: The director allocates materials, equipment, and facilities to accomplish instructional goals.

Measurable Indicators of Task 2: The director, based on information gathered from appropriate instructional leaders, determines distribution of equipment/supplies. Factors such as days involved, amounts of equipment available, times of classes, and so forth, all have to be factored in to optimize fair allocation of resources on hand.

Task 3: The director directs the identification and selection of appropriate necessary materials, equipment, and facilities for instruction.

Measurable Indicators of Task 3: Through interaction with staff, the director determines desired supplies/equipment requested by the program leaders. Through application of budget and materials on hand or available elsewhere around the district, the director works to meet each program's requirements. Working with on-site support groups (PTO, PTA) as well as fund-raising efforts, the director helps to coordinate efforts to acquire needed materials.

Task 4: The director coordinates the redesigning of instructional facilities to facilitate the accomplishment of instructional goals as needed.

Measurable Indicator of Task 4: The director, for example, may order the installation of a room divider to accommodate a new preschool program on a temporary basis due to lack of classroom space.

Task 5: The director provides for the development or modification of instructional materials to meet the unique needs of the instructional program.

Measurable Indicator Task 5: The director, remaining in close communication with instructional and support staff, recognizes the need for program and/or equipment modification.

Example: When mainstreaming a child with special needs into a regular classroom, the director may authorize a change of equipment, modified instructional materials, or the purchase or addition of new equipment to facilitate learning for the child.

CONCEPT: COORDINATES SUPPORTING NONINSTRUCTIONAL SERVICES

The director coordinates supporting noninstructional services to accomplish instructional goals.

Task 1: The director inventories the changing needs for counseling services in order to facilitate accomplishment of instructional goals. For example, the director is aware of the changing needs for counseling services such as increased use of district staff, the peak time of use, population, scheduling, the type of materials used, availability of materials, space, and so forth.

Measurable Indicators of Task 1: Survey of all grade levels questionnaire to coordinators for each grade level.

Task 2: The director organizes and coordinates counseling services to optimize the accomplishment of instructional goals.

Measurable Indicators of Task 2: The director makes available enough counseling to account for the increase in student population. He or she organizes the schedule in such a way that there is no conflict in schedules and expands the size of the counseling facility as needed.

CONCEPT: DEVELOPS POSITIVE SCHOOL-COMMUNITY RELATIONS

The director develops positive school-community relations to accomplish instructional goals.

Task 1: The director establishes communication with the various school constituencies for the purpose of assessing needs and setting broad instructional goals.

Measurable Indicators of Task 1: The director, in order to develop positive community relationships, communicates effectively in decision making. In order to assess needs to set broad instructional goals, he or she seeks their help by sending newsletter to parents; inviting room mothers to contribute suggestions; seeking ideas at PTA meetings.

Task 2: The director explains school and school district instructional policies and procedures and reports instructional problems and achievements to the school constituencies.

Measurable Indicators of Task 2: The director informs the parents and key members of the community about the school district's instructional policies and procedures. He or she reports instructional problems right in the beginning of the school year and later as there is need through a newsletter, formal meetings after school and at night and to selected PTA members.

Task 3: The director provides an adequate system for reporting students' performances to parents and others (consistent with privacy of information laws).

Measurable Indicators of Task 3: The director feels it is necessary to report to the parents how their children are progressing in their studies at school using report cards, progress sheets, parent conferences.

Task 4: The director provides for the communication to the professional staff at school and district levels about the feelings and desires of the school constituencies as they bear on the instructional program.

Measurable Indicators of Task 4: The director keeps the staff at school and the professionals at district level aware of the feelings and desires of the parents about the instructional program. She or he organizes an informal or a formal meeting with the community and parent representatives to discuss their feelings or problems with the instructional program that the school offers to children, discussion during staff meetings and offering of possible solutions, meetings at the school level.

CONCEPT: DEVELOPS APPROPRIATE IN-SERVICE TRAINING

The director develops appropriate in-service training programs to improve instruction.

Task 1: The director provides for in-service training programs for teachers designed to improve instruction in relation to school goals.

Measurable Indicators of Task 1: In order to improve the quality of instruction, the director provides as many in-services as possible appropriate to their needs including in-service rendered by experts in an area appropriate to those teachers who want it, workshops during staff development, and meaningful conferences.

Task 2: The director guides individual teachers toward appropriate participation in in-service training activities.

Measurable Indicator of Task 2: The director arranges for in-services with the cooperation of the teachers. Therefore the director feels confident that the teachers would make use of the opportunity to learn more about attendance and at-risk students, involving the teachers in the decision making, making commitments of one's time carefully.

Task 3: The director organizes and coordinates in-service training programs so as to make maximally effective use of personnel, time, materials, space, and money.

Measurable Indicator of Task 3: The director arranges for in-services with the cooperation of all the personnel, arranges the schedule appropriately, meeting place convenient to everyone, topic relevant to everyone keeping in mind that the schedule is made collectively and a questionnaire is created to select topic, place, and materials.

Task 4: The director models appropriate instructional methods when leading in-service training sessions for teachers.

Measurable Indicators of Task 4: The director, with the joint cooperation from the staff, prepares for his or her in-service. The director concentrates on the materials that would be meaningful to the staff. She or he prepares materials ahead of time, uses ideas put succinctly on paper, and prepares adequate hand-outs.

Task 5: The director trains other members of the professional staff to assume leadership roles in the in-service and instructional improvement program.

Measurable Indicators of Task 5: The director sends staff member to attend various conferences, workshops, and in-services to come back and share with the other teachers. They then offer staff development and mini-workshops.

Task 6: The director assesses the effectiveness of in-service training activities and makes appropriate revisions.

Measurable Indicators of Task 6: The director makes note of key events and gives the teachers an opportunity to evaluate the in-service to improve or revise it using evaluation forms asking pointed questions that will help in the revision and suggestions from the staff members attending.

CONCEPT: ASSESSES THE NEEDS OF THE SCHOOL

The director assesses the needs of the school in relationship to its goals and evaluates the process and products of instruction in order to provide for the improvement of instruction.

Task 1: The director collects, organizes, analyzes, and interprets data concerning the performance of teachers.

Measurable Indicator of Task 1: It is necessary for the director to help the teachers to improve their performance. Therefore, any data he or she could get to analyze and interpret would help her in helping the teachers using school-wide surveys, self-analysis, self (director) evaluation, teacher evaluation, peer evaluation, questionnaires.

Task 2: The director collects, organizes, analyzes, and interprets data concerning other-than-teacher influences on learning.

Measurable Indicator of Task 2: The director collects information such as student attitude toward school, desire of the parents to participate in their children's school affairs, and their interpersonal relationships to see if the data will help the children learn better using questionnaires, a survey, interviews.

Task 3: The director collects, organizes, analyzes, and interprets data concerning the performance of students.

Measurable Indicators of Task 3: The director is interested in the progress of the students. Since he or she cannot be present in every classroom to observe, the director needs to rely on some other means to collect, organize, analyze, and interpret data concerning their performances including CTBS test scores, SABE test scores, report cards, CLAS test scores.

Task 4: The director collects, organizes, analyzes, and interprets data concerning former students that is indicative of the effectiveness of the instructional program.

Measurable Indicators of Task 4: The director seeks to base his or her decisions on evidence in addition to present students' performance. Therefore, the director uses former students to study the effectiveness of the instructional program for comparison purposes. He or she utilizes former students' records and interviewing of former students' teachers.

Task 5: The director utilizes the data effectively in design and modification of the instructional program for improvement of instruction.

Measurable Indicators of Task 5: Based on all these data the director feels ready and confident to make changes or to create a new improved program design. Procedures may call for redesign of the program altogether, making necessary modifications, use of an expert to design the new program.

NOTE

1. J. Culbertson, *Performance Objectives for School Principals* (Berkeley, Calif.: McCutchan Publishing Corporation, 1974).

Chapter Thirteen

Planning and Supervising the Use of Technology

Teachers shouldn't be forced to change their curriculum just for the purpose of using technology. Any time there is change in instruction, whether it's technological or simply a teaching technique, it should not be imposed, but gradually integrated into the teaching process as teachers come to see its value. Technology is an integral part of teaching in today's society. The goals of the questionnaire for teachers, seen later in this chapter, are first, to develop an idea of the skills of faculty and the types of training that need to be implemented, and second, to determine the attitude of the faculty in terms of the appropriate use of technology. Parent and student questionnaires are also included in the survey effort.

Key Concepts:
Teacher Questionnaire: Skills and Attitude
Teacher Questionnaire: Usage
Student Survey
Parent Questionnaire
Conclusions and Recommendations
Technology Plan—Teachers
Technology Plan—Students
Teacher Competencies
Results

When I first started at Cheerful School (adapted from the work of Curtis Marcel) the school had sixteen Apple IIe computers and one dot matrix printer hooked up to a Corvus system. Since then the administration conducted an extensive needs assessment, involved staff, administrators, and parents, and upgraded the computer lab. Cheerful School now has seven Color Macintosh Classics, nine Macintosh Classics, eight Performa 5200 Power PCs, and one Mac Se30, all hooked up to a LaserWriter Select 360 printer. The Macintosh Classics are on an AppleTalk network daisy chained to the printer on a twenty-four port hub, and the Performas and Color Classics now have 10baseT ethernet connections to the hub. We presently use a Power Mac 7200 as the file server.

The following questionnaires were developed as part of our technology needs assessment. The questionnaires were distributed at a faculty meeting. They evaluate the types of software the faculty uses, the availability of the software, and the amount of expertise in other multimedia equipment on campus. The data from the questionnaires will be evaluated so we can locate faculty to help other faculty with software and equipment they know how to use.

TEACHER QUESTIONNAIRE: SKILLS AND ATTITUDE

As our ongoing process for technology continues, I would like to thank you for taking the time to fill out this questionnaire. Please rate the statements below according to the following scale. Circle the number which best reflects your opinion on each item.

TEACHER QUESTIONNAIRE: USAGE

This questionnaire is a very important part in evaluating the ongoing process of technology at Cheerful. Please fill out the questionnaire and return it to the front office no later than Friday. Thank you for your time!

Please read the Instructional Technology Plan Indicators and check the box that represents your current level of technology usage. Answer "No Access" if you do not have access to the technology, or select "Don't use" if the technology is available but you do not use this particular technology. Check only one box for each category.

Table 13.1. Teacher Questionnaire: Skills and Attitude

No Opinion	Strongly Disagree	Disagree	Agree	Strongly Agree
0	1	2	3	4

	No Opinion	Strongly Disagree	Disagree	Agree	Strongly Agree
I am familiar with computers and use them in the classroom.	0	1	2	3	4
I feel some anxiety using a computer.	0	1	2	3	4
I feel a great deal of anxiety when trying to use the computer in the delivery of instruction.	0	1	2	3	4
Computer-assisted instruction is a valuable experience for children.	0	1	2	3	4
Computer-assisted instruction is valuable in delivery of science instruction.	0	1	2	3	4
Computer-assisted instruction is valuable in delivery of math instruction.	0	1	2	3	4
Computer-assisted instruction is valuable in delivery of reading instruction.	0	1	2	3	4
Computer-assisted instruction is valuable in delivery of thinking-oriented instruction.	0	1	2	3	4
Computer-assisted instruction is valuable in delivery of writing instruction.	0	1	2	3	4
The textbook should be how we learn ideas.	0	1	2	3	4
Computers provide an addition to textbook learning that is valuable.	0	1	2	3	4
Knowledge of technology is important in today's society.	0	1	2	3	4
Computers and other technology are important tools and will probably replace books in some areas of education.	0	1	2	3	4

Please add any additional comments:

Table 13.2. Teacher Questionaire: Usage

	No Access	Don't Use	Beginner	Novice	Proficient
Word Processing					
Databases					
Spreadsheets					
CD-ROMs					
VCRs and Videocassettes					
Instructional Software					
Grading Software					
Laser Discs					
Desktop Publishing					
Telecommunications/E-mail					

STUDENT SURVEY

The questionnaire for the students was passed out the last week of the semester and collected before their last day in the lab. The questionnaire is designed to see if the students developed skills of keyboarding and word processing and had a positive experience when using the computer lab.

As our ongoing process for technology continues, I would like to thank you for taking the time to fill out this questionnaire.

Please rate the statements below according to the following scale. Circle the number which best reflects your opinion on each item.

Table 13.3.   Student Survey

No Opinion 0	Strongly Disagree 1	Disagree 2	Agree 3	Strongly Agree 4

Statement	No Opinion	Strongly Disagree	Disagree	Agree	Strongly Agree
The computer lab was organized in a useful way.	0	1	2	3	4
The computers and printer are in good working order.	0	1	2	3	4
I feel a great deal of anxiety when using a computer.	0	1	2	3	4
I learned proper keyboarding skills.	0	1	2	3	4
There was adequate time doing keyboarding skills.	0	1	2	3	4
I learned proper word processing skills.	0	1	2	3	4
There was adequate time doing word processing.	0	1	2	3	4
I was able to print several writing assignments.	0	1	2	3	4
Computer-assisted instruction is valuable in delivery of reading instruction.	0	1	2	3	4
The software was interesting and made learning fun.	0	1	2	3	4
The time spent in the computer lab was beneficial to my learning.	0	1	2	3	4
Computers provide an addition to textbook learning that can be valuable.	0	1	2	3	4
Knowledge of technology is important in today's society.	0	1	2	3	4
Computers and other technology are important tools and will probably replace books in some areas of education.	0	1	2	3	4

PARENT QUESTIONNAIRE

Parents are critical in developing an effective use of technology in schools. If they are supportive and have been part of the decision process, they can make sure that computers are (a) purchased for school, and (b) purchased for use at home.

In our ongoing process of improving our use of technology, we ask that you fill out this survey and return it as soon as possible. Thank you for your time.

Table 13.4. Parent Questionnaire

No Opinion 0	Strongly Disagree 1	Disagree 2	Agree 3	Strongly Agree 4
I am familiar with computers and use them.	0	1	2	3	4
I am unfamiliar with computers and would like to use them.	0	1	2	3	4
I feel a great deal of anxiety when using a computer.	0	1	2	3	4
I would like to be able to work with a computer frequently.	0	1	2	3	4
Computer-assisted instruction is a valuable experience for children.	0	1	2	3	4
Computer-assisted instruction is valuable in delivery of science instruction.	0	1	2	3	4
Computer-assisted instruction is valuable in delivery of math instruction.	0	1	2	3	4
Computer-assisted instruction is valuable in delivery of reading instruction.	0	1	2	3	4
Computer-assisted instruction is valuable in delivery of thinking-oriented instruction.	0	1	2	3	4
Computer-assisted instruction is valuable in delivery of writing instruction.	0	1	2	3	4
The textbook should be how we learn ideas.	0	1	2	3	4
Computers provide an addition to textbook learning that is valuable.	0	1	2	3	4
Knowledge of technology is important in today's society.	0	1	2	3	4
Computers and other technology are important tools and will probably replace books in some areas of education.	0	1	2	3	4

CONCLUSIONS AND RECOMMENDATIONS

The surveys and questionnaires indicate that there is a desire among the parents, teachers, and students of the school community to bring technology to the school.

Technology must not replace the importance of the teacher but instead, augment the teaching process. Schools should be cautious about technology that is not designed to promote interaction between the student and teacher. Technology is often promoted as a stand-alone learning tool; however, learning also depends on social interaction. An effective multimedia tool will enhance the interaction between student and teacher and reinforce the value of the teacher instead of replacing the teacher.

Parent views are critical. Research conducted in a charter school in Vermont indicated that student performance in reading showed seven months growth (for nine months attendance) for students who perceived their parents were negative about school. Neutral students grew nine months and students who perceived a positive parent view grew fourteen months. The study compared equal groups of students based on test scores and gender.[1]

Cheerful currently has implemented a technology mission statement: "The academic goals established by the School's philosophy statement vows to provide a multifaceted and holistic educational experience which assists each student in the full development of his gifts and talents through a challenging academic program." In order to meet these goals, Cheerful is committed to vast improvements and developments in the area of technology. Because the use of technology is neither an end in itself, nor an add-on, but rather a tool for improving and transforming teaching and learning, technology is an integral part of a comprehensive improvement plan that will move all students toward high academic standards.

The following recommendations are separated into categories for teachers, students, and the new building.

TECHNOLOGY PLAN—TEACHERS

One Year

Four computers—Two Power Macs, one Pentium, and obtain second IBM Compatible 486 from business office for faculty workroom.

Have all four computers hooked to the Internet using at least 54.6 modems

One color ink jet printer

Purchase software

Obtain laminator, 24" wide

Two Years

Obtain one more Power Mac and Pentium computers for faculty work-room

One black/white laser printer

Multimedia computer on TV stand. Instead of purchasing a monitor, purchase TV monitor

Purchase two laptop computers (Macintosh) for teacher checkout

One laser/video disc player w/bar-code reader

Make video camera, scanner, microphone, and so forth, accessible to teachers

Three Years

One more Mac and one more Pentium for faculty workroom. This will bring the total to eight computers

Every classroom with one computer for teacher use with the capability for Internet hookup and multimedia usage

Minimum collection of CD-ROM discs available for teachers (i.e., CD-ROM library for each department including *Collier's* or *Groliers Encyclopedias*)

Two laser/video disc players w/bar-code reader or comparable technology

Four Macs and three Windows-based laptops for teacher checkout

Five Years

Continue building collection of CD-ROMs and laser discs, or comparable technology

Evaluate and update all equipment

One more laser disc player w/bar-code reader, bringing the total to four

TECHNOLOGY PLAN—STUDENTS

One Year

All students are able to word process

Have present lab hooked up to the Internet

Acquire nine more Power Macs for present lab. The goal is to slowly bring the lab to a complete Power Mac lab

Give old computers to teachers for classroom use

Make lab accessible to students either after or before school

Two Years

Acquire eight more Power Macs for present lab. This will bring the lab to twenty-five Power Macs

Evaluate curriculum for graduation requirements in technology

Three Years

Two full labs up-to-date. One Mac lab (present), one Pentium

Both labs with access to the Internet and multimedia capabilities

Students doing research on the Internet

Students using e-mail (this should come much earlier; you need a server to do it)

Students having access to either lab

Five Years

Two classroom sets of laptop computers for student use

Library collection of CD-ROMs

Long Term:

Every student with a computer at their desk with up-to-date technology

TEACHER COMPETENCIES

Teacher Competency Goals for Year One

These goals are divided into several phases. Phase I goals are considered to be basic and should be attained by all teachers. Phase II goals are more intermediate in nature and allow for the school to select the technology area or areas they are concentrating on for the year. Phase III and IV goals allow for a further expansion of skills by teachers. All teachers should make a conscious effort to learn one or more new technologies a year.

In order for these competencies to be met, appropriate software must be available.

Phase I—Basic Skills Attainment

Goal 1: Demonstrates basic word processing skills

1. Creates a memo, knows how to include graphics
2. Uses a computer to create a worksheet or test
3. Saves a file on a diskette and/or file server
4. Can edit a file as needed

Goal 2: Selects and uses appropriate technology when teaching:

1. Includes appropriate software as part of regular lesson plans
2. Computer is used for teacher demonstrations and as a student workstation
3. Works with technology coordinator to integrate lesson plans with all activities
4. Uses available multimedia equipment including: VCR and tapes, LCD panel or large display monitor, CD-ROMs

Goal 3: Uses available grading software on a regular basis

Phase II—Intermediate Skills Attainment
   Goal 4: Accesses and uses network

1. Can successfully use e-mail (internal and/or Internet)
2. Creates and replies to messages
3. Can delete messages
4. Knows how to use the Help command
5. Knows how to make a group mailing

Goal 5: Uses the Internet

1. Can access the World Wide Web and use search tools (e.g., Yahoo!)
2. Understands appropriate use of the Internet
3. Participates in Electronic Field Trips as appropriate
4. Able to research over the Internet

Goal 6: Uses some multimedia hardware such as:

1. Laser disc player
2. Video camera
3. Digital camera

4. Scanner
5. Computer
6. MIDI (music creation) keyboard
7. Microphone for recording sound

Phase III—Advanced Skills Attainment
   Goal 7: Uses the Internet regularly and can:

1. Save graphics from the Internet
2. Transfer text from a website to word processing
3. Print a Web page
4. Identify the difference in types of sites available (collaborative, search, publication)
5. Use bookmarks

   Goal 8: Engages in multimedia production

1. Integrates motion, sound, and graphics
2. Performs video capturing and editing
3. Hooks up camera, VCR, and computer
4. Understands hypertext presentation styles (tutorials versus reports) and when to use them

Phase IV—Future Goals
   Goal 9: To share developed projects and tools via:

1. Web pages
2. Computer-based presentations
3. Video conferences

Appendix to Teacher Competencies

Evaluate all software that we have.
Department chairs will select someone in their respective departments to evaluate and choose software.
Make sure there is software to meet competencies for teachers.
Start in-service training.

Develop a mandatory date for selected competencies.

Provide an in-service for teachers. They may choose to go elsewhere for training.

Start training certain personnel in grant writing.

Train teachers in technology ethics.

Departments should incorporate an ongoing process to evaluate wants and needs for technology specific to department needs.

Budgeting: Four different accounts will be developed within the technology budget. They shall include: hardware (computers, etc.), software, networking, training.

RESULTS

Parents

The technology use plan survey for parents was given to find out whether parents believe that their child was getting adequate training in technology. Forty-nine parents took part in the survey with positive results.

Teachers

Thirty-three teachers participated in both surveys. The first survey for teachers was to indicate the ability of the faculty in the usage of technology and software. The results of the survey were listed in the format seen here.

Table 13.5. Teacher Questionaire: Usage

	No Access	Don't Use	Beginner	Novice	Proficient
Word Processing					
Databases					
Spreadsheets					
CD-ROMs					
VCRs and Videocassettes					
Instructional Software					
Grading Software					
Laser Discs					
Desktop Publishing					
Telecommunications/E-mail					

Students

The student survey was conducted in the same fashion as the teacher survey on attitude. The survey asked questions to decide whether the students developed skills and acquired a positive attitude relative to technology. Eighty students participated in the survey, and the data were analyzed in the same way as the teacher survey with no opinion selections not counted in the average. The results were positive also.

NOTE

1. William Callison, *A Study of the Effect of Parent Involvement on Reading Performance* (Plainfield, Vt.: Goddard College, 1974).

Chapter Fourteen

Identifying At-Risk Students Using Risk Assessment

This chapter presents a model for using the risk assessment system to place at-risk students into appropriate interventions and, more importantly perhaps, to keep track of their progress. Most teachers know which of their students are at-risk but they often cannot accurately remember which interventions, if any, have been delivered. This is critical to know since a director and the teachers involved need to know what was delivered in order to know if it worked. Instructional improvement rests on knowing which interventions are successful and changing or deleting them if they are not. Schools can create their own approach or adapt the Students-at-Risk (SAR) Risk Assessment approach to their existing situation.

Key Concepts:
A Model Risk Assessment Questionnaire
The Questionnaire and Suggested Interventions
Attendance

A MODEL ELEMENTARY RISK ASSESSMENT QUESTIONNAIRE

Explanation of the Levels of Intervention

(1) The interventions suggested are in order of intensity, Level I requiring the least intensive intervention and Level III the most intensive.

(2) Teachers, resource people, or administrators could provide most Level I or Level II responses as a part of their usual and expected interactions with students and parents. Level III interventions may include specialized programs and outside agencies.

(3) In every instance that the student's response to the Risk Assessment Questionnaire has triggered a suggested intervention, it is strongly recommended that you make at least a Level I response, which typically means a one-to-one interview with the student.

(4) Level I interventions will suggest an individual meeting or interview with the student to gather more information. Suggestions for discussion will be offered. The Level I interview will help to ascertain whether Level II or Level III interventions will be most beneficial.

(5) Level II interventions may suggest ongoing support by a teacher, resource person, or mentor, to monitor the student's situation. Ideas for skill building through particular programs may be noted as well as possible referral to outside agencies for family counseling.

(6) Level III interventions may be more immediate and acute. Specialized skills will be noted with interventions provided by school resource people or outside agencies, depending on the need and resources available at your site.

In schools with resource people, Level III interventions might typically be provided by them. However, with special programs, training, and support, interventions could also be provided by teachers. For example, many schools already have programs in place to provide drug and alcohol education as well as programs to foster self-esteem and communication skills.

If a suggested Level III intervention does not seem to fall within any program you presently have, you may be able to use the intervention description and the material in the training videos to design your own intervention, you may want to consult the "Sample Programs" referenced, and/or you may want to refer the student/family to an outside agency.

It is highly suggested that educators consult with others before undertaking Level III responses. Depending upon your school situation, you might consult with another teacher, with an appropriate administrator, with the school resource person and/or psychologist, or with the student study team.

(7) Note: Because it is the student who decides how to respond to each question, it is also helpful for educators to use their knowledge and experience in interpreting the responses.

For example, Question 1 asks: How frequently are you angry? The responses include: never, sometimes, frequently, and very frequently. What one student considers frequently may seem to peers and teachers to be very frequently, or, on the other hand, to be only sometimes. It all depends on the student's frame of reference. In deciding what level of intervention is necessary, it is helpful to look at what you know of—and can learn about—the student, in addition to the student's responses to the questionnaire.

The Questionnaire and Suggested Interventions

QUESTION 1
The first question students respond to is:
1. How often are you angry?
   (0) never
   (1) sometimes
   (2) frequently
   (3) very frequently
If the student responds with a (2) score or higher, you should use a Level II intervention (preceded, as always, by a Level I intervention).

Level I

Interview the student for reasons, in order to select the appropriate intervention(s).

First, establish a caring and helpful environment/relationship with the student so that the student will trust you to give you information.

You may share some information about yourself, that you care about students, that you work on special programs, that you experienced some challenging times growing up, etc. (whatever may be appropriate).

Suggestions for discussion topics include the following: Tell me about your day. Is there a particular time of the day you notice anger? Is there a particular situation/person (teacher, peer, parent, important relationship, etc.) that triggers anger for you? Have you gone through any family or relationship changes in the past few years?

This initial interview may show you what additional interventions, if any, are needed. For example, if a student's anger is a result of inadequate social skills, identifying and teaching particular skills may be helpful. If the anger is due to a family crisis, other responses will be more appropriate (see examples below).

Level II

If indicated by the computer recommendation or information gathered in the interview, assign the student to a mentor or resource person who can provide ongoing support and monitoring of the student's situation. If your school does not have a mentoring program in place, this may be done informally. The mentor needs to have regularly scheduled contact with the student and provide "evidence" that there is someone who cares. This might involve help with schoolwork or other problems, sending a birthday card and other little notes, and occasional activities together.

Level II interventions may also include informal discussion and brainstorming of alternative behaviors and teaching of social skills or self-esteem fundamentals.

If no mentors are available at your site, consider referral to an outside group that offers mentors. (Sample programs may include Big Sisters/Brothers, College or Business Mentoring Programs, etc.)

Level III

Level III interventions will vary according to the reasons for the student's anger. Possible interventions are as follows:

(1) If the student's anger is due to a crisis in his or her personal life—birth of a sibling, divorce, serious illness, or death in the family, etc.—teach coping skills, such as recognizing feelings of anger, control issues, and depression; coming to terms with problems; and learning to hope.

(2) Teaching stress management skills may also be helpful.

(3) If the student's anger is due to lack of social skills, teach communication skills, skills for making friends, etc., as appropriate.

(4) If the student's anger is due to deep-seated family or social problems, consider referral for individual and/or family counseling.

QUESTION 2

The second question on the questionnaire is:

2. I understand what the teacher says.
   (0) always
   (1) usually
   (2) seldom
   (3) never

If the student's response is (1) or higher, the following interventions may be recommended on your computer read-out.

Level I

Interview the student for reasons, in order to select the appropriate intervention(s).

First, establish a caring and helpful environment/relationship with the student so that the student will trust you to give you information.

You may share some information about yourself, that you care about students, that you work on special programs, that you experienced some challenging times growing up, etc. (whatever may be appropriate).

Topics for discussion: What do you think of/feel about why you don't understand what your teacher says? Do you speak a language other than English? What do you do to try to understand your teacher? Is there a student who helps you understand what your teacher says? Do you have several students who help you understand your teacher? What is your favorite subject? Least favorite? Tell me what happens after school/in the evenings/on the weekends. Have you and/or your family gone through any big changes? Whom do you hang around with at school? What is the hardest thing about school? Is there anyone to help you at home? What year in school was your best/most difficult? (You may need to check cum file, especially for younger students.) Is there a learning difficulty? Responses to these questions will identify what, if any, interventions may be helpful.

Level II

If indicated by the computer recommendation or information gathered in the interview, assign the student to a mentor or friend who speaks his or her language who can provide ongoing support and monitoring of the student's situation. If your school does not have a mentoring program in place, this may be done informally. The mentor needs to have regularly scheduled contact with the student and provide "evidence" that there is someone who cares. This might involve help with schoolwork or other problems, sending a birthday card and other little notes, and occasional activities together.

Parent conference: Explore the same topics you covered in the interview with the student. In addition, does the student have someone at home who can help with language skills and/or who has training in how to help a child with schoolwork? You may be able to do this parent education during the conference. If more help is needed, refer the parent to school parenting and/or homework workshops, if available. Refer to outside programs if needed and available.

Provide academic assistance: Assign a tutor, if available, or guide student to outside tutoring programs. Arrange for or provide instruction in English as a Second Language, if needed.

Consider using a behavior modification program with the student, such as a daily contract for getting work done on time and correctly, with an appropriate system of positive responses.

Level III

Refer student to the student study team for evaluation and recommendations, if there appear to be severe academic problems.

Refer student for counseling, if the academic problems seem to be a function of personal problems. If the student is experiencing a life crisis, consider teaching skills for coping: recognizing feelings of anger, control issues, and depression; coming to terms with problems; and learning to hope. (Sample programs may include STAGES, small group counseling, PAL, etc.)

QUESTION 3

The third question on the questionnaire is:
3. I usually do what the teacher wants in class.
    (0) always
    (1) usually
    (2) seldom
    (3) never

If the student's response is (2) or higher, the following interventions may be recommended on your computer read-out.

Level I

Interview the student for reasons, in order to select the appropriate intervention(s).

First, establish a caring and helpful environment/relationship with the student so that the student will trust you to give you information.

You may share some information about yourself, that you care about students, that you work on special programs, that you experienced some challenging times growing up, etc. (whatever may be appropriate).

Suggestions for discussion topics: Tell me about your day. What situations bring you to not do what your teacher wants? What do people do that really bothers you? How do you think people usually experience anger? What do you think about students who disobey? What happens when people don't obey the teacher? What is the worst thing you can think of that might happen to a person who doesn't obey the teacher? What do people do when they are really upset? Have you gone through any family changes in the past few years? What changes has your family experienced? This initial interview may show you what additional interventions, if any, are needed.

Level II

If a student's inability to obey the teacher seems to be primarily a function of confusion about misunderstood emotion, inadequate modeling, and/or information, provide education on appropriate and inappropriate expressions of resistance to authority. Explain that disobeying the teacher is understandable; brainstorm healthy ways of expressing resistance to authority; model appropriate behavior, etc. Infuse such modeling and discussion into the daily life of the classroom, monitoring the student's progress informally.

You may want to consider the appropriateness of a simple behavior modification program for the student, such as a system of "rewards" for appropriate reactions to the teacher. (Remember that an elaborate program need not be designed—The system may be as simple as an agreement between you and the student that you will send him or her a private signal of congratulations when she expresses appropriate response to the teacher.)

Level III

If the student needs to learn to communicate thoughts and feelings assertively, use a communication skills program to teach these skills.

If the student's resistance to the teacher continues, refer to appropriate personnel and agencies school administration, resource person, and/or psychologist; Child Protective Services, etc. keeping in contact with the student as he or she goes through this often confusing process.

QUESTION 4

The fourth question on the questionnaire is:

4. How often do you argue with teachers?
   (0) never
   (1) sometimes
   (2) frequently
   (3) very frequently

If the student's response is (2) or higher, the following interventions may be recommended on your computer read-out.

Level I

Interview the student for reasons, in order to select the appropriate intervention(s).

First, establish a caring and helpful environment/relationship with the student so that the student will trust you to give you information.

You may share some information about yourself, that you care about students, that you work on special programs, that you experienced some challenging times growing up, etc. (whatever may be appropriate).

Suggestions for discussion topics: Tell me about your day. Is there a particular time of the day you notice that you argue? Is there a particular teacher that triggers argument for you? Have you gone through any family or relationship changes in the past few years where there has been a lot of arguing?

This initial interview may show you what additional interventions, if any, are needed. For example, if a student's arguing is a result of inadequate social skills, identifying and teaching particular skills may be helpful. If the arguing and anger is due to a family crisis, other responses will be more appropriate (see examples below).

Level II

Assign the student to a mentor or resource person who can provide ongoing support and monitoring of the student's situation. If your school does not have a mentoring program in place, this may be done informally. The mentor needs to have regularly scheduled contact with the student and provide "evidence" that there is someone who cares and who can work with him or her to reduce the tendency to argue with teachers. This might involve help with schoolwork or other problems, sending a birthday card and other little notes, and occasional activities together.

Level II interventions may also include informal discussion and brainstorming of alternative behaviors and teaching of social skills or self-esteem fundamentals.

If no mentors are available at your site, consider referral to an outside group that offers mentors. (Sample programs may include Big Sisters/Brothers, College or Business Mentoring Programs, etc.)

Level III

Level III interventions will vary according to the reasons for the student's argumentative tendencies. Possible interventions are as follows:

(1) If the student's argumentative behavior is due to a crisis in his or her personal life—birth of a sibling, divorce, serious illness, or death in the family, etc.—teach coping skills, such as recognizing feelings of anger, control issues, and depression; coming to terms with problems; and learning to hope.
(2) Teaching stress management skills may also be helpful.
(3) If the student's behavior is due to lack of social skills, teach communication skills, skills for making friends, etc., as appropriate.
(4) If the student's behavior is due to deep-seated family or social problems, consider referral for individual and/or family counseling.

QUESTION 5
The fifth question on the questionnaire is:
5. Do your parents know your whereabouts after school?
    (0) always
    (1) usually

(2) seldom

(3) never

If the student's response is (2) or higher, the following interventions may be recommended on your computer read-out.

Level I

Interview the student for reasons, in order to select the appropriate intervention(s).

First, establish a caring and helpful environment/relationship with the student so that the student will trust you to give you information.

You may share some information about yourself, that you care about students, that you work on special programs, that you experienced some challenging times growing up, etc. (whatever may be appropriate).

Topics for discussion: Does the family have a childcare problem? Have the parents indicated that they don't care where the student is? Is there evidence that the parents feel they can't control the student, etc.? What would happen if your parents did know what you are doing? Has your family gone through any major changes in the past few years? How do people in your family feel? What do people in your family think about? What would happen if something happened to you while you were out? How does your family feel about your friends? At what age do you think kids can take care of themselves? How do you know that? Etc. The responses will tell you what additional response, if any, is required.

Level II

Interview parents. The family may need referral to after-school care programs such as latch key programs operated by the YMCA/YWCA, local colleges, or the district, Girls' Club/Boys' Club, etc. Parents may need referral to district or outside programs for parent effectiveness training—need for setting limits, communicating with children, etc.

If indicated by the computer recommendation or information gathered in the interview, assign the student to a mentor or resource person who can provide ongoing support and monitoring of the student's situation. If your school does not have a mentoring program in place, this may be done informally. The mentor needs to have regularly scheduled contact with the student and provide "evidence" that there is someone who cares. This might involve help with schoolwork or other problems, sending a birthday card and other little notes, and occasional activities together.

Level III

Lack of supervision may be so serious that a referral to Child Protective Services is indicated because of neglect. Involve administrators and other appropriate and available personnel in this decision. If there is evidence for such a referral from your initial interview with the student, you need to proceed directly to this level of intervention after the interview.

Students may need close monitoring at school, having someone to "check in" with several times a day. The mentor would show care and concern in a benevolent manner.

QUESTION 6
The sixth question on the questionnaire is:
6. How often do you feel all alone?
   (0) never
   (1) seldom
   (2) usually
   (3) always
If the student's response is (2) or higher, the following interventions may be recommended on your computer read-out (note that the numbering is different on this question).

Level I

Interview the student for reasons, in order to select the appropriate intervention(s).

First, establish a caring and helpful environment/relationship with the student so that the student will trust you to give you information.

You may share some information about yourself, that you care about students, that you work on special programs, that you experienced some challenging times growing up, etc. (whatever may be appropriate).

Topics for discussion: Tell me about your day. Is the student lonely due to problems making friends? If that is the problem, is it shyness, being new, or the fact that something about the student's behavior causes his or her peers to reject him or her? Has your family gone through any changes in the past few years? How does it feel for you to be alone? What do you think about? What happens when you get home from school? What do you and your family do after school/in the evening/on the weekend? What kinds of things make people sad? What happens when people feel sad? Etc. (If you sense the student may be depressed, check with resource people, school psychologists, etc., for intervention on Level III.) Choose appropriate Level II and/or Level III interventions according to the results of this interview.

Level II

Assign the student to a mentor or resource person who can provide ongoing support and monitoring of the student's situation. If your school does not have a mentoring program in place, this may be done informally. The mentor needs to have regularly scheduled contact with the student and provide "evidence" that there is someone who cares. This might involve help with schoolwork or other problems, sending a birthday card and other little notes, and occasional activities together.

It may also be helpful to assign a "special friend" to the student. Your school may have a mechanism for doing this: leadership team, peer assistance team, PAL, etc. If not, make use of your contact with and knowledge of the other students to find students who would enjoy doing this and who would also be in contact with you or other mentors, so that the peer does not feel responsible for the identified student's behavior.

Level III

If the student has been through family changes and is feeling sad, he or she may not understand this natural emotion. The need may be in the area of social skills.

If the student seems depressed, referral of student to school/ community counseling services may be necessary. Family referral to outside agencies may also be helpful. If the family has been through a major change, parenting resources such as grief adjustment or loss programs may be helpful.

QUESTION 7

The seventh question on the questionnaire is:

7. Do your parents/guardians listen to you and attempt to understand your problems?
    (0) always
    (1) usually
    (2) seldom
    (3) never

If the student's response is (2) or higher, the following interventions may be recommended on your computer read-out.

Level I

Interview the student for reasons, in order to select the appropriate intervention(s).

First, establish a caring and helpful environment/relationship with the student so that the student will trust you to give you information.

You may share some information about yourself, that you care about students, that you work on special programs, that you experienced some challenging times growing up, etc. (whatever may be appropriate).

Topics for discussion: Whom do you share your thoughts and feelings with at school/home? What happens when you get home from school/in the evening/on the weekends? When do people in your family talk? What happens when people in your family talk together? How do you feel during the day? Check to see if parents' hectic work scheduling makes it difficult to provide support. Has your family been through any big changes in the past few years? Is there evidence that parents are unaware of the importance of listening to their children? The student's response to these questions will suggest what level of intervention would be beneficial, if any.

Level II

It may be helpful to conduct a parent conference. The content will be a function of the results of the student interview and the responses the parent makes during this conference. It may be that the family is experiencing a crisis or has many demands and needs referral to outside agencies. The parent may need/desire parent education. This education may simply take the form of the communication that occurs at this conference—the parent becomes aware of the student's feelings and understands the significance of his or her responsiveness. If more education is needed, it might be provided by the school resource person or psychologist, or by a district parenting class.

Teaching the student social skills to express thoughts and feelings may be beneficial. Modeling sharing and teaching social conversation and listening skills may be needed.

Level III

The student may be experiencing some kind of life crisis—birth of a sibling, serious illness or death of a family member or other significant person, family financial crisis, divorce, etc. If so, provide support and instruction in coping skills, such as recognizing feelings of anger, control issues, and depression; coming to terms with problems; and learning to hope.

Referral to counseling: If the student is angry or depressed, it may be helpful to spend time with the school resource person or psychologist for additional support. It may also be important to refer the student and/or family for individual and/or family counseling or district/city/county programs.

QUESTION 8

The eighth question on the questionnaire is:

8. Have you ever been sent to the principal's office for a behavior problem?

(0) no

(1) yes

If the student's response is (1), the following interventions may be recommended on your computer read-out.

Level I

Interview the student for reasons, in order to select the appropriate intervention(s).

First, establish a caring and helpful environment/relationship with the student so that the student will trust you to give you information.

You may share some information about yourself, that you care about students, that you work on special programs, that you experienced some challenging times growing up, etc. (whatever may be appropriate).

Topics for discussion: How many times have you been sent to the principal's office? What is your version of what happened (choose one or more occasions)? Tell me about the kids at school. What happens during your day/after school/in the evenings/on the weekends? Have you and/or your family gone through any big changes in the past few years? What kinds of things make you angry? How do people usually express anger? What happens to them? How are you doing in class? What do you think about your teacher? What does your teacher think about you? What subject(s) do you like/not like? What consequences do you have at school/home for seeing the principal? The responses will guide your choice of any additional interventions.

Level II

If indicated by the computer recommendation or information gathered in the interview, assign the student to a mentor or resource person who can provide ongoing support and monitoring of the student's situation. If your school does not have a mentoring program in place, this may be done informally. The mentor needs to have regularly scheduled contact with the student and provide "evidence" that there is someone who cares. This might involve help with schoolwork or other problems, sending a birthday card and other little notes, and occasional activities together.

Consider referral to school resource person, if available. Consider a behavior modification program focused on reducing number of incidents of misbehavior and/or referrals, rewarding the student for appropriate behavior, etc.

Hold a parent conference. Is behavior the same at home? If not, what does the parent think is wrong at school? If behavior is the same at home, offer help. If appropriate, discuss some of the options described below, as possible steps the family might take.

Provide new responsibilities as alternative activities to replace the patterns that have gotten the student into trouble. Provide opportunities for involvement in clubs, scouts, etc. give the student a special responsibility (something active) at school and recognition for completion.

Provide academic assistance, if behavior problems are related to academic problems. (Sample programs may include tutoring, peer tutoring, ESL, changing student's program, referral to the student study team, or help for parents on how to work with the child at home.)

Level III

Provide instruction in social skills, if student's misbehavior reflects lack of knowledge in interpersonal communication and or lack of social skills that leads to aggressive responses. Consider special instruction in these areas: understanding own personality style, making friends, being a friend, communicating needs, etc.

If the behaviors seem connected to a lack of interpersonal skills and relationships with peers, consider assigning a student "special friend" to give the student recognition and extra attention.

Consider referral for individual and/or group counseling for the student and family within the district/city/county, if the student's behavior is due to deep-seated family or social problems.

Monitor frequency and severity of referrals to the principal to see if problems persist.

QUESTION 9

The ninth question on the questionnaire is:

9. How many Ds and Fs did you receive last semester?

   1

   2

   3

   4

   5

   6

If the student's response is (1) or higher, the following interventions may be recommended on your computer read-out.

Level I

Interview the student for reasons, in order to select the appropriate intervention(s).

First, establish a caring and helpful environment/relationship with the student so that the student will trust you to give you information.

You may share some information about yourself, that you care about students, that you work on special programs, that you experienced some challenging times growing up, etc. (whatever may be appropriate).

Topics for discussion: What do you think of/feel about school? What do you think of your teacher? What is your favorite subject? Least favorite? Tell me what happens after school/in the evenings/on the weekends. Have you and/or your family gone through any big changes? Whom do you hang around with at school? What is the hardest thing about school? Is there anyone to help you at home? What year in school was your best/most difficult? (You may need to check cum file, especially for younger students.) Is there a language or other learning difficulty? Responses to these questions will identify what, if any, interventions may be helpful.

Level II

Assign the student to a mentor or resource person who can provide ongoing support and monitoring of the student's situation. If your school does not have a mentoring program in place, this may be done informally. The mentor needs to have regularly scheduled contact with the student and provide "evidence" that there is someone who cares. This might involve help with schoolwork or other problems, sending a birthday card and other little notes, and occasional activities together.

Parent conference: Explore the same topics you covered in the interview with the student. In addition, does the parent appear to need help with parenting skills and/or training in how to help a child with schoolwork? You may be able to do this parent education during the conference. If more help is needed, refer the parent to school parenting and/or homework workshops, if available. Refer to outside programs if needed and available.

Provide academic assistance: Assign a tutor, if available, or guide student to outside tutoring programs. Arrange for or provide instruction in English as a Second Language, if needed.

Consider using a behavior modification program with the student, such as a daily contract for getting work done on time and correctly, with an appropriate system of positive responses.

Level III

Refer student to the student study team for evaluation and recommendations, if there appear to be severe academic problems.

Refer student for counseling, if the academic problems seem to be a function of personal problems. If the student is experiencing a life crisis, consider teaching skills for coping: recognizing feelings of anger, control issues, and depression; coming to terms with problems; and learning to hope.

QUESTION 10

The tenth question on the questionnaire is:

10. Have you ever been suspended or expelled from school?

    (0) no

    (1) yes

If the student's response is (1), the following interventions may be recommended on your computer read-out.

Level I

Interview the student for reasons, in order to select the appropriate intervention(s).

First, establish a caring and helpful environment/relationship with the student so that the student will trust you to give you information.

You may share some information about yourself, that you care about students, that you work on special programs, that you experienced some challenging times growing up, etc. (whatever may be appropriate).

Topics for discussion: What do you think of/feel about school? What happened to cause you to be suspended? How are things at home? When did things get tough here at school? How are your relationships going? (Friends, family, etc.) Is there anything you feel really angry about now? Have you or your family been through any big changes in the past few years? This year? (Check cum file.) How many times have you been suspended? What happens at home when this occurs? The student's response will guide you in deciding which additional interventions, if any, are needed.

Level II

If indicated by the computer recommendation or information gathered in the interview, assign the student to a mentor or resource person who can provide ongoing support and monitoring of the student's situation. If your school does not have a mentoring program in place, this may be done informally. The mentor needs to have regularly scheduled contact with the student and provide "evidence" that there is someone who cares. This might involve help with schoolwork or other problems, sending a birthday card and other little notes, and occasional activities together.

Assign student to a peer advisor if your school offers such a program, particularly if the suspension may be partially a function of a poor choice of friends.

Parent conference: Explore the same topics you covered in the interview with the student. In addition, does the parent appear to need help with parenting skills and/or training in how to help a child with behavior/anger management, etc.? You may be able to do this parent education during the conference. If more help is needed, refer the parent to school parenting and/or district/city/county workshops, etc. Refer to outside programs if needed and available.

Level III

If indicated, arrange for instruction in social skills if student's misbehavior reflects lack of knowledge in interpersonal communication and/or lack of social skills. Consider special instruction in these areas: understanding own personality style, making friends, being a friend, communicating needs, etc.

Refer student to the student study team for evaluation and recommendations, if there appear to be severe academic/behavior problems.

Refer student/family for individual or group counseling, if the expulsions or suspensions seem to be a function of personal problems. If the student is experiencing a life crisis, consider teaching skills for coping: recognizing feelings of anger, control issues, and depression; coming to terms with problems; and learning to hope.

QUESTION 11

The eleventh question on the questionnaire is:

11. How many times last semester were you absent?

 1–10
 11–20
 21–30
 31–40
 41–50
 51–60

If the student's response is (11) or higher, the following interventions may be recommended on your computer read-out.

Note: This number is designed for schools where a high absence rate is typical. The critical number may be less than 11 in some schools; consider the normal attendance profile for your school.

Level I

Interview the student for reasons, in order to select the appropriate intervention(s).

First, establish a caring and helpful environment/relationship with the student so that the student will trust you to give you information.

You may share some information about yourself, that you care about students, that you work on special programs, that you experienced some challenging times growing up, etc. (whatever may be appropriate).

Topics for discussion: What kinds of things keep you at home? (Check cum file or other records for a pattern of excessive absences.) What do you think of school this year? What do you like/dislike? Tell me about your friends. What do you think of your teacher this year? What does your teacher think about you? Have you or a family member been through any big changes—new baby, financial, divorce, loss, moving, etc.? What happens when you get sick? Who takes care of you? (Does the student have a neglected or undetected health problem? If indicated, consider additional interventions, working with your school nurse or community health programs.) How are things at home? (Check for any signs of abuse and make appropriate reports to your school team and Child Protective Services.) Responses in this interview will direct you to other interventions, if any.

Level II

Monitor student absence. Consider a behavior modification program to improve attendance. Some schools have special attendance clubs; individual teachers can also design a program of attendance incentives.

Assign student to an adult mentor, to increase student's bonding to school. Many students are convinced that, "Nobody cares whether I'm here or not. They probably don't even notice." If indicated by the computer recommendation or information gathered in the interview, assign the student to a mentor or resource person who can provide ongoing support and monitoring of the student's situation. If your school does not have a mentoring program in place, this may be done informally. The mentor needs to have regularly scheduled contact with the student and provide "evidence" that there is someone who cares. This might involve help with schoolwork or other problems, sending a birthday card and other little notes, and occasional activities together.

Refer student or family to school nurse or outside health provider, if student has (or may have) unmet health needs.

If the behaviors seem to be a cry for attention, consider assigning a student "special friend" to give the student recognition and extra attention.

If the student indicates that he or she was absent for reasons other than illness or for very minor complaints, the following interventions are recommended:

Level III

If student absence due to parental neglect, babysitting, etc., hold a parent conference, possibly refer to district or site attendance personnel.

If absences seem related to emotional problems, consider referral for counseling. If student is experiencing a life crisis—serious illness or death in the family, divorce, birth of a sibling, etc.—consider teaching skills for coping. This includes learning to recognize feelings of anger, control issues, and depression; learning to come to terms with problems; and learning to hope.

QUESTION 12

The twelfth question on the questionnaire is:

12. How many times have you moved or changed schools in the previous year?

    1

    2

    3

    4

    5

    6

If the student's response is (1) or higher, the following interventions may be recommended on your computer read-out.

Level I

Interview the student for reasons, in order to select the appropriate intervention(s).

First, establish a caring and helpful environment/relationship with the student so that the student will trust you to give you information.

You may share some information about yourself, that you care about students, that you work on special programs, that you experienced some challenging times growing up, etc. (whatever may be appropriate).

Topics for discussion: Sometimes, it's hard for people to move. What is moving like for you? Which move did you like? What was the hardest move? A lot of people have a hard time making new friends. How have you done with making friends? What do you like to do with your friends? What kind of things do friends like to do here at this school? How are things going at home? What do you think of school/your teacher? Have you or other family members been through other big changes in the past year? When there are lots of changes, it is sometimes hard on families. How are you doing? How is your workload here at school? How long do you spend on homework? The student's responses will determine the interventions you select, if any.

If indicated by the computer recommendation or information gathered in the interview, assign the student to a mentor or resource person who can provide ongoing support and monitoring of the student's situation. If your school does not have a mentoring program in place, this may be done informally. The mentor needs to have regularly scheduled contact with the student and provide "evidence" that there is someone who cares. This might involve help with schoolwork or other problems, sending a birthday card and other little notes, and occasional activities together.

Level II interventions may also include informal discussion and brainstorming of alternative behaviors and teaching of social skills or self-esteem fundamentals.

If no mentors are available at your site, consider referral to an outside group that offers mentors.

It may also be helpful to assign a "special friend" to the student. Your school may have a mechanism for doing this: leadership team or peer assistance team. If not, make use of your contact with and knowledge of the other students to find students who would enjoy doing this and who would also be in contact with you or other mentors, so that the peer does not feel responsible for the student's behavior.

Level III

If the student has been through family changes and is feeling sad, he or she may not understand this natural emotion. The need may be in the area of social skills.

Individual or group counseling programs may help this student to talk with others who have been through changes and learn coping skills.

If the student seems angry or depressed, referral of student to school/community counseling services may be necessary. Family referral to outside agencies may also be helpful.

Risk assessment software for PC computers is available from: Students at Risk, 1260 Brangwyn Way, Laguna Beach, CA 92651, e-mail: bcallison@cox.net.

We suggest that each school invest in one or more copies of the *Pre-Referral Intervention Manual* by Stephen McCarney and his colleagues[1] to supplement our suggestions.

RISK ASSESSMENT QUESTIONNAIRE
EXPLANATION OF THE LEVELS OF INTERVENTION

The interventions suggested are in order of intensity, Level I requiring the least intensive intervention, and Level III the most intensive.

Teachers, resource persons, or administrators could provide most Level I or Level II responses as a part of their usual and expected interactions with students and parents. Level III interventions may include specialized programs and outside agencies.

In every instance where the student's response to the risk assessment questionnaire has triggered a suggested intervention, it is strongly recommended that you make at least a Level I response, which typically means a one-to-one interview with the student.

Level I interventions will suggest an individual meeting or interview with the student to gather more information. Suggestions for discussion will be offered. The Level I interview will help to ascertain whether Level II or Level III interventions will be most beneficial.

Level II interventions may suggest ongoing support by a teacher, resource person, or mentor to monitor the student's situation. Ideas for skill building through particular programs may be noted as well as possible referral to outside agencies for family counseling.

Level III interventions may be more immediate and acute. Specialized skills will be noted with interventions provided by school resource persons or outside agencies, depending on the need and resources available at your site. In schools with resource persons, Level III interventions might typically be provided by them. However, with special programs, training, and support, interventions could also be provided by teachers. For example, many schools already have programs in place to provide drug and alcohol education as well as programs to foster self-esteem and communication skills. If a suggested Level III intervention does not seem to fall within any program you presently have, you may be able to use the intervention description and the material in the training videos to design your own intervention, you may want to consult the "Sample Programs" referenced, and/or to refer the student/family to an outside agency. It is highly suggested that educators consult with others before undertaking Level III responses. Depending upon your school situation, you might consult with another teacher, with an appropriate administrator, with the school resource person, and/or psychologist, or with the student study team.

Note: since it is the student who decides how to respond to each question, it is also helpful for educators to use their knowledge and experience in interpreting the responses. For example, Question 1 asks: How frequently are you angry? The responses include: "never," "sometimes," "frequently," and "very frequently." What one student considers frequently may seem to peers and teachers to be very frequently, or, on the other hand, to be only sometimes. It all depends on the student's frame of reference. In deciding what level of intervention is necessary, it is helpful to look at what you know of, and can learn about, the student, in addition to the student's responses to the questionnaire.

THE QUESTIONNAIRE AND SUGGESTED INTERVENTIONS

The first question students respond to is: How frequently are you angry? If the student responds with a (2) score or higher, you should use a Level II intervention (preceded, as always, by a Level I intervention):

Level I

Interview the student for reasons, in order to select the appropriate intervention/s.

First, establish a caring and helpful environment/relationship with the student so that the student will trust you to give you information.

You may share some information about yourself, that you care about students, that you work on special programs, that you experienced some challenging times growing up, etc. (whatever may be appropriate).

Suggestions for discussion topics include: Tell me about your day. Is there a particular time of the day you notice anger? Is there a particular situation/person (teacher, peer, parent, important relationship, etc.) that triggers anger for you? Have you gone through any family or relationship changes in the last few years?

This initial interview may show you what additional interventions, if any, are needed. For example, if student's anger is a result of inadequate social skills, identifying and teaching particular skills may be helpful. If the anger is due to a family crisis, other responses will be more appropriate (see examples below).

Level II

If indicated by the computer recommendation or information gathered in the interview, assign the student to a mentor or resource person who can provide ongoing support and monitoring of the student's situation. If your school does not have a mentoring program in place, this may be done informally. The mentor needs to have regularly scheduled contact with the student and provide "evidence" that there is someone who cares. This might involve help with schoolwork or other problems, sending a birthday card and other little notes, and occasional activities together.

Level II interventions may also include informal discussion and brainstorming of alternative behaviors and teaching of social skills or self-esteem fundamentals. Many teachers use *The Pre-Referral Intervention Manual*. Although it is written for special education it is very appropriate for any student with learning or behavior problems. It lists three hundred interventions in an easy to use format with the problem, say poor attendance, at the top of the page, and twenty-five interventions line by line on the page.

If no mentors are available at your site, consider referral to an outside group that offers mentors. (Sample programs may include: Big Sisters/Brothers, College or Business Mentoring Programs, etc.)

Level III

Level III interventions will vary according to the reasons for the student's anger. Possible interventions are as follows:

If the student's anger is due to a crisis in her/his personal life—birth of a sibling, divorce, serious illness or death in the family, etc.—teach coping skills, such as recognizing feelings of anger, control issues, and depression; coming to terms with problems and learning to hope.

Teaching stress management skills may also be helpful.

If the student's anger is due to lack of social skills, teach communication skills, skills for making friends, etc., as appropriate.

If the student's anger is due to deep-seated family or social problems, consider referral for individual and/or family counseling.

ATTENDANCE

Following are a list of suggestions from the *Pre-Referral Intervention Manual* on how to deal with students who have frequent unexcused absences.

1. Communicate with parents, agencies, or appropriate parties in order to inform them of the problems, determine the cause of the problem, and consider possible solutions to the problem.
2. Record or chart attendance with the student.
3. Begin the day or class with a success-oriented activity that is likely to be enjoyable for the student.
4. Give the student a preferred responsibility to be performed at the beginning of each day or each class (e.g., feeding the classroom pet, helping to get the classroom ready for the day).
5. Reinforce the student for getting on the bus or leaving home on time.

There are 26 more suggestions on their list for this category and there are 219 categories!

NOTE

1. Stephen B. McCarney, Kathy Wunderlich, and Angela Bauer, *The Pre-Intervention Manual* (Columbia, Mo.: Hawthorne Educational Services, 1993).

Chapter Fifteen

Establishing a Climate for Staff Acceptance of Assessment and Evaluation

Assessment often means the application of agreed-upon standards to use in judging student work; typically, rubrics are developed to describe these standards as in direct writing assessments. Portfolios are primarily an assessment tool. Students who perform better are rewarded and poor performance is made visible in this approach. The purpose of evaluation is to provide timely, useful information for decision making. Organizations that have clear objectives and administrators that focus on performance related to their objectives are the most effective. I have worked directly in many schools at elementary, middle, and senior high levels and know personally the difficulty of gaining agreement about what to emphasize and how to measure it. What I have learned is that the great effort involved in carrying out effective assessment and evaluation has a big benefit that can be seen in improved student performance and higher teacher morale and satisfaction. Good teachers expect serious assessment and evaluation because they understand it is the primary means the director has to improve instruction.

Every person that reads this chapter has his or her own ideas about the fundamental problems in our schools. Sanford Dornbusch and Richard Scott at Stanford University have studied organizational behavior in schools, churches, businesses, football teams, and several other organizations and they have found that organizations that have clear objectives and managers that focus on performance related to their objectives are the most effective.[1] This sounds like common sense but it is especially hard to accomplish in schools where there is continuing debate about which objectives (not goals; there is often agreement there) to emphasize. Even when the administrator guides a credible

163

needs assessment and gains a solid consensus about which objectives to emphasize, there is another big debate over how to measure the objectives.

Key Concepts:
Power and Authority
Legitimate Power through Group Support
Power Can Be Converted to Authority
Evaluation
Proper Control Systems
Evaluation Requirements
Good Teachers Like Strong Evaluation
Soundly Based Evaluations
Visibility of Work

POWER AND AUTHORITY

Administrators develop the capacity to lead by offering school staff greater benefits for complying with their directives than this compliance costs the staff in terms of paperwork and meeting time. The road to a leadership position with staff is paved with contributions to goal attainment. This is good news, for everyone wants to be helpful whenever possible. The bad news is that staff often resist the needed contributions to goal attainment at the time they are being made. These contributions may include making suggestions about improving instruction, evaluating teacher performance honestly and accurately, forming committees to work on unpleasant problems like decreasing period absences and fighting on the playground, and negative secretarial telephone behavior.

Research with laboratory groups indicates that there are two means of achieving a position of informal group leadership. One is to be a "task specialist" by helping staff stay with the problem at hand until a solution has been worked out. The other approach is to be a "feeling specialist" by attending to people's personal and social needs as they work. Some people can combine both of these roles, but most of us who develop a capacity for leadership emphasize one or the other.

LEGITIMATE POWER THROUGH GROUP SUPPORT

Since most people resent the use of force that comes from the authority of an administrative position, it is incumbent upon the administrator to legitimate her or his power through group support. This is done by gaining a consensus for our decisions, which provides group endorsements for an administrator's authority. This authority from the group allows the administrator to rely on consent rather than force, such as direction from the superintendent, to achieve important objectives.

Dornbusch and Scott define power as "the ability and willingness of one person to sanction another by manipulating rewards and punishments which are important to the other." More simply it is the ability of person A to get person B to do what he or she wants. The term sanction refers both to rewards—a positive sanction—and punishment—a negative sanction. Directors have the ability to sanction because it comes with their position; they may, however, be unwilling to use it. This creates a power vacuum, which aggressive staff such as the director's secretary or teachers then move in to fill. This "dual authority" at the top tends to diminish staff morale and reduce organizational focus on key objectives.

POWER CAN BE CONVERTED TO AUTHORITY

Power can be converted to authority either by legitimization from above or by normative group support from below. Thus, a powerful teacher may be designated assistant director by the superintendent and gain formal authority. Alternatively, a director who gains the support of most teachers in transferring a staff member to another school thus legitimates the move. This authorized power, Dornbusch and Scott term authority. It is critically different from power because it is subject to group consensus and support. The experienced administrator learns it is preferable to go slow and gain confirmation of his or her authority from above as well as endorsement from a majority of the staff before making decisions. If they offer more benefits than costs to staff, as previously mentioned, obtaining staff authorization can be easily achieved. When costs exceed benefits, authorization from staff can be very difficult to achieve, even on minor decisions.

EVALUATION

Evaluation is the means used by administrators to control staff behavior and thus achieve school goals and objectives. Without meaningful evaluation teachers tend to pursue a great variety of objectives, thus diminishing focus. This dissipation of energy and resources on too many objectives results in lower school achievement levels and leads to the minimal public support presently being experienced. This is one of the most important problems facing U.S. schools and my experience verifies that administrators can do much to improve the situation at no additional cost to the public. Further, a director who is willing to make distinctions about the quality of teaching on the staff and to back them up with good data from clinical supervision is respected by teachers.

It is difficult to think of any organization in our society other than a school where the staff are allowed to ignore the stated organizational goals and objectives to the extent that teachers do in public schools. Society is paying a heavy price for this behavior with unimpressive achievement levels in our schools. A desire for improved school accountability on the part of the public is forcing administrators to tighten their control of teacher performance. If this tightening is to improve schools' performance, that is, to result in student growth, sound evaluation practices must be utilized. If they are not, teachers will resist the unfair procedures and their performance will not improve.

PROPER CONTROL SYSTEMS

Control systems that are perceived as proper by teachers lead to higher levels of performance and increased morale. Improper systems may cause staff to leave the system, change their conception of what is proper and adjust to the system, or create pressure to change the system. A sound evaluation system is one where: better performance produces more highly valued outcomes; higher quality outcomes produce higher evaluations; and effort is reflected in evaluations received.

These conditions are frequently not met in administrative evaluations of school staff. More typically better teacher performance receives no special recognition because administrators fear having to defend their judgment to teachers who are not top performers. Therefore, higher performance receives the same evaluation as an average performance. This causes teachers to feel the administrator either doesn't know the difference or is afraid of hurting teacher morale. Actually, teacher morale goes up when distinctions are made, much like it does in businesses. As for the third condition, rarely, if ever, does a teacher evaluation form have any item that allows consideration of or focus on teacher effort.

It is hard to overestimate the negative impact of these evaluation errors on staff. Alternatively, when teachers are evaluated soundly, teachers feel great respect for administrators and become strongly supportive of the evaluation system.

Most schools meet these evaluation requirements, at least to some extent. If your school does not you should make it an immediate priority to initiate whatever changes are needed so that it does meet the conditions. They in effect require that teacher performance be taken seriously and that teachers are evaluated on the basis of their work.

EVALUATION REQUIREMENTS

1. The school must distribute rewards and penalties on the basis of evaluations of staff performance as professionals.

Positive Example: Two teachers whose classes consistently score high in meeting their objectives are selected to go to a conference on application of Piaget's learning theories to teaching.

Negative Example: An attractive teacher who is rewarded for being friendly with the director, not his or her teaching.

2. Staff evaluations must be based on performance of school tasks.

Positive Example: A second-grade teacher who is bilingual and consistently teaches Spanish-speaking children to read first in Spanish and then in English when the first-grade teachers who are not bilingual have not taught the children to read.

Negative Example: A teacher who receives positive evaluations from the director because he employs the director's wife in his lucrative summer swim camp.

3. The evaluators, typically administrators, must themselves be subject to evaluation of their performance by people they are not attempting to control, typically, district office administrators.

Positive Example: The superintendent gives serious attention to how well each director monitors teachers' objectives for each class.

Negative Example: An administrator whose main evaluator is a teacher in their school whose wife is on the school board.

4. Staff consider the sanctions, or rewards and punishments, that results from evaluations important.

Positive Example: An administrator provides a list of the top 25 percent of classes in terms of achieving measurable objectives.

Negative Example: An administrator gives most teachers outstanding annual evaluations causing the teachers to feel the annual evaluations are meaningless and that the administrator does not understand clinical supervision.

One of the paradoxical findings of the Dornbusch–Scott research is that school staff who are convinced that better effort leads to better evaluations buy into the system and are more controlled or influenced by the evaluations.

GOOD TEACHERS LIKE STRONG EVALUATION

It is often found that good teachers prefer strong evaluation; this is evident when an effective teacher agrees with an evaluation and proceeds to change his or her behavior. The teacher might agree to contact each student that was late to his or her class daily, for example, if an evaluation showed an increase in unexcused tardies was occurring.

A corollary to the preceding principle relates to the amount of effort that is involved. If a staff member believes better effort leads to better evaluations he or she will further believe that these evaluations are more important than evaluations that do not take into account the teacher's effort.

SOUNDLY BASED EVALUATIONS

Staff believe that their effort improves their evaluation if the evaluation is soundly based. This occurs when the quality of the work is improved by better effort and when this stronger effort in turn receives a higher evaluation.

If, for example, the reading scores of children in grade one go up and no other teacher has taught the children, then the grade-one teacher may assume her effort made the positive difference. This better effort then must receive a higher evaluation from the director than he or she gives the teacher across the hall whose scores improved half as much with comparable children.

Making such distinctions is contrary to much practice in administration. One might believe that a director should treat all the teachers alike and not single out the best for special mention. Research at Stanford indicates this differentiation is exactly what causes teachers to grow in respect for their administrator.

VISIBILITY OF WORK

When a teacher knows his or her evaluator has seen the key aspects of her or his performance or the results of the performance, the teacher will trust the evaluation to a greater extent. This leads the teacher to be more influenced by the administrator's evaluation. This principle is easy to understand but difficult to achieve. Close monitoring is a key element in success and the best directors find time to do it. Some directors call it "management by walking around."

School staff prefer evaluation systems where great effort leads to more positive evaluations. If the tasks teachers perform are active or nonroutine, they will need more autonomy in their work to be effective. Key efforts should receive the most positive evaluations. (For an additional resource see appendix D—Evaluation Competencies.)

NOTE

1. Sanford Dornbusch and Richard Scott, *Evaluation and the Exercise of Authority* (San Francisco: Jossey-Bass, 1975).

Chapter Sixteen

Self-Evaluation for Director and Teachers

A director's effectiveness is evaluated yearly by the district/governing board. How does one obtain self-evaluation feedback on a regular basis to obtain a pulse on the job being done at school? Quick surveys based on your governing board's requirements as well as how to set personal goals, measure success, and determine next steps for personal and professional growth can give the director invaluable feedback.

For teachers there are extensive self-evaluation forms that follow in this chapter. Some teachers may decide to share their data with the director and some may not.

Staff development days that are pupil-free are also an effective way to provide professional growth at minimal cost. For example, each year a staff development plan can be developed with days determined based on identified school needs. Professional articles from educational journals are shared with staff and discussed at staff meetings. Many new teachers have personal professional teacher portfolios that show samples of strategies and projects completed in their classrooms. Increasingly these are in an electronic form. Student work is entered into these portfolios to show work in progress, not only student work, but evidence of students at work. Consider encouraging teachers to have personal journals to reflect on what is being done in their classroom. Journals and personal portfolios can also be helpful in fall and spring teacher planning.

Key Concepts:
Staff Development
Self-Evaluation for Staff

SELF-EVALUATION FOR STAFF

The tables that follow are from the Teacher Ability Assessment Instrument for teachers to use in self-assessment. It was developed by a team of researchers headed by Ellen Moir of the University of California at Santa Cruz and was funded by the California State Department of Education.

This chapter is intended as a combination self-evaluation and supervisor evaluation of teaching abilities. The user may photocopy four copies of the instrument, which is the balance of this chapter.

The method for using this instrument would be for the director to complete the first copy based on his/her own perception of present competence. The second copy is for the teachers to rate what they believe the director's abilities level ought to be.

DEVELOPMENT OF TEACHER ABILITIES

The Continuum of Skills, Knowledge, and Attitudes from Beginning to Advanced Levels of Teaching has been designed for two primary purposes: First, to guide support providers as they assist teachers' professional growth, and second, to assist teachers to assess their own development and identify areas for growth. When using the continuum, recognize that an individual teacher's placement will vary from category to category depending on the situation and over time. This continuum provides descriptors of beginning and advanced teaching abilities derived from both research and practice. The descriptors are intended to be used as a guide to define each of the categories in tables 16.1 through 16.6 but are not all-inclusive.

Table 16.1. Organizing and Managing the Classroom: Creating a Positive Learning Environment

Beginning Abilities		Advanced Abilities
Promotes a Positive Learning Environment Recognizes the importance of a positive learning environment, and applies some strategies that support and foster self-esteem.	++ ++ ++ ++	Promotes a positive learning environment through modeling and developing strong relationships with and among students.
Classroom Arranged to Facilitate Learning Uses a structured room environment to maximize teacher control and maintains it regardless of the learning activity. May experiment with various grouping strategies.	++ ++ ++ ++	Arranges the classroom to facilitate teacher movement, proximity, and student engagement. Varies the groupings to accommodate learning activities and regroups when appropriate.
States Expectations Clearly States expectations for student behavior on occasion and generally restates them in the same way in different situations.	++ ++ ++ ++	States expectations clearly and explains them in several ways. Draws upon a variety of strategies for assisting students to understand and meet expectations.
Develops Flexibility for Efficiency Establishes routines and procedures to accomplish regular classroom tasks and has transitions between activities.	++ ++ ++ ++	Develops a flexibility in the use of routines, procedures, and transitions that both provides for efficiency and is sensitive to the needs of individuals and groups.
Encourages Positive Student Behavior Tries to handle disruptive student behavior by ignoring it or by frequently interrupting the instruction.	++ ++ ++ ++	Monitors student behavior during a lesson and responds to students to encourage positive behavior. Rarely interrupts lesson to deal with discipline.
Demonstrates Rapport toward All Students Works to develop relationships with students. Uncertain of appropriate role.	++ ++ ++ ++	Demonstrates rapport, empathy, and supportiveness toward all students.
Uses Time Efficiently on Academic Task Focuses time and energy on classroom routines, procedures, and behavior management thus decreasing time on academic tasks.	++ ++ ++ ++	Uses efficient and effective classroom management and organization which maximizes the time that students are actively engaged on meaningful academic activities.

Promote a Positive Learning Environment

1	2	3	4	5

Classroom Arranged to Facilitate Learning

1	2	3	4	5

State Expectations Clearly

1	2	3	4	5

Develop Flexibility for Efficiency

1	2	3	4	5

Encourage Positive Student Behavior

1	2	3	4	5

Demonstrate Rapport toward All Students

1	2	3	4	5

Efficient Use of Time on Academic Task

1	2	3	4	5

Using the performance statements on table 16.1, assess your own development from 1–5 on the continuums, then answer the following: What will I do to get there? What help do I need? How will I know when I get there?

Table 16.2. Planning and Designing Instruction

Beginning Abilities		Advanced Abilities
Planning Plans day-to-day or a few days in advance with some consideration given to previous or future instructional outcomes.	‡ ‡ ‡ ‡	Plans well in advance and uses current information about students' progress to guide planning. Planning is connected and builds upon previous learning and future outcome
Appropriateness of Lessons Plans individual lessons and units with some sense of the appropriateness of content in relation to student development and exposure.	‡ ‡ ‡ ‡	Plans lessons and units that are conceptually clear, developmentally appropriate, and experientially relevant to future outcomes.
Sensitivity to Diversity Begins to develop sensitivity to students' diverse backgrounds, experiences, understandings, interests, and dispositions. Incorporates their understanding in the design of the lesson.	‡ ‡ ‡ ‡	Designs instruction that consistently displays sensitivity to students' diverse background, experiences, dispositions, understandings, and interests.
Lesson Plan Flexibility Follows lesson plan closely with some awareness of need to adapt to unexpected opportunities or problems.	‡ ‡ ‡ ‡	Uses the lesson plan flexibly as a guide and modifies plans during a lesson to capitalize on unexpected opportunities or problems. Draws upon a repertoire of contingency plans.
Lessons Reflect Outcomes and Success Plans activities with some awareness of the learning outcome and success indicators for each lesson.	‡ ‡ ‡ ‡	Identifies specific learning outcomes and success indicators for each lesson.
Variety of Materials Uses the textbook as the primary source for planning instruction.	‡ ‡ ‡ ‡	Draws upon and adapts extensive supporting materials and enrichment activities to enhance instructional units.
Variety of Lesson Formats Designs lessons using a whole group lecture format as the primary mode of instruction. Focuses learning outcomes primarily at recall and comprehension of information.	‡ ‡ ‡ ‡	Designs lessons to engage students in learning by discovery, so they can search for problems, patterns, and solutions. Focuses learning outcomes on problem solving and critical thinking.

		Planning		
1	2	3	4	5

		Appropriateness of Lessons		
1	2	3	4	5

		Sensitivity to Diversity		
1	2	3	4	5

		Lesson Plan Flexibility		
1	2	3	4	5

		Lessons Reflect Outcomes and Success		
1	2	3	4	5

Using the performance statements on table 16.2, assess your own development from 1–5, then answer the following: What will I do to get there? What help do I need? How will I know when I get there? Who can help me to get there?

Table 16.3. Delivering Instruction to All Students

Beginning Abilities		Advanced Abilities
Lesson Design Explains instructional materials to be used and/or the steps to be carried out to complete academic tasks.	‡ ‡ ‡	Models clearly instructional materials to be used and steps to be followed. Demonstrates, models, provides for guided practice, and then checks for understanding.
Teaching Strategies Relies on a limited range of instructional activities to respond to the diversity of learning styles and needs.	‡ ‡ ‡	Selects a variety of activities and media to respond to the diversity of learning styles and needs in the class.
Concept Review Introduces or reviews concepts or skills orally, using few, if any, visuals or other demonstration techniques.	‡ ‡ ‡	Introduces and reviews concepts and skills in a clear and complete manner using oral, visual, and other demonstration techniques (e.g., metaphors, explanations, illustrations, examples, models).
Grouping for Interaction of All Students Employs a limited range of grouping techniques for encouraging involvement and interaction of all students.	‡ ‡ ‡	Creates structures that encourage involvement by individuals, pairs, and small groups. Uses a variety of strategies for engaging students in discourse.
Reference to Students' Knowledge Presents/discusses concepts or skills with little reference to students' prior knowledge or skills.	‡ ‡ ‡	Presents/discusses skills and concepts in the context of what the students have already mastered, showing how they build on prior knowledge.
Instructional Strategies Begins to develop a repertoire of instructional strategies, relying most often on the one or two strategies that are most familiar.	‡ ‡ ‡	Uses a variety of instructional strategies (e.g., direct instruction, cooperative learning, individualized instruction, inquiry) to engage students. Selects appropriate strategy to maximize the learning outcome.
Instructional Cues Attempts to alter instruction based on cues related to student interest or success. May have difficulty interpreting cues.	‡ ‡ ‡	Uses student cues to alter instruction during the lesson. Discriminates important student cues from unimportant cues.

		Lesson Design		
1	2	3	4	5

		Teaching Strategies		
1	2	3	4	5

		Concept Review		
1	2	3	4	5

		Grouping for Interaction of All Students		
1	2	3	4	5

		Reference to Students' Knowledge		
1	2	3	4	5

		Instructional Strategies		
1	2	3	4	5

		Instructional Cues		
1	2	3	4	5

Using the performance statements on table 16.3, assess your own development from 1–5, then answer the following: What will I do to get there? What help do I need? How will I know when I get there? Who can help me to get there?

Table 16.4. Demonstrating Subject Matter Knowledge

Beginning Abilities		Advanced Abilities
Level of Subject Matter Sophistication Acquires the subject matter knowledge and attempts to link and convey the concepts with accuracy and coherence.	‡ ‡ ‡	Understands subjects taught and shows how this knowledge is created, organized, linked to other disciplines, and applied to real-world settings.
Variety of Subject Matter Materials Uses textbooks and commercially prepared worksheets as the primary source for teaching.	‡ ‡ ‡	Critiques and adapts content in the textbook and other resources to represent concepts and principles at various levels of complexity to match students' development.
Evaluation of Subject Matter Resource Materials Begins to collect resource materials in the discipline(s), but has limited criteria for evaluating their usefulness.	‡ ‡ ‡	Keeps current with the growing body of curricular materials available for his/her specific discipline(s) and constantly evaluates the usefulness of those materials for the students.
Relate Subject Matter to Student Interests Attempts to consider knowledge, skills, abilities, and interests students bring to the subject matter.	‡ ‡ ‡	Builds upon knowledge, skills, abilities, and interests students bring to the subject matter and tailors curricular materials and instruction to students.
Multiple Strategies to Convey Information Anticipates that students will comprehend the subject matter and presents content in the same way to all students.	‡ ‡ ‡	Knows subject matter in such a way that enables thorough explanations. Understands and predicts possible student conceptions and misconceptions of particular topics in a subject area.

Level of Subject Matter Sophistication

1	2	3	4	5

Variety of Subject Matter Materials

1	2	3	4	5

Evaluation of Subject Matter Resource Materials

1	2	3	4	5

Relate Subject Matter to Student Interests

1	2	3	4	5

Multiple Strategies to Convey Information

1	2	3	4	5

Using the performance statements on table 16.4, assess your own development from 1–5, then answer the following: What will I do to get there? What help do I need? How will I know when I get there? Who can help me to get there?

Table 16.5. Diagnosing and Evaluating Student Learning

Beginning Abilities		Advanced Abilities
Flexibility of Lesson Knows when the lesson is not going well but may not be able to identify the variables that are affecting the instruction. Continues with lesson as planned.	‡ ‡ ‡ ‡	Recognizes the appropriateness and consequences of teaching actions and makes in-progress changes in instruction.
Reflection on Own Teaching Reflects on student characteristics more frequently than on own instruction when evaluating outcomes of a lesson.	‡ ‡ ‡ ‡	Reflects on own teaching in terms of effects on students and sees what the teacher does as the main influence on learning rather than student characteristics (e.g., motivation, intelligence, behavior).
Adjusts Instruction Appropriately Targets lessons to meet the needs of the whole class and stays with the panned academic task even if it is too easy or too difficult for the students.	‡ ‡ ‡ ‡	Monitors student progress and adjusts instruction appropriately, both for individuals and for the whole class.
Uses a Variety of Assessment Strategies Employs a few assessment strategies. Communicates with parents regarding student progress to meet school requirements.	‡ ‡ ‡ ‡	Uses a repertoire of assessment strategies to determine what students have learned. Provides constructive feedback frequently and in a variety of ways to students and parents.

		Flexibility of Lesson		
1	2	3	4	5

		Reflection on Own Teaching		
1	2	3	4	5

		Adjusts Instruction Appropriately		
1	2	3	4	5

		Uses a Variety of Assessment Strategies		
1	2	3	4	5

Using the performance statements on table 16.5, assess your own development from 1–5, then answer the following: What will I do to get there? What help do I need? How will I know when I get there? Who can help me to get there?

Table 16.6. Participating as Members of a Learning Community

Beginning Abilities	Advanced Abilities
Ability to Work with Staff Works primarily in own classroom. Participates on occasion in school-wide planning or curriculum work.	Participates as part of a collaborative team and contributes to the overall school effectiveness. Shares curricular and instructional ideas with the staff.
Knowledge of School Community Recognizes the value of working with the community but tends to focus on day-to-day life in the classroom.	Uses knowledge of school's community as a powerful resource for delivering instruction.
Professional Relationships Begins to build professional relationships with other teachers in the school. May feel too vulnerable to ask for help.	Establishes professional relationships with other teachers in the school. Shares ideas and looks to peers for ideas and support.
Development of Knowledge and Skill Identifies areas of need and begins to explore professional development opportunities.	Sees self as a lifelong learner, seeking to expand own repertoire and deepen knowledge and skill.
Judgment of Individual Student Problems Relies on own judgment about individual student problems. May be uncertain about when and from whom to seek guidance.	Works with other teachers, resource specialists, and community agencies for help with an individual student.
Interpersonal Communication Skills Begins to develop effective interpersonal communication and human relations skills.	Demonstrates effective interpersonal communication and human relations skills.
Interaction with Parents Interacts with parents at prescribed times (e.g., open house, report cards). Begins to experiment with other forms of contact.	Understands the impact of family culture, expectations, and environment on student learning. Uses a variety of strategies to connect with parents.

		Ability to Work with Staff		
1	2	3	4	5

		Knowledge of School Community		
1	2	3	4	5

		Professional Relationships		
1	2	3	4	5

		Development of Knowledge and Skill		
1	2	3	4	5

		Judgment of Individual Student Problems		
1	2	3	4	5

		Interpersonal Communication Skills		
1	2	3	4	5

		Interaction with Parents		
1	2	3	4	5

Using the performance statements on table 16.6, assess your own development from 1–5, then answer the following: What will I do to get there? What help do I need? How will I know when I get there? Who can help me to get there?

Chapter 17

Assessing Student Progress

A strong focus is placed on authentic or performance-based assessment, the use of portfolios, and holistic scoring with rubrics to demonstrate student progress. Assessment often means the application of agreed-upon standards to use in judging student work; typically, rubrics are developed to describe these standards as in direct writing assessments. Portfolios are primarily an assessment tool. Students who perform better are rewarded and poor performance is made visible in this approach.

Assessment is a subcategory of evaluation, a general term used in education to refer to any effort to gather data, analyze the data, and report them in a timely fashion to those who need to use that information to make decisions. The purpose of assessment is to identify levels of curriculum attainment, and especially, changes that may lead to a need for improvement. There are many types of assessment beyond various kinds of tests. These may include, among others, portfolios, journal entries and free-writing, an autobiography, references, audiotapes, notes from conferencing, art work and graphics, or reading logs.

Equally valuable would be a thoughtful sample of the student's work with an explanation of the selection process or documentation of student progress in skill development such as self-assessment, thinking and problem solving, and employment skills.

Any information that shows a student has engaged in self-reflection, providing evidence the student is learning about learning, could aid assessment, as would information that illustrates growth: a series of examples, changes on interest inventories, reading records, or attitude measures. Self-reports of student analysis and assessment of his or her own proficiency as well as learning logs with student responses to class work, organizational tasks, or readings or connections among learnings can also be used for assessments.

Key Concepts:
What Is a Portfolio?
How Can the Portfolio Help Students Reflect on Their Learning?
How Do You "Manage" a Portfolio?
A Guide to Self-Assessment
Assessment Lingo

WHAT IS A PORTFOLIO?

A portfolio is a purposeful collection of student work that tells the story of a student's efforts, progress, or achievement. It is a longitudinal collection of ideas, drafts, and questions for a storehouse of possibilities for later work. It is a collection of student-produced artifacts that serve as evidence of proficiency, achievement, capability, or performance. It must include student participation in the selection of portfolio content, criteria for selection, criteria for judging merit, and evidence of student self-reflection.

In order for the classroom to support the use of portfolios students must be immersed in reading, writing, speaking, and listening. They need to be given time to do so in large blocks and they must be given choices about what they are doing, and they must receive a positive response to their ideas.

There are many purposes of portfolios. They show progress on the goals represented in the program, mastery of objectives, growth as a literate human being, how relationships have changed, and how the student has matured. They present a student's history through a personal collection of work and encourage self-reflection and writing across the candidate's assignments. They also increase communication among subject areas, grade levels, teachers, parents, and other students and provide an additional measure of achievement. They can be helpful for placing students in particular curricular assignments and for examining growth over time. They can be used as a gauge to a student's ability to solve problems or to provide more than one right answer.

HOW CAN THE PORTFOLIO HELP
STUDENTS REFLECT ON THEIR LEARNING?

Environments that promote reflection include opportunities to talk with others; opportunities to think about decision making; opportunities to listen to others; the use of explicit, specific language; the introduction of models and practice of strategies for reflecting with feedback; and permission to reflect with judgment or qualification.

It is important for students to identify what they have learned. Students need to realize that they can learn on their own and develop confidence in their own abilities to read and write, to revise and to edit, to respond and to articulate their thoughts.

Here is an exercise to help a student develop a better portfolio: Review the items in your portfolio and reflect in writing on how your portfolio documents what you have learned, how you have grown, and what you have come to understand. Write an introduction to your portfolio. Consider what you have learned about your own learning process. Discuss assignments you enjoyed the most, the ones that were the most difficult, and the ones from which you learned the most. Write a letter to the reader of your portfolio identifying your best piece of work. Explain what standards or criteria you used to select the work and provide illustrations that show how this work meets the standards or criteria. Generalize about what "learning" is using examples from your own papers. Write several "I Learned . . ." statements after taking time to reflect on your portfolio, or write a summary sheet that reviews the things you learned as you developed your portfolio. Complete the following sentences:

- I do my best work when . . .
- When I look at my portfolio, I feel . . .
- This portfolio reveals that I . . .
- By looking at this collection of my work, you will be able to tell . . .

To say it another way, teachers need to feel that the administrator is stressing the supervision part of the task and not the evaluation portion. If they do learn to trust the supervisor, real progress can be made in helping them to improve instruction. This is especially true for groups of students that are difficult to teach, such as those at risk of dropping out of school.

An effective instructional leader should also be able to accurately describe current leading theories of human development, learning, and motivation, and to evaluate the strengths and limitations of the theories as they are applied to classroom teaching. This type of knowledge is often acquired in university courses and through professional organizations.

Key Concepts:
Planning Instruction
Staff Evaluation
Contingency Supervision
Clinical Supervision

PLANNING INSTRUCTION

Learning is ultimately the student's responsibility when the school staff have provided a relevant curriculum and effective instruction. Twenty years ago many directors assumed that if a student was not learning it was the student's fault. Directors were trained to use individual tests and test results led to working with the student and his or her problem.

Ten years ago the director was trained to think about the nature of her or his school and to consider student problems to be the result of some need to improve school services and effectiveness. We can think of this as an organizational approach to problem solving. The content area is called organizational behavior.

Today directors should think increasingly about the school's need to network with other agencies in the community and businesses to provide effective services and instruction for students. These can include social services, mental health, law enforcement, and, perhaps, one-on-one mentoring of students by volunteers from businesses and the local service clubs such as Kiwanis. This expansion is called the interorganizational approach to problem solving.

In addition to seeking community resources, an instructional leader needs to acquire an experiential attitude that influences the future behavior of the staff in ways that lead them to seek classroom applications of new knowledge about human learning, development, and motivation.

Planning instruction involves the development of school and course goals and the conversion of goals into objectives that can be taught using a variety of instructional strategies. Teachers need to learn to assess student skills in ways that help them deliver instruction effectively. To be effective, the instruction should take account of the differing learning styles of students as well as their special needs in a time of full inclusion efforts.

STAFF EVALUATION

A director should become familiar with several models for staff evaluation. In order to understand how staff evaluation operates in your district, locate the following documents:

- The contract between the teachers association and the district;
- A description of the evaluation procedures to be used;
- A statement of the policies issued by the district pertaining to teacher evaluation;
- A set of the forms developed in the district personnel office for evaluating certificated personnel;
- A statement of the terms and definitions that relate to teacher evaluation;
- A copy of the State Education Code, which deals with evaluation of certificated employees.

Sample evaluation forms have been included in this chapter as tables 18.1–18.3.

Table 18.1.   Documentation Model: Oral Conference

Date:
To: (Name of Employee)
From: (Name of Evaluator and Title)
Topic: (Summary of Oral Conference)
This is to summarize our conference on (date) concerning (topic of concern). Those present at our meeting were (list those present). During the conference the following concern was discussed:

I reviewed your non-compliance with regard to this (rule, policy, directive, law) in connection with the above-mentioned conduct:

I also informed you that your behavior had negatively impacted the (students, staff, parents; whoever is affected most directly) in that it:

During the conference, I provided you with the following directive and assistance to take effect (date).

You were also informed that your failure to comply with any of the directives mentioned above will result in:

This document will be placed in your personnel file after (date). Before this time, you may prepare a response which will be attached to this memo and placed in your personnel file.

CONTINGENCY SUPERVISION

Contingency supervision has several other names including developmental supervision and holistic supervision. It is a problem-solving process that suggests that supervisors may employ any of three leadership orientations with teachers including: directive, collaborative, and nondirective.

The directive approach to contingency supervision would be best utilized, for example, with a teacher who is low on commitment and low on abstract thinking. Alternatively one can use nondirective strategies with a teacher who is high on commitment and high on abstract thinking. The collaborative approach would work with teachers who are average in both commitment and abstract thinking.

Table 18.2.   Documentation Model: Written Warning

Date:
To: (Name of Employee)
From: (Name of Evaluator and Title)
Topic: (Written Warning)
It was reported to me by (name and title) on (date) that you were engaged in the following:

This conduct is a violation of (state source: Ed Code, contract, law) which requires:

As discussed on (date), you violated this (law, policy, contract condition, etc.) previously on (date). A copy of the memo documenting this conversation is attached.
   Your conduct negatively impacted (students, staff, parents; name who has been most affected) in that it (list effect caused).

Effective immediately, you are (directed, required, expected) to (state directive). Failure to comply with this directive will result in (list next step).

To assist you in complying with this (directive, requirement, expectation), I offer the following (suggestions or assistance).

This document will be placed in your personnel file after (date). Before this time, you may prepare a response which will be attached to this memo and placed in your personnel file.

CLINICAL SUPERVISION

Clinical supervision is a process that includes a number of stages such as: establishing the teacher-supervisor relationship, planning a lesson (unit) with the teacher, planning the strategy for observation, observing the instruction, analyzing the teaching-learning process, planning the teacher-supervisor conference, and conducting the conference. This model, or one that is similar, is used by many school districts and may well be presented in detail in your district teacher evaluation packet. The typical contents of an evaluation packet are listed above under the "Staff Evaluation" heading. Clinical evaluation includes the above mentioned activities and adds writing up an evaluation report.

   Several of our students have developed a documentation approach, which is presented in appendix E. This is reprinted with permission from *Improving the Job Performance of Staff Members through Effective Evaluation and Documentation Procedures* by Yolanda Finley, Lisa A. Hinshaw, and Janet Olsavsky.[1]

Table 18.3.   Documentation Model: Letter of Reprimand

Date:
To: (Name of Employee)
From: (Name of Evaluator and Title)
Topic: (Letter of Reprimand)
It was reported to me by (name and title) on (date) that you were engaged in the following:

This conduct is a violation of (state source: Ed Code, contract, law) which requires:

Your conduct negatively impacted (students, staff, parents; name who has been most affected) in that it (list effect caused):

Effective immediately, you are (directed, required, expected) to (state directive). Failure to comply with this directive will result in (list next step).
   To assist you in complying with this (directive, requirement, expectation), I offer the following (suggestions or assistance).

This document will be placed in your personnel file after (date). Before this time, you may prepare a response which will be attached to this memo and placed in your personnel file.

NOTE

1. Yolanda Finley, Lisa A. Hinshaw, and Janet Olsavsky, *Improving the Job Performance of Staff Members through Effective Evaluation and Documentation Procedures* (Fullerton: Department of Educational Administration, California State University, 1980).

Chapter Nineteen

Evaluation of Program Effectiveness

The purpose of evaluation is to help the administrator develop quantitative and qualitative information useful in decision making. Evaluation studies tend to fall into two categories: for programs of one year or less in length, or those in place for more than one year. The program evaluation approach used here is from the conceptual work of Novak and Dougherty.[1]

Key Concepts:
Why Evaluate?
Some Purposes of Evaluation
A Sample Evaluation Method

WHY EVALUATE?

The answer to the question as to why educators evaluate is that without effective evaluation educators would not know what works for students or why. Sometimes, even after evaluation analysis, educators are not sure what works due to the complexity of the program, the effect of intervening variables, or poor evaluation design strategies. However, the probability is that more will be known than if evaluation was not done. The goal of evaluation is to bring the information about many varied activities together in a form so that it can be assessed or compared and then reported in a timely manner that will assist decision makers to make sound decisions. A director should use both quantitative (measures like tests) and qualitative (narrative) types of evaluation.

SOME PURPOSES OF EVALUATION

In designing an evaluation of a program, the first question to ask is, What is the purpose of this evaluation? Some purposes include:

- Were the objectives and activities completed?
- Is the program effective (summative/quantitative evaluation)?
- How did the program achieve its effectiveness, or lack thereof (process/qualitative)?
- How cost effective are the program services?
- Was any change due to the program?
- Would the program be effective with other groups?

A SAMPLE EVALUATION MODEL

The following evaluation model was developed by Novak and Dougherty. One way to use this evaluation model is to give each item two ratings on a 1 (low) to 10 (high) basis. The first rating is the extent to which the programs were implemented; the second is the extent the rater believes each should be implemented. This then provides the administrator in charge with a sense of needed changes to improve the program with those items with the highest discrepancy receiving priority in the future. This model is written from the point of view of a director who wishes to help a student who has been determined to be having serious problems in school.

The broad goal of any program or intervention effort is to help students by increasing program effectiveness, such as a combined whole language and phonics reading program. An effective evaluation could focus on formal assessment of the student utilizing grades, test data, and staff entries in the student's permanent record. Informal assessment might be developed from observation of student behavior, school record analysis, and teacher interviews.

Grades

Grades provide a convenient way to quickly identify students who are in academic difficulty. Grades also allow us a convenient way to measure student improvement, individually and for the program as a whole.

Scoring: Rating 1 to 10 (as described above) for "is now being implemented" ____; rating 1 to 10 (as described) for "ought to be implemented" ____ .

Test Scores

Test scores serve the same function as grades in that educators can readily see which students are in difficulty (using district proficiency scores) and, at the same time, record scores pre- and post- to find out if they are improving. These data can then be used to analyze individual students and the program as a whole.

Scoring: Rating 1 to 10 (as described above) for "is now being implemented" ____; rating 1 to 10 (as described) for "ought to be implemented" ____.

Staff Entries in Permanent Record

The written notes that teachers and other staff make in the student's cumulative record are a fine indicator of student progress and, especially, difficulties. The staff member can then begin to build a student case history from information in the cumulative folder.

Scoring: Rating 1 to 10 (as described above) for "is now being implemented" ____; rating 1 to 10 (as described) for "ought to be implemented" ____.

Student Behavior

Student behaviors of discipline incidents, truancy, and so forth are helpful in assessing progress of interventions.

Scoring: Rating 1 to 10 (as described above) for "is now being implemented" ____; rating 1 to 10 (as described) for "ought to be implemented" ____.

counseling to help work on personal problems, testing to identify areas of competence and interest, as well as developing a supportive learning environment. Here are several examples for each category of service.

Instruction in Basic and Social Skills

Special offerings of basic/social skills;
Flexible curriculum with basic/social skills offering;
Individualized courses with basic skills options;
Resource teachers who offer basic/social skills.

Scoring: Rating 1 to 10 (as described above) for "is now being implemented" ____; rating 1 to 10 (as described) for "ought to be implemented" ____.

Give tutoring in areas of individual need utilizing peers to:

Listen to the student read;
Provide individualized content help;
Play instructional games;
Work through programmed materials;
Drill on a specific academic skill;
Assist with development of a motor skill.

Scoring: Rating 1 to 10 (as described above) for "is now being implemented" ____; rating 1 to 10 (as described) for "ought to be implemented" ____.

Give counseling on personal problems giving special attention to:

Involving the student's parents;
Providing a relaxed atmosphere;
Being a responsive listener;
Discussing strengths as well as weaknesses;
Starting and ending conferences with a positive comment.

Scoring: Rating 1 to 10 (as described above) for "is now being implemented" ____; rating 1 to 10 (as described) for "ought to be implemented" ____.

Testing to identify areas of competence and interest through:

1. Achievement tests: Norm-referenced where the student's score can be compared with a national mean score; criterion-referenced where the student's score can be looked at with reference to a specific instructional objective.
2. Questionnaires: Used to measure attitudes, opinion, or judgments.
3. Observation instruments: Used to measure involvement or process behaviors.
4. Logs, records, and checklists: Used to record informal but key information.

Scoring: Rating 1 to 10 (as described above) for "is now being implemented" _____; rating 1 to 10 (as described) for ought to be implemented _____.

Supportive learning environment, which offers:

Academic tutoring by referral;
Flexible placement in regular school, school within a school, or some other appropriate setting;
Variable time/day scheduling;
Opportunity classes that move at a slower pace;
Fifth year of four-year high school option;
Pregnant teenager and childcare option;
Small group instruction option;
Big Brother/Sister connection.

Scoring: Rating 1 to 10 (as described above) for "is now being implemented" _____; rating 1 to 10 (as described) for "ought to be implemented" _____.

Coordinates Resources and Personnel

The comprehensive services suggested in the previous section may all be available through a school district, but a student with serious problems often would not know about them or how to get them. Hence, there is need for a staff member to coordinate the efforts of teachers, librarians, counselors, health staff, and contact persons in business and other agencies who can provide mentoring and tutoring. The following areas of coordination between the program for students with serious problems and school staff presently exist.

Administrators

Support and participate in in-service efforts pertaining to the program;
Visit program activities frequently;
Allow program staff access in a timely manner.

Scoring: Rating 1 to 10 (as described in above) for "is now being implemented" ____; rating 1 to 10 (as described) for "ought to be implemented" ____.

Special Education Coordinator

Discusses students of mutual interest (serious problems and special education) on a regular basis;
Develops educational plans for students of mutual interest;
Develops in-service on special education topics for project staff;
Shares administrative and instructional materials of interest;
Exchanges information about students of mutual interest on a timely basis;
Jointly selects materials that would be of use to both programs.

Scoring: Rating 1 to 10 (as described above) for "is now being implemented" ____; rating 1 to 10 (as described) for "ought to be implemented" ____.

Resource Staff (reading specialist, speech therapist, social worker, language/math specialist, bilingual specialist, job placement coordinator, work experience coordinator, and vocational education coordinator)

Discusses students of mutual interest on a regular basis;
Develops educational plans for students of mutual interest;
Develops in-service on relevant topics for project staff;
Shares administrative and instructional materials of interest;

Exchanges information about students of mutual interest on a timely basis;
Jointly selects materials that would be of use to both programs.

Scoring: Rating 1 to 10 (as described above) for "is now being implemented" ____; rating 1 to 10 (as described) for "ought to be implemented"
____.

*Out of School Resources (parents, advisory committees, citizens,
organizations, business-industry-labor, social agencies, and other
education providers)*

Improving the school's public image;
Providing services to help meet the needs of at-risk students; and
Providing feedback to increase the quality of the program.

Scoring: Rating 1 to 10 (as described above) for "is now being implemented" ____; rating 1 to 10 (as described) for "ought to be implemented"
____.

Incorporates Feedback and Evaluation into the System

The evaluation aspect of the evaluation plan is critical in that so much of
the effort is one-on-one by its nature. It is very difficult to keep staff informed about what is working and what isn't unless a strong effort to evaluate is implemented. A case system is one way to organize the effort where
each student with special needs is dealt with by a team of professionals
who diagnose needs and suggest treatment and/or remediation as appropriate. All of these efforts are recorded in a permanent folder or computer
record. The following materials can be taken from the student's permanent
record or gathered separately if needed: basic personal data; home background; school background and progress; attendance record; entrance and
withdrawal information; health and physical development reports; academic record; test results; data explaining the differences between test results and classroom achievement; social and personality characteristics; interests and activities (in school and out of school); vocational interests and
plans; educational interests and plans; work experiences; comments, observations, and summarization; guidance notes; and follow-up data.

Scoring: Rating 1 to 10 (as described above) for "is now being implemented" ____; rating 1 to 10 (as described) for "ought to be implemented" ____.

NOTE

1. J. Novak and B. Dougherty, *Staying in . . . a Dropout Prevention Handbook K–12* (Madison: University of Wisconsin Press, 1986).

Chapter Twenty

Legal Responsibilities of the Director

This chapter focuses on understanding the legal responsibilities of the job of director, including federal and state laws as well as district and school policy. It gives the legal basis for education and the responsibilities for which site administrators must be aware. Discussion is directed to the topic of due process and how it relates to the management of personnel as well as students and parents. Legal and regulatory applications are directed to acting in accordance with federal and state constitutional provisions, statutory standards, and regulatory applications. They also pertain to working within local rules, procedures, and directives, recognizing standards of care involving civil and criminal liability for negligence and intentional torts, and administering contracts and financial accounts. This material is adapted from Scott D. Thomson (1993) *Principals for Our Changing Schools: Knowledge and Skill Base* and was written by experts from the field of school law for the National Policy Board for Educational Administration.

Key Concepts:
Legal Errors Can Be Costly
Constitutional Issues Apply to Schools
A Preventive Law Approach
Individual Freedoms
Federal Statutory Requirements
State Constitutional and Statutory Provisions
Civil and Criminal Law Liability
Administration of Contracts and Accounts

Key Behaviors
What a Director Should Be Able to Do

LEGAL ERRORS CAN BE COSTLY

Directors require knowledge of these materials in order to address a range of complex and sensitive problems that arise in the school setting. Operating within the constraints of our system of laws requires both technical knowledge of the law as well as awareness of the fundamental values that undergird legal and regulatory standards. Experienced directors pay careful attention to legal matters because errors in this area can lead to law suits that cost large amounts of money for your district.

CONSTITUTIONAL ISSUES APPLY TO SCHOOLS

As the U.S. public school system has evolved, so, too, has the state and federal regulation of it. School boards have the power to sue, be sued, and to ratify and execute contracts. School boards and their employees are subject to the principles of contracts and torts. Compulsory attendance, finance and taxation schemes, and a governance structure for public education are firmly established within state laws. Federal constitutional issues increasingly have come to be applied to public school systems beginning with the landmark school desegregation case of *Brown v. The Board of Education of Topeka* (1954). In the early 1960s and 1970s, courts and legislative bodies expanded personal and civil rights and limited the authority of school officials in favor of the individual's freedom from governmental intrusion. Educational equity and the enforcement of individual rights presented powerful social issues that fueled litigation and compelled change in the U.S. public education system. Directors must pay increased attention to these issues as well as newer legal mandates ranging from student performance standards to teacher performance evaluations.

Today's directors are confronted with a wide range of constitutional, statutory, and regulatory constraints. These include federal legislative mandates like the Civil Rights Act of 1964 and the Education of All Handicapped Children Act of 1974, as well as present-day state-initiated accountability efforts.

A PREVENTIVE LAW APPROACH

The costs of litigation, monetary and otherwise, suggest that directors adopt a preventive law approach to professional practice. Knowledge of legal issues and competence in managing school risk are essential to avoid legal liability and to provide effective on-site leadership. With this knowledge, directors can identify legal issues, foresee potential legal liability, and act to reduce or mitigate risks.

Competency for directors in this area would reflect knowledge of the following:

• Federal constitutional provisions (like First Amendment free speech rights) applicable to a public education system;
• Federal statutory standards (laws like Title IX) and regulatory applications relevant to public schools;
• State constitutional provisions, statutory standards, and regulatory applications related to public school operation in a selected state;
• Standards of care applicable to civil or criminal liability for negligent or intentional acts under a selected state's common law and school code;
• Principles applicable to the administration of contracts, grants, and financial accounts in a public school setting (like not commingling funds from grants with different purposes).

INDIVIDUAL FREEDOMS

The director, as an agent of the state, must be mindful of the range of individual freedoms articulated within the U.S. Constitution, including, but not limited to First Amendment rights to free speech and association, free exercise of religion, press freedom, and the separation of church and state; Fourth Amendment rights to privacy, particularly as they apply to search and seizure in a public school setting; and Fourteenth Amendment rights to due process of law and equal protection of the law as applied to a wide range of issues, including disciplinary and academic policies and their implementation on site.

FEDERAL STATUTORY REQUIREMENTS

The director must be aware of federal statutes and accompanying regulations that directly implicate the operation of public schools. Among these statutes are federal antidiscrimination provisions such as Titles VI and VII of the Civil Rights Act of 1964, Title IX of the Education Amendments of 1972, Section 504 of the Rehabilitation Act of 1973, the Americans with Disabilities Act, and the Age Discrimination in Employment Act.

STATE CONSTITUTIONAL AND STATUTORY PROVISIONS

Because education is a primary function of state government and is mandated in provisions of the state constitution, there are a wide variety of state constitutional, statutory, and regulatory standards applicable to public school operation. All states, for example, provide for a system of public education and define the duties of officers, school boards, and directors. All states make provision for personnel administration, including statutory and regulatory requirements related to certification, selection, evaluation, dismissal, reprimand, and nonrenewal of employees.

CIVIL AND CRIMINAL LAW LIABILITY

A substantial body of law affecting school operation and the duties of administrators arises under common law and state statutory codes specifying civil or criminal penalties for the breach of a duty of care. Tort law provides actions in damages for negligence and/or intentional acts that cause injury to students, employees, or third persons. State statutes increasingly prescribe the reporting of child abuse and neglect as well as adequate supervision, proper instruction, and reasonable maintenance of school equipment and facilities.

ADMINISTRATION OF CONTRACTS AND ACCOUNTS

Although the degree of authority and discretion varies by state and district, directors must know the limits of managerial authority in negotiating and managing contracts, grants, and other financial accounts. Site-based management and decentralization within school systems has been accompanied by delegation of responsibility for management of contracts for goods and services. Negotiated agreements with organized employees place obligations on the director for contract administration.

KEY BEHAVIORS

The director should keep the following issues in mind to be legally safe:

- Articulate the legal issue(s) that arise from alternative policy options involving practice. For example, in the area of federal constitutional provisions, a director, when considering whether to conduct a search of a student's purse in a public school setting, would be able to explain that any search by a school official would implicate a student's right to privacy under provisions of the Fourth Amendment to the U.S. Constitution.
- Delineate a legal rationale that guides conduct in resolving a controversy with legal implications and for which action is required by law. To illustrate, the director would indicate that such a search must be based on a reasonable suspicion standard requiring that a search be justified at inception and limited in scope.
- Justify a course of conduct or position in light of the degree of conformity to legal principles. For instance, the director could justify a decision to search (or not to search) on the basis of weighing actual facts available at the time of the search.

WHAT A DIRECTOR SHOULD BE ABLE TO DO

To sum up our presentation, it is clear that legal issues should be of great interest to successful directors, and that lack of attention to them can cause severe district reprimand. One of the most common problem areas, for example, pertains to the supervision of staff. To illustrate, which of the following is not one of the functions of the supervision/staff development aspect of staff supervision?

1. Seeks to enhance the personal and professional lives of the staff;
2. Supplies the means to remediate unsatisfactory performances of staff;
3. Allows a clean, linear approach to evaluation of innovation;
4. Sets the groundwork for implementation for district and school goals.

Item 3 is the inappropriate choice. What the director needs to know is not just this list of requirements, but, rather, where these requirements are listed when the need to know them arises. Therefore, what the director should be doing is understanding how staff evaluation operates in his or her district and be able to quickly locate (have in your office) the following documents as a reference for legal issues:

- The contract between the teachers association and the district;
- A description of the evaluation procedures to be used;
- A statement of the policies issued by the district pertaining to teacher evaluation;
- A set of the forms developed in the district personnel office for evaluating certificated personnel;
- A statement of the terms and definitions that relate to teacher evaluation;
- A copy of the State Education Code that deals with evaluation of certificated employees.

In a more general sense, a director should visit the nearest law library and practice looking up several cases relating to schools so he or she would be prepared and knowledgeable of accessing this information should the need arise. Directors can also access information pertaining to school law using the Internet; this information would typically be found on your state's Department of Education website.

Chapter Twenty-one

Public Relations and Media Relations

This chapter focuses on developing common perceptions about school issues; interacting with internal and external publics; understanding and responding skillfully to the electronic and printed news media; initiating and reporting news through appropriate channels; managing school reputations; enlisting public participation and support; recognizing and providing for various markets. This material is adapted from Scott D. Thomson (1993) *Principals for Our Changing Schools: Knowledge and Skill Base* and was written by experts from the field of public relations for the National Policy Board for Educational Administration.

Key Concepts:
Working with the Media
Building Relationships that Change Attitudes
Dodge the Tough Ones and Morale Goes Down
Role Conflict
Two-Way Communication
Key Components of Effective Programs
Two Essential Theories of Public Relations
Effective and Ineffective Behaviors

WORKING WITH THE MEDIA

It is important for the director to be familiar with the complexities of the critical area of public relations. Like school law, this is an arena fraught with danger for the new administrator. Representatives of the media are interested

213

in items that interest or amuse the general public. They are not trying to protect the schools of their community or to explain school programs in a sympathetic way. To say it another way, bad news dominates the media because it sells. Hence, the director needs to be friendly, wary, and organized in advance to deal with the media. A clever director learns to use the media to her or his advantage by preparing press releases that focus on what sells, like animal stories or topics that draw large numbers of parents to a meeting.

BUILDING RELATIONSHIPS THAT CHANGE ATTITUDES

Public relations is more than writing press releases that communicate a positive school image. It is more than producing newsletters that keep parents abreast of organizational goals and activities or creating programs that reward student and staff performance. Ultimately it centers on building relationships that change attitudes. That is the positive side of it. The darker side is the fierce competition for sales among the print and electronic media. This leads reporters and editors to focus on primarily negative stories. And these stories may be about schools.

Public relations, like other challenging aspects of the director's life, such as violence and gangs, has to be addressed in a manner that deals directly with the problem. This means working with staff to look at activities taking place in your school from the media's point of view. Perhaps there are topics that are controversial, such as bilingual education, that the director can prepare a press release on and get approval from the district office. If the director approaches the task from the reporters' viewpoint it is indeed possible to get articles into print and sometimes picked up by local television. This is especially true of grants that a director has been funded to carry out.

DODGE THE TOUGH ONES AND MORALE GOES DOWN

Directors need to be able to change negative attitudes and build on positive ones to develop public support for education in general and schools in particular. This support must be earned each day and school year, and public relations is the vehicle through which this occurs. There is one more preliminary point that may have been overlooked. If a director does not deal with his or her school's most difficult problems in a direct fashion, the morale of the staff goes down. Alternatively, if the director works with staff to address the tough issues, they will appreciate it and support him or her, even as they complain. To develop trust from the staff a director should help them learn why some administrators "speak out of both sides of their mouths" or words to that effect.

ROLE CONFLICT

Experienced teachers learn to be philosophical about a superintendent's vagueness because they have an intuitive sense that there is no other way to deal with what sociologists call "role conflict." Role conflict occurs when a person is forced by circumstances to take positions that are not consistent. For example, the teachers' association demands a 4 percent cost of living raise and the school board knows without question that critical instructional expenses would be eliminated if they gave the teachers a 4 percent raise. At the same time the PTA is adamant that a successful new reading curriculum used in a nearby district be purchased and implemented. Each of these groups will punish the superintendent in a severe manner if he or she does not support them. This is role conflict and it causes people in political jobs to be quite vague and sometimes misleading just to survive, in the case of superintendents, an average of about three years in each superintendency. Sophisticated teachers may not know about role conflict but they know the superintendent has to sometimes be misleading to keep her or his job and have a positive impact in other areas.

What teachers are not willing to accommodate is an administrator who is unwilling to address serious problems at the school level such as violence, substance abuse, dropout rates, gangs, and public relations. These are tough issues and they don't go away. They just fester and destroy the otherwise good work of the director.

TWO-WAY COMMUNICATION

As a systematic management function, public relations requires sensitivity and careful planning. The National School Public Relations Association notes that one needs to rely on two-way communication between schools and their internal and external audiences in order to successfully interpret public attitudes, identify and shape public policies and procedures, organize involvement activities, and disseminate information. Taken together, these initiatives stimulate a better understanding of the role, objectives, accomplishments, and needs of the school.

KEY COMPONENTS OF EFFECTIVE PROGRAMS

As increased public interest in education draws schools and their directors into the spotlight, public relations has become an essential leadership tool. Literature on educational public relations identifies the following key components of effective programs:

- *They are built on a plan.* Public relations activities cannot be successful if implemented on a hit-and-miss basis.
- *They require a community focus.* Effective school programs have a community focus that is based on open and honest relationships. This focus is created by two-way communication with targeted audiences (e.g., opinion leaders, businesspeople, senior citizens, and so forth). Within these audiences are "key communicators," individuals whose opinions carry considerable weight within their communities. Generally, they are longtime residents who have many acquaintances and personal and professional contacts. Savvy directors communicate with these individuals consistently.
- *They are low cost, practical, and functional.* Some corporations spend millions of dollars or more on public relations activities. By contrast, many of the best and most effective ideas in school programs are low cost and practical in their focus. Directors can build community support by publicizing school themes, implementing staff and student recognition projects, turning bulletin boards into communication vehicles, and having secretaries keep logs of incoming calls to determine parents' concerns. All of these activities can be powerful components of a school public relations plan.
- *They require that parents play a key role in relationships with any school.* Parents are their children's first teachers and remain a powerful

influence on student attitude and performance throughout the school years. Yet, despite being strong partners in quality education, parents too often are taken for granted. A study of a community school in Vermont showed that otherwise equal students who perceived their parents as positive about their school outperformed neutrally perceived parents by five months of reading growth and negatively perceived parents by seven months in a single year of reading instruction.[1] Effective public relations activities draw parents into the schools by keeping them abreast of programs and policies and by providing them with opportunities to voice their concerns and contribute their ideas and energies. (For a wealth of ideas on developing and strengthening relationships with parents, see Lee Canter's *Parent Conference Book* and *Parents Make the Difference*, a monthly newsletter published by the Parent Institute.)[2]

- *They recognize staff communication as the starting point for all public relations activities.* Many directors mistakenly believe that public relations is geared solely toward external audiences. Effective programs, however, emphasize staff relations and communications. School staff— be they teachers, secretaries, custodians, or bus drivers—are key communicators within their own communities. Directors, therefore, should share information openly with them in order to develop greater understanding and support among them. This is especially important if staff are to present and communicate a positive image of their schools to others.

- *They manage crises to limit damage to a school's reputation.* Crises are inevitable. If improperly handled, however, they can destroy overnight the favorable public opinions directors have worked long and hard to establish for their schools. As a preventive measure, directors must be prepared to handle crisis communications. This requires that they designate a spokesperson to handle inquiries under fire, identify the key audiences whom they must contact immediately in a crisis, and determine how information and data will be collected and communicated to the media. These plans should be formulated and tested in advance.

- *They require that directors work effectively with the media.* All directors are likely to have dealings with the news media. Although they cannot control the outcome of these interactions, they can influence what will be reported and how it will be presented by establishing their credibility with reporters, editors, and publishers. In addition, directors can use numerous techniques to convey a positive image of themselves and their schools. These techniques include using appropriate dress and body language, inviting reporters to special events, and being prepared for interviews. For example, directors should enter interview situations ready to convey—forcefully, if necessary—important points related to the issue at hand. Basic media training is useful in this regard and helps directors maintain some control during media interactions.

• *They utilize technology to improve their effectiveness.* Technology can speed up and improve communications. Today's desktop publishing programs, for example, allow schools to create more attractive and effective publications; new telephone technologies offer directors quick and innovative ways to communicate with parents, staff, and students. Leading word processing software programs now offer school staff the opportunity to create their own World Wide Web pages by converting standard narrative to HTML, the format used on the Web. For example, if you have Microsoft Word 6.0 (or later) for either the Macintosh or PC you can convert to HTML very simply with the click of your mouse. For directors who inherit schools that have no public relations programs in place, there are several texts available that will help in this area.[3]

Directors engage in numerous one-way communications every day (e.g., when they notify parents of an upcoming PTA meeting or contact radio stations during a snow emergency). However, two-way communication is at the heart of a successful public relations program. It not only helps frame messages, but helps elicit responses to them.

TWO ESSENTIAL THEORIES OF PUBLIC RELATIONS

Directors have no choice but to engage in public relations because, ultimately, they are responsible for building and maintaining the reputations of their schools. If their schools are to be viewed in a positive light, they must develop and implement effective programs. Because directors lack the resources available in the private sector, it is crucial that their programs be low-cost, practical, and based on proven theory. The two essential theories of public relations are the Four-Step Public Relations Process and the Diffusion Process. Familiarity with each enhances a director's success in reaching internal and external audiences.

The Four-Step Public Relations Process consists of research, planning, communicating, and evaluating. During the research stage, directors identify key internal and external audiences, ascertain their level of knowledge, choose the most appropriate medium to reach them, and collect the information that will be communicated to them. During the planning stage, directors set measurable objectives, establish timelines and resources, and assign responsibilities for implementing the planned activities. During the communication stage, directors deliver their messages via brochures, newsletters, meetings, and through other appropriate media. Finally, during the evaluation stage, directors determine whether or not their messages have been received and their objectives met.

The Diffusion Process allows directors to do more than communicate information; it enables them to change attitudes by identifying the five information-processing steps people take when making major decisions:

1. Awareness: People first become aware of an idea, service, or product. General mass communication vehicles such as newsletters, public service announcements, and ads are effective here.
2. Interest: People next want to find out details about the program, product, or idea. Mass communication, especially those of detail, are still effective.
3. Evaluation: People now want to hear personal experiences about the program, product, or idea and may ask trusted friends about their specific experiences. Communication during this step must become interpersonal if it is to be effective.
4. Trial: At this point people want to experience the program, product, or idea personally. In a school setting, directors should encourage parents and community members to visit the school and see programs first-hand. These direct experiences move the visitor past the "trial" phase into something more substantial.
5. Adoption: During the adoption phase, people make a decision to act. For example, parents and interested community members might assist the school by volunteering or by participating in other activities. If school choice is involved, parents may decide to enroll their students.

One-way communication works well during the first and second steps of the Diffusion Process; two-way communication must be employed during subsequent steps if public relations activities are to be effective.

EFFECTIVE AND INEFFECTIVE BEHAVIORS

When it comes to public relations, directors must be knowledgeable and committed. Too many directors maintain that public relations activities are unnecessary. Because they believe their work is admirable and that their mission is worthy, they assume public support will come automatically. Such an attitude invites trouble.

Effective directors take an active stance in creating and maintaining positive reputations for their schools; they view public relations as an essential leadership tool and are willing to learn the skills necessary to implement successful programs. Effective directors are honest and open in their communications. They understand that the more information people have, the more likely they will feel valued, and the more likely they will support their schools.

Key behaviors of effective directors include: identifying the advantages and disadvantages of mass and interpersonal communications techniques; and identifying appropriate interpersonal and mass communications techniques for each step in the Diffusion Process.

Data Collection

Directors must be able to assess the knowledge level and attitudes of their various constituencies. Formal research is not necessarily required to accomplish this; however, directors should be skilled at interviewing, conducting focus groups, and designing simple questionnaires. More specifically, they should be able to identify the types of information they need to develop effective public relations programs and the types of data collection methods available to them. Some of these methods are simple and easy to implement, such as having secretaries log incoming phone calls by topic area.

Other key behaviors of effective directors include: identifying key types of information before constructing a public relations plan; and identifying the three ways to collect data.

Communications Psychology

Directors must know what makes people tick if they are to change attitudes and motivate others to act. They also must be aware of the kinds of behaviors that create negative reactions in others.

Additional key behaviors of effective directors include: understanding the communications models such as those found above; and understanding the concepts of source reliability, credibility, and barriers to communications.

Written and Oral Communications

To share information, directors must use the printed and spoken word. They must be able to write memos, letters, and other materials, as well as deliver speeches, lead group discussions, and communicate with others on a one-on-one basis.

More key behaviors of effective directors include: communicating in clear, concise, and appropriate language that is free of educational jargon; and writing understandable memos, business letters, newsletter articles, and news releases.

Staff Relations

Effective public relations begins with effective director–staff communications. Directors must be skilled at communicating with all members of the school family: teachers, secretaries, custodians, and food service personnel, as well as volunteers, students, and district personnel. All of these individuals have daily contact with schools and can deliver positive or negative messages to others within and outside the school community. Their messages are more likely to be positive if directors provide them with adequate information, listen to their concerns, answer their questions, and make them feel like team players.

Key behaviors of effective directors include: identifying ways to provide complete, accurate information to all staff members in a timely manner; and implementing a program to obtain feedback from staff and to establish effective two-way communication.

Community Relations

A school is an important part of its community, and to a great extent, its reputation is built on its relationships within that community. Positive relationships evolve when a school is responsive to its constituencies and handles concerns in an honest and humane manner. Effective directors implement public relations programs that involve all segments of their communities. In addition, they serve on and work with numerous civic and community groups.

Key behaviors of effective directors include: identifying community opinion leaders and establishing a network of key communicators; identifying written and oral techniques for transmitting information to and from their various constituencies; and identifying the three ways to receive information from the community.

News Media Relations

Because of the public nature of education, directors will be involved with the news media throughout their careers. Accordingly, they should know how to work with and maintain positive relationships with reporters, editors, and publishers. Directors should know how to establish ground rules before interviews (e.g., when and where interviews will take place, whether they will be live or taped, what subjects they will cover, and so forth). They should know how to anticipate questions and formulate answers that deliver the messages they want communicated; how to convey important information, even if it has not been requested; how to shift reporters' questions away from or toward certain subject areas; how to handle interruptions; and how to present a positive image through proper dress and body language. In addition, directors must understand the differences between the print and broadcast media.

Key behaviors of effective directors include: writing news releases and public service announcements; preparing and following the procedures for placing op-ed articles; and identifying at least one use of today's telephone or desktop publishing technology.

Crisis Communications

Because of societal pressures on today's schools, directors must be skilled at developing and implementing specific crisis communication plans. Such plans must be developed in advance to ensure that communications will be handled properly and that the school's reputation will be protected.

Key behaviors of effective directors include: identifying key elements in a crisis communications plan.

Technology

Today's technology makes it easier for directors to implement their public relations objectives. For example, a newsletter designed on a desktop publishing system will likely be more attractive and widely read than using software without clip art and graphics.

NOTES

1. William Callison, *A Study of the Effect of Parent Involvement on Reading Performance* (Plainfield, Vt.: Goddard College Occasional Paper, 1974).

2. The Parent Institute (accessed February 2, 2002) www.parent-institute.com/.

3. Donald Bagin, *How to Start and Improve a Public Relations Program* (Alexandria, Va.: National School Boards Association, 1975); L. Kindred, Donald Bagin, and D. Gallagher, *The School and Community Relations* (Englewood Cliffs, N.J.: Prentice-Hall, 1990); S. Cutlip, A. Center, and J. Bloom, *Effective Public Relations* (Englewood Cliffs, N.J.: Prentice-Hall, 1985).

Chapter Twenty-two

Understanding Different Political Positions in Schools

If we attempt to fool ourselves into believing that education is not highly political we hurt the educational chances of the children we are responsible for because we will not gather their fair share of resources for them. Some nations use force to divide resources. Democratic nations tend to use politics to accomplish this job. One of the prime tasks of the school administrator is resource gathering for his or her staff, and political skills are crucial in the competition. This chapter concentrates on creating an understanding of the different characteristics within the school organization including influence, control, attitudes and feelings, trust, discontent, and dissatisfaction.

Key Concepts:
Authorities Make Decisions
Influence Perspective
Control Perspective
Loss of Trust in Director
Increased Support Stimulates More Effective Influence
Negative Influence or Backlash
Ways to Influence
Types of School Decision Making

AUTHORITIES MAKE DECISIONS

Authorities make decisions and look at them from a control perspective; influentials seek to influence decisions and look at them from a "lobbying" perspective. See if you can spot the authorities and the influentials in the following case study from a California school district.

The Adapted Physical Education (APE) specialists at USD recently decided to modify the criteria for the admittance of preschoolers into the APE program. Children of this age group and category will henceforth receive guidance from the APE specialists for play-therapy activities in specially designed programs for the special day class (SDC) teachers to incorporate into their own programs. In the past a pull-out approach was used, which sometimes offered services to the whole class.

Various pre-K teachers are concerned that their "at-risk" population will be overlooked if APE specialists alter their past practice of assessing preschoolers in September and pulling them out in small groups or with the whole class. Meetings have been held involving administrators, teachers, and psychologists to plan, present, and invite response to the redefined preschool assessment philosophy and procedures. (Note: The APE specialists have the primary responsibility for interpreting program philosophy and implementing APE services under the law; therefore, they are "the administrators" for the purposes of this example.)

It is important to learn to distinguish between the influence and control perspectives. The following material may help the director improve his or her skills in order to make this distinction.

INFLUENCE PERSPECTIVE

Task One

The administrator can identify those members of the organization who look at decisions in the organization from an influence perspective. There are four criteria used to locate "influence members."

1. Note who, at various staff meetings, have people gathering around them, asking questions.
2. Note who the union leaders are.
3. Identify teacher group leaders through director's cabinet (i.e., a small group of "leader" teachers who have been chosen or who take on the role of bringing information back to the others from the administrator).

4. Note those who have been historically successful in persuading others to their point of view (who have gained credibility with others through their influence in successfully aligning themselves with programs or procedures that have been adopted). They are vocal, assertive, and have time/experience on the job.

CONTROL PERSPECTIVE

Task Two

The administrator can identify those members of the organization who look at decisions in the organization from a control perspective. The administrators recognize that they (the APE specialists)—the director of special education and the coordinator of special education—are the "controllers" in this situation. (Note: Authorities control those below them in the pecking order; these same authorities become partisans [attempt to influence] when dealing with those above them.) There are four criteria used to locate "control" members:

1. Those who make binding decisions
2. Those who formally evaluate performance
3. Those who are on the administrative flow chart, including the school board
4. Those who "control" by unofficial authority

The "control members" in the case study here and the criteria that apply to them are: director of special education, under criteria 1, 2, 3; the coordinator of special education, under 1, 2, 3; and the APE specialists, under 4.

Now, still looking at our case study, define power as it relates to school goals. The administrator recognizes that power is the capacity to mobilize resources of the community for the attainment of school goals. (Note: Resources may include money, people, time, energy, and facilities.) There are two indicators that the administration in the case study recognized this. The APE specialists presented a plan to make "more efficient" use of people utilizing the special day class (SDC) teachers. And the APE specialists presented a plan to make better use of teacher/student time, thus freeing the APE staff to better service their caseloads, and allowing the student to remain in an integrated, nonfragmented SDC program.

Using the case study as an example, when should a director "go public" in a political struggle? The administrator recognizes that private conflicts are taken into the public arena because someone wants to make certain that the power ratio among the private interests most immediately involved shall not prevail. To say it another way, one moves from a behind-the-scenes struggle to open conflict when one sees no other way to win.

The administrators (APE staff) are aware that two of the SDC teachers affected by the program change have tried to mobilize the community (parents) in defense of their past approach. The pre-K teachers operated their classrooms with APE services filling (typically) two thirty-minute time slots per week with the APE specialist administering the effort. The APE specialists proposed a new plan that provided more limited special education services in a time of decreasing special education funds. The pre-K teachers could mobilize parents to demand additional APE services for their children.

Using the case study as an example, can you name the faculty from your school who are alienated, neutral, or allied with the present administration? Orientation toward the school may be classified as allegiance when attitudes, feelings, and evaluations are favorable to the school; as apathy or detachment when attitudes, feelings, and evaluations are neutral; and as alienation when attitudes, feelings, and evaluations are negative. For example, Teacher A is followed by everyone and has credibility; he is positive about the school. Teacher B has the perception that he has some influence, but really doesn't. At times he recognizes this and is usually neutral. Teacher C eats lunch alone, dislikes administrators, who have been out to get him for years, and is negative.

Looking at your school in particular who from your faculty wanted to influence and who felt they could, in fact, influence? The administrator wants to influence the staff and recognizes that for his or her authority to be effective he or she must have a good deal of freedom to commit resources without the prior consent of the staff. For example, an administrator, along with a group of math teachers, plans for the expenditure of funds for "math manipulatives" in September. Freedom is needed for the administrator to make various purchases later on for specific items as necessary without having to get a line-item okay on each occasion from the original group. She is successful in the influence attempt and is given the freedom to move ahead without prior consent.

LOSS OF TRUST IN DIRECTOR

Some directors will receive a large amount of goodwill from his or her faculty and others will not. The administrator should recognize that it is possible for the loss of trust to encourage a downward spiral. In the case study presented the administrators (APE specialists) realized that continued dedication to program quality in everyone's eyes would help maintain credibility when changes are necessary. All staff were aware that special education funds were increasingly being channeled to support "full inclusion" lawsuits where parents had won the right to place their children in private facilities that offered services not available through public schools. Therefore, special education had to make reductions in services wherever it was possible.

A director realizes control/credibility is negatively impacted when loss of trust or confidence occurs. The indicators of declining trust include: low morale; tension in staff meetings; and lack of response in staff meetings.

INCREASED SUPPORT STIMULATES
MORE EFFECTIVE INFLUENCE

There are some things a director who has obtained goodwill among the staff can do while negotiating a new project for a school that one who has not obtained goodwill in his or her school cannot. The administrator recognizes that successful influence stimulates member support and increased support stimulates more effective influence. In the case study the administrators (APE specialists) discussed redefining their program with key psychologists and administrators prior to presenting modifications at a general meeting. Following the announcement of intended APE program modifications at the general meeting, support for the changes was given by the special education administrators when queried by the affected teachers. Realizing the "tide had turned" and that reductions had to be made, most of the teachers eventually accepted the changes positively. A "positive wave" had been formed.

Think of a situation where you have seen a "downward spiral of trust" when a director caused the staff to lose faith in her or his judgment. The administrator understands that dissatisfaction begins to be generalized when an undesirable outcome is seen as a member of a class of decisions with similar results. If an administrator takes a stand on a number of issues that ultimately fail, his or her lack of judgment might be seen as pervasive.

For example, a director is advised by the district administration that a certain high school would be a good candidate for a year-round program. The director likes the idea and begins to initiate it. He fails to poll the community, and it resists the concept en masse. The district office refuses to back him up. He loses credibility. The same director earlier had banned certain hairstyles on campus and had been confronted with a large (and publicized) protest. The director was eventually transferred to a small, remote school.

So how can successful influence lead to increased staff support? The administrator recognizes individuals with differing levels of trust in the district/school administration including persons who have confidence; are neutral; and are alienated. For example, Director A enters a new school. She requests feedback from each English teacher in the form of a private, one- or two-sentence note asking how they feel about a new idea for the English curriculum. She then knows who is amenable to the new idea, who is not, and who may be neutral. She shows the list to her secretary and confirms her idea about which English teachers are most influential, in this case the positive ones. She moves ahead with the curriculum change and it gains general support.

A conscientious administrator will be looking for ways to lead to greater respect not only in his or her own school but at other schools too. Authorities control and partisans influence as their primary means of utilizing power. The administration recognizes that a partisan (influence) group can be said to have exercised influence only if there is a difference in an outcome that can be traced to the group's efforts.

In the case study the APE staff realized that gaining approval from the controlling administrators(s) in advance would greatly increase their chances of implementing desired program changes smoothly. The APE staff researched the need for program modifications in several schools and presented a series of positive reasons for change. Program restructure was accomplished.

Dissatisfaction, if followed by a series of decisions favoring the same group, can lead to general loss of trust. The administrator recognizes that a negative influence or backlash may occur when partisans' efforts turn authorities against their preferred outcome. In the present case the top administrators knew they had not granted recent favors to the APE staff.

In the case study the APE specialists had received two new Macintosh computers. In order to maximize their impact, in this example who should have gotten the computers—those with allegiance, the neutrals, or the alienated? A director recognizes that there are three ways to influence: constraints can be introduced, inducements offered, or persuasion offered. Careful analysis suggests the computers in the case study should have gone to the neutrals. Those with allegiance can be brought along with a few kind words about their children; hence, persuasion for them. The negatives will not support the cause even if they had been given the computers; hence, use constraints such as loss of parking privileges with them. The neutrals may, however, be tipped into the support column with a Macintosh nudge.

NEGATIVE INFLUENCE OR BACKLASH

Authorities should control and partisans should seek to influence as the appropriate use of power. The administrator recognizes the cost of influence, including the sacrifices that a would-be influencer must make in exercising influence and, in particular, the alternative use of foregone resources. In the case study the director of special education made a judgment that control would not work because the key teachers were not under her authority but were regular classroom teachers. Hence, she supported the APE staff in giving the computers to key neutrals, a direct (and successful) influence effort.

Sometimes partisans go too far and this can lead to backlash. Certain parents have expressed disappointment with the loss of a traditional program. These parents have been encouraged to observe the changes and gain assurance, hopefully, that their children are not going to receive less than they should on the next important resource decision.

The art of influence is often a matter of knowing who to offer an inducement to. In the example if the neutrals who received the computers were disliked by many teachers, the strategy might well have backfired.

Certainly the cost of influence in the example was the hurt feelings of some of the positive teachers who had a hard time understanding why an administrator would give computers to teachers who were neutral rather than their longtime supporters. With patient conversation over time they could no doubt be helped to understand.

WAYS TO INFLUENCE

Often the job of the director is to "manage discontent" and/or to "contain influence." For example, a supportive director was confronted by a group of angry parents who didn't like the decision and demanded that a fence be placed completely around the charter school or they would go to the school board. They intuitively knew that even though they had asked for this in the past without success they might win this time. The director agreed that the fence should have been built completely around from the beginning. She asked the group for help in determining how much additional fencing was needed (giving them some input and control over the situation) and agreed to assist them in going through the appropriate channels. She managed their discontent and contained their influence.

What is meant when a director says he or she has "modified the content of the decision" in order to build trust? A supportive director, in her hiring of two new teachers, had a disagreement among her staff about whom to select. She modified her decision to favor the teachers who had just lost on the APE decision in order to build trust that she was evenhanded and played no favorites on the staff.

Sometimes the most discontented staff have the least opportunity to influence a decision. For example, the discontented parents at Campus A have not been influential in the past. On the other hand, the chairperson of the parent teacher organization at Campus A has been around for years, wielding a great deal of influence. She has a great deal of control as to what direction her organization's resources may take and she was able to swing her school to support the APE decision, even though she was loudly opposed by the discontented parents.

So by saying that the director "offered conciliatory measures in a timely fashion to head off a rebellion" meant that those who believe that the head of the parent teacher organization persuaded a friend to propose the fencing of the school mentioned above in order to head off a rebellion of a large group of parents at her school.

A director can "offer differential access to staff in order to win the support of key neutrals" on an important decision. At another school the director readily allowed a group of parents to publish some mathematics curriculum materials and influence the parents and staff of the school because he knew these parents could help him gain the support of several neutrals from his staff on the APE decision (which he supported).

A director can "absorb new people into the leadership group" as a strategy for heading off an insurrection by including a neutral teacher on a key committee in order to win the support of other neutrals whose support was needed on a vote.

For example, a director understood that if the teachers who were for and against the new math curriculum were stalled, the neutral teachers would vote for no change and the discontented groups would be quieted, if not pleased.

If a group has received more than its share of resources it is more likely to be more aggressive to seek more resources. As in other aspects of life, the teachers who have garnered the most favors pursue more relentlessly. Give them kind words but no more resources.

The more liquid a group's resources are, the more they will attempt new influence. Just as it is easier to save money if it is not easily available.

Confident groups will try to influence decisions constantly but so will alienated groups. These are the teachers who care, and they will be busily attempting to achieve their objectives.

All three means of influence are likely to be employed by partisan groups, but any given group will tend to rely on one more than the other two. For instance, confident groups will rely on persuasion. Neutrals will offer inducements and the alienated will threaten. Well-trained directors will use these concepts in decisions they control with confident, neutral, and alienated groups. The confident teachers get affectionate comments, the neutrals the new modems, and the alienated will be isolated.

TYPES OF SCHOOL DECISION MAKING

There are four types of school decision making:

- Organizational: To use this model you must demonstrate that (1) staff objectives are different from board objectives, and (2) staff objectives are not the best way to meet board goals. For example, the board wants improved reading scores. An easy test is purchased with the thought that no one on the board will know the difference.
- Rational: The three criteria to use in deciding if this model is in use are: (1) board members agreed in writing on certain objectives, (2) reference to these objectives was made in the course of decision making, and (3) outcomes were consistent with objectives. About the only time such rationality is used in decision making is when there is a severe penalty for not following agreements to the letter, as in a federal or state grant.
- Pluralist: Pluralist groups will (1) concentrate their energies on those issues having the greatest impact on their interests, (2) develop new alliances as the issues and tactical situations change, and (3) migrate from one political faction to another as political leaders' positions on matters of group concern are modified. This type of horse trading is typical of people who don't care about the content of a decision but are trying to avoid criticism. They will be owed a vote or two to use in the future.
- Ideological: Ideologues will (1) be very reluctant to compromise, especially on their favorite issues, and (2) push their favorite issue or issues relentlessly. This type of decision is typical of people with little political experience who were elected on one salient issue like "no bussing."

Chapter Twenty-three

Utilizing Federal, State, and Community Resources

We have passed the point where a director can rely on federal or state resources to supplement the operation of a good charter school. He or she must turn to all available sources including foundations and businesses, especially those in the local area.

Key Concepts:
Regional Occupational Programs
Greater Avenues for Independence Program
Health Services Western Unified School District
Special Education Program
Resource Specialist Program
Designated Instruction and Services

The Western Charter High School, Western, California, is a model for the utilization of federal, state, and community resources. It uses support from the Sierra Health Foundation (private) to augment health services. It operates a Tobacco Use Prevention grant (state) and a Safe and Drug-free School grant (federal). Also offered are special education (federal), an Extended School Year Program (district), and linkage to residential schools that are funded in some cases by state funds and in others by private sources.

The Regional Occupational Programs (ROP) experience is planned to help the students gain the readiness skills needed for success in their careers. The program focuses on building self-esteem and confidence in problem solving. Health evaluations are done in hearing, vision, and physical health. Students and families are referred to agencies within the community that can meet specific needs. Community services like the fire department, police department, health services, and local businesses are used both in the classroom and as field trips. Parents participate on the parent advisory committee, which works with the program and budgets. These experiences prepare parents to participate in their students' education.

The Sierra Health Foundation provides early intervention and prevention services that improve a student's readiness to learn and succeed. It is also believes that family-centered services help families meet their immediate needs and in the long run strive to be more self-sufficient.

By providing social, health, and economic services to families and children in need, they are addressing the National Education Goals that relate to:

- Readiness to learn;
- School completion;
- Student achievement and citizenship;
- Teacher education and professional development;
- Adult literacy and lifelong learning;
- Safe, disciplined, and alcohol/drug-free schools;
- Parental participation.

To support school safety efforts the foundation provides physicals, immunizations, treatment for minor illnesses and injuries, and health-care guidance and referrals. The dental association has agreed to provide free dental assessments, and community sponsors provide free dental services.

Family counselors and interns provide student and family crisis assistance, which guides and assists teachers in understanding and handling family crisis situations appropriately. Social workers and interns provide family maintenance services to dysfunctional families designed to strengthen families and keep children in school. Eligibility workers provide economic, homeless, guidance, and referral services to strengthen families and keep children in school.

REGIONAL OCCUPATIONAL PROGRAMS

Regional Occupational Programs (ROP) teach students how to find and keep a job. All ROP courses include instruction on self-directed job search. Instruction includes filling out job applications, interviewing techniques, and locating potential employers. Job referral assistance is provided by individual high schools. There are approximately 420,000 students in ROP in California; about half are high school students and half are adults seeking specific job training.

GREATER AVENUES FOR INDEPENDENCE PROGRAM

The Greater Avenues for Independence Program (GAIN) teaches, trains, counsels, and helps people on Aid to Families with Dependent Children (AFDC, now TANF) find a job. When people become self-supporting, they and their children will enjoy a higher income and a better way of life. GAIN provides supportive services such as childcare, transportation, and funds for work- or training-related expenses. It also helps people get the skills needed in today's workforce. GAIN recipients can become technicians, salespersons, assemblers, or any of hundreds of professional occupations. The entire staff also makes many referrals to a wide variety of other community organizations who assist families and children in their efforts to survive and become successful.

HEALTH SERVICES OF
WESTERN UNIFIED SCHOOL DISTRICT

Department of Health Services includes one nursing services coordinator and one part-time and six full-time nurses. Some of the mandated services include vision and hearing testing, scoliosis testing, immunizations, CHDP and HIV prevention education. Health services coordinates the Tobacco Use Prevention grant and the Safe and Drug-free School grant. Health services is responsible for all health education for students and staff, including HIV/AIDS, Family Life.

The coordinator of health services contributes to district-wide health programs and is involved with wellness, safety, insurance, and charter and secondary curriculum advisory committees. Staff in-services include blood-borne pathogens, child abuse, first aid, and employee assistance program. The health services coordinator serves on many community committees to bring wellness and health programs to the district personnel.

MediCal billing provides additional health services to the district personnel. The health services coordinator is a member of the Healthy Start Collaborative and is also chairperson of a committee to oversee all family life materials presented to students. At Western health services is active in the school nursing organization (CSNO) within the state and generously shares its expertise with others.

SPECIAL EDUCATION PROGRAM

Special education programs offered through Western Unified School District (WUSD) includes resource specialist program, designated instruction and services, special classes and centers, nonpublic schools, state special schools, and instruction in settings other than classrooms where specially designed instruction may occur. These program options are provided to eligible students ages birth to twenty-two years as appropriate to the implementation of an individualized education program.

RESOURCE SPECIALIST PROGRAM

Resource students are individuals with less intensive needs who are assigned to regular classroom teachers for the majority of the school day. The resource specialist program (RSP) provides instructional planning, special instruction, tutorial assistance, and other services to individuals with disabilities in regular classrooms and/or special programs in each school as specified in the individualized education plan (IEP). The plan provides information, assistance, consultation, resource information, and materials regarding individuals with exceptional needs to parents and staff. An instructional assistant is assigned to help each resource specialist provide necessary instruction.

DESIGNATED INSTRUCTION AND SERVICES

Designated instruction and services are provided as prescribed in the IEP. Designated instruction and services are provided by the regular teacher, special class teacher, resource specialist, or a variety of other qualified specialists. Designated instruction and services are provided in a variety of settings that include regular and special education classrooms, the home, hospitals and institutions, or other settings as appropriate.

Chapter Twenty-four

Using the Internet and CD-ROMs

Every school director is looking for a teacher who can create a nice Web page to tell about her or his school. In this chapter we suggest the use of top-of-the-line word processors that typically have the capability to convert text to HTML format, which is the format used on the Web. But to use the Web you need to be on the Internet and to be on the Internet you typically use a browser. The most common is Microsoft's Explorer. Netscape Navigator is its rival. Several instructional examples taken from the Internet and CD-ROM encyclopedias are discussed.

Key Concepts:
Common Files Can Be Databases, Programs, or E-Mail
Compact Disks Are a Fine Resource
Developing an Instruction and Learning Knowledgebase
Professional Development for Using Technology in Secondary Schools

A computer network is the interconnection of many individual computers, much as a road is the link between the homes and the buildings of a city. Having many separate computers linked on a network provides many advantages to organizations such as schools, businesses, and universities. People may quickly and easily share files; modify databases; send memos called e-mail, or electronic mail; run programs on remote mainframes; and get access to information in databases that are too massive to fit on a small computer's hard drive. Networks provide an essential tool for the routing, managing, and storing of huge amounts of rapidly changing data.

The Internet is a network of networks: the international linking of tens of thousands of businesses, universities, agencies, schools, and research organizations with millions of individual users. It is what has been referred to as the information superhighway. What is now known as the Internet was originally formed in 1970 as a military network called ARPAnet (Advanced Research Projects Agency network) as part of the Department of Defense. The network opened to nonmilitary users in the 1970s, when universities and companies doing defense-related research were given access, and flourished in the late 1980s as most universities and many businesses around the world came online. In 1993, when commercial providers were first permitted to sell Internet connections to individuals, usage of the network exploded. Millions of new users came on within months, and a new era of computer communications began.

COMMON FILES CAN BE
DATABASES, PROGRAMS, OR E-MAIL

Most networks on the Internet make certain files available to other networks. These common files can be databases, programs, or e-mail from the individuals on the network. With hundreds of thousands of international sites each providing thousands of pieces of data, it's easy to imagine the mass of raw data available to users.

The Internet is by no means the only way in which computer users can communicate with others. Several commercial online services provide connections to members who pay a monthly connect-time fee. These firms provide a tremendous range of information and services, including online conferencing, electronic mail transfer, program downloading, current weather and stock market information, travel and entertainment information, access to encyclopedias and other reference works, and electronic forums for specific users' groups such as PC users. One of the most economical is Webbox, by MicroSoft, which offers five e-mail accounts for a nominal price, making it an fine option for schools use in labs and classrooms. Each student can then learn to communicate privately with her or his teacher and to use the Internet.

COMPACT DISCS ARE A FINE RESOURCE

There are exciting and varied instructional resources (encyclopedias) on compact discs selling for less than $40 through sources such as America Online. They may contain the standard twenty-plus volumes of information; 7,000 images, maps, and graphs (many on a separate CD using pictures from space, in color); fifty minutes of sounds (like bird calls), music, and speeches; ninety multimedia videos (President Kennedy's assassination); 5,000 charts and diagrams, and the complete *Webster's Intermediate Dictionary*.

There is a CD titled *A Small Blue Planet*, which is an atlas using thousands of pictures from space taken at different altitudes so that you can move down to an earthbound perspective as if you were flying in a small plane. It also includes pictures of the major cities of the world and information about each country, its people, and its language(s).

DEVELOPING AN INSTRUCTION
AND LEARNING KNOWLEDGEBASE

Directors who are effective instructional leaders find ways to spend more time on instruction than directors who are not as effective. They learn about new approaches to powerful learning such as uses of technology including the Internet and *Compton's Interactive Encyclopedia*.

Using access to the Internet I carried out a search with the following descriptors: technology/elementary schools. This is an excellent way for a director to build her or his knowledgebase of current innovations and practices. For example here is one of our search results:

Garden City Elementary, a twenty-first-century school, has a variety of technology. Since 1992 our students have been interacting with the latest developments in educational multimedia equipment. Computers, discourse lab, the Internet with long-distance learning (in every classroom), laser disc materials, and a state-of-the-art media production studio are a few of the most advanced materials available to both students and teachers.

The computer lab is a special place for the students at Garden City to learn about and have hands-on experience with different technologies. We will be turning this area into a "Technology Lab" during the school year with the introduction of more technology such as CD burning, scanning into applications, multimedia production, and video conferencing.

Another fabulous teaching tool, uniquely available at Garden City Elementary, is the Discourse Electronic Classroom. This classroom presents a nonthreatening environment in which all students are actively engaged in the learning process. Thirty-one student terminals allow every student the opportunity and motivation to interact simultaneously to teacher-designed materials.

The teacher's station monitors all responses, prints reports and data, and can publicly display student work on the television screen. Students are unable to hide or fall through the cracks because every student's name and his or her response appears on the teacher's monitor. Student feedback is immediate! This integration of technology supports and empowers teachers as students work at their own pace on reading, math, and science material appropriate to their skill and grade levels. Our students love it! They have developed "Discourse Fever!"

Students in fourth and fifth grade are given the opportunity to become "real" reporters and camera people. Garden City has a "live" newscast every morning where the student body is led in the Pledge of Allegiance, Mission statements, and student creed. The reporters read announcements to the rest of the student body and give weather reports daily. After the announcements are read, Mrs. Johnson addresses GCE and introduces students with birthdays, special awards for students, and any other important announcements.

The "newscast" is entirely run by the students. This includes the mixing board, camera shots, weather reports, announcements, and reporting. Leadership and cooperation are cultivated and developed here in media production.

Access to the Internet from every computer at Garden City Elementary was the goal of several of the technology upgrades completed last summer. We are well on our way to that goal with every classroom computer having Internet access. Students and teachers are able to find information and interesting enhancements to lessons using cutting-edge and extremely fast Internet connections.

GCE is excited to bring the Internet to the classroom and expose our students to a great learning tool of the twenty-first century.

PROFESSIONAL DEVELOPMENT FOR USING TECHNOLOGY IN SECONDARY SCHOOLS

Search the Internet for "technology secondary schools" to locate the following model from the Northwest Regional Educational Laboratory.

Presentations

Short presentations of one-hour or less can focus on one classroom by viewing one video and demonstrating some of the Web site materials related to that classroom. A short session can be sufficient for engaging teachers' interest in further independent review of the Web site resources.

Workshops

Longer workshops allow hands-on learning with better transfer to a teacher's own context through group discussion of instructional strategies. Workshops can target a group of teachers by grade level or subject and focus on one classroom or learning project. For a mix of K–12 teachers, a workshop can cover more than one of the classroom projects and include a survey of strategies across the grades and projects at the site. Workshops might also focus on instructional components, such as assessment in the Assessing Learning sections of each project or on project learning design in Learning that Works.

Getting Started

Audience

These products will best meet the needs of K–12 classroom teachers who are using technology for student learning and recognize the organization and management issues that arise when integrating technology. They have a working knowledge of computer use and are familiar with applications such as e-mail, Internet searching, spreadsheets, databases, and CDs for information retrieval.

Goals

Teachers learning from classrooms@work resources will explore authentic models of technology integration to:

- Develop more focused and personalized visions of technology integration
- Identify new strategies for technology-supported project learning
- Find and adapt classroom-tested materials that support integration of technology
- Consider new methods to meet technology integration challenges

Suggested Workshop Agenda

Agenda

The agenda below briefly outlines sections of a 1 1/2 to 2-hour hands-on workshop. It includes a few helpful pointers and time estimates.

1. Preliminaries

Check the facilities and equipment:

Presentation station: Computer (Macintosh or Windows), with T-1 Internet connection or with a CD drive; high quality projection (for both video and computer); and VCR

Participant Workstations: T-1 Internet connectivity or CD drive; current browser with plug-ins installed (*Adobe Acrobat* reader, *QuickTime* 4.0)

Test Equipment

Connect to Web site; www.netc.org/classrooms@work; test projection; adjust display, if needed

Cue video; test video projection

Check workstations for plug-ins (*Adobe* and *QuickTime*)

2. Openers

Following the welcome, introductions, and any get-acquainted activities; review the goals, agenda and the classrooms@work resources. If workshop time is less than 1 1/2 hours and if participants come from several grade and subject levels, you may need to poll the participants for their preferences on which classroom video to view. (10–20 minutes)

3. Show a Video

The videos give a visual overview of an individual class and a learning project and are intended to introduce the Web site. The video and the Web site are organized into the same segments which makes the video a good "table of contents" for the extensive Web site materials. Prior to showing a video, prompt teachers with the following:

• As you view the video, make (mental or written) notes of what interests you:
• What do you want to know more about? What would you like to have?
• What would you want to explore further on the Web site? (20 minutes)

4. Discuss Video

Share and discuss answers to the above questions. Make notes about the areas of particular interest to the group to use in the next demonstration. (10–15 minutes)

5. Demonstrate the Web site

A quick demonstration of the Web site should focus on introducing a few organization and navigation basics and not on content. With monitors off, walk participants through a few preliminary features of the Web site.

Point out opening page options, such as the Introduction and Ordering links

Show the Site Map (Note: This site map is for organization overview and is not used for navigation)

Select Explore, then choose the classroom associated with video

Show that there are four orientation sections for background information on a classroom

Review the five main organizers on the Contents page and how they align with the video

Select Learning That Works and demonstrate some secondary pages and show navigation back with the back button of the browser

Demonstrate navigation buttons at the bottom of the main section pages

Return to opening page for selecting classrooms and select site map to review and end (10–20 minutes)

6. Explore the Web site

Get teachers started by having them type in the complete URL: www.netc.org/classrooms@work. Depending on time available, structure the hands-on time with pauses for group discussions. It may be helpful to use a prepared handout with questions to prompt discussion.

Encourage participants to start with the contextual information before moving to the project description. When the majority have moved through this material, pause and discuss:

- How is this classroom similar to or different from your classroom(s)?
- What aspects of the project are appropriate for your classrooms?
- What project ideas does this classroom bring to mind? (10–15 minutes)

Review management and organization strategies

The Working Together and Using Workspaces sections contain a lot of material on specific strategies and activities. A discussion of these strategies generate a lot of variations and new possibilities among a group of teachers. Pause and discuss strategies:

- What strategies does this teacher use to keep students organized and managing their group work? What do you use?
- How are computer and non-computer activities scheduled in this classroom and in your own? How do students rotate or move from activity-to-activity?
- What are the advantages and disadvantages of the workspace arrangements in this classroom? In your own classroom? (10–15 minutes)

Review monitoring and assessment practices

The Assessing Learning section contains many student work samples, scoring guides, and description of assessment for the project. After reviewing the materials, pause and discuss:

- Extended projects often result in a culminating performance assessment, what kinds of performance assessment do your students do? How do you assess final projects?
- In what ways are the scoring guides and student monitoring tools useful for projects you do or may do?
- In what ways has technology supported student learning? (10–15 minutes)

Review of school support

The final section, Supporting Success, addresses school leadership and structure that supports classroom use of technology.

In your school, what structures are in place that support your use of technology? What has helped you the most? What support would you like to have? (10–15 minutes)

7. Wrap up and evaluation

Participants can use the Web site to complete an online evaluation of the classroom@work resources or to order copies of the videos or CD from the Web site.

Afterword

The charter school innovation redefines the role of districts, allowing them to move from a command and control structure to one where the district holds individual schools accountable for student achievement results, while providing them the flexibility to run their schools in a manner that those at the school believe will allow them to meet these expectations.

This new public school governance structure has been described by the Education Commission of the States in their report, "Governing America's Schools: Changing the Rules—Report of the National Commission on Governing America's Schools" (1999), as one where "in return for greater accountability, schools and professional staff ideally receive more flexibility and autonomy to make strategic decisions. With accountability, state officials prescribe outcomes and leave choices about instructional methods and practices to professional educators in the schools."

A recent study, "California Charter Schools Serving Low SES Students: An Analysis of the Academic Performance Index" (2002), shows that student achievement in low-income charter schools is improving at a faster rate than in their noncharter counterparts. Over a two-year period, charter schools serving very high poverty children (75 percent or more free and reduced lunch eligible students) saw test score growth of 28.1 percent, while noncharters serving similar students grew 23.8 percent. Charter schools face many other challenges. These include addressing issues of economies of scale, as charter schools are smaller in

This afterword is excerpted from an article titled "The Charter School Option" by David Patterson (*Leadership*, Association of California School Administrators [September/October 2002]: 26–38).

order to be educationally effective, but individually are too small to have important cost efficiencies. There are the continuing attempts to reregulate charter schools. And finally there is the sheer difficulty of creating and sustaining a start-up school, which gives too many otherwise interested educators pause.

Make no mistake about it, charter schools are no panacea. The freedom charter schools have does allow the development of very powerful and effective schools. At the same time this freedom provides an opportunity to fail. And a small number of schools have failed, and others are struggling. However, the critical difference between a charter school and a noncharter school is that a failing charter school, if it does not improve, can and should be shut down.

Too many public school educators in California, both administrators and teachers, are overworked, demoralized and fundamentally frustrated with their ability to effectively educate children. Charter schools offer hope to educators; the opportunity to create successful schools and places that work for children, their families, and educators. They offer the opportunity to reconnect schools and their communities. And they offer educators the opportunity to work in something other than large, impersonal bureaucracies.

We must encourage educators to take up the challenge of being responsible for educational results and provide them with the support necessary so they can create, through charter, many new "options" in communities throughout the state.

Multiple Intelligence Instructional Activities Manual

Teacher Name_____
Student Name_____
You should order a new manual each year since we revise and add new activities each year.

1. How frequently do you like to write stories?

   never (0)
   sometimes (1)
   frequently (2)
   very frequently (3)
   always (4)

Suggested Activities (several adapted from *Seven Ways of Knowing* by David Lazear)

The grade-level suggestions have been left off these activities because special needs students at many grade levels may benefit from a given suggestion.

   a. Read a story and write a new ending; teacher reads story, children tell ending orally.
   b. Listen to a friend's idea and then discuss how you think about it.
   c. Learn a new word each day and use it that day (record it).
   d. Make a short speech to your class on your favorite TV program.
   e. Write down the main things that happen to you each day in a notebook.
   f. Exercises involving the meaning of words.

g. Exercises involving the order of words in a sentence.

h. Exercises involving the sound and rhythm of words.

i. Make a list of five things you did yesterday. Now describe how you could have a dream that would take you into the future. How will you do one of these things ten years from now?

j. Write down a short story telling about the most important thing that has happened to you in your life.

k. Create an imaginary conversation between two people you know.

l. Pick a time when you are alone and list all of the things you were not thinking about such as smells, sounds, thoughts, feelings, and tastes.

m. Start a journal and write down all of the things you think about when you are alone each day.

n. At the end of the week write down ten big things that happened to you that week.

o. Open a dictionary and randomly place your finger on a word. Read about it and then give a one minute explanation of it to the class.

p. Pick a topic you know about and give a three minute presentation on it to a group.

q. Take the opposite position from what you believe on a topic and give a one minute presentation on it.

r. Tell a friend about an idea you had that might be impossible.

s. Select a big decision you have ahead. Write down a conversation between two people you know as they talk about the topic.

t. Select a TV program you remember and write down why you remember it.

u. Write down what you think your first job will be. Write down what you think your second job will be.

v. Write a short story with a villain and a hero or heroine.

w. What was the hardest part of writing the short story?

x. Change the story and make the villain turn into a good person at the end.

y. Change the story so one of the characters has an amazing dream.

Reprinted with permission from Students at Risk, 1260 Brangwyn Way, Laguna Beach, CA 92651; telephone and fax: 949-497-1331.

2. I like to observe and be "scientific."

never (0)
sometimes (1)
frequently (2)
very frequently (3)
always (4)

Suggested Activities (several adapted from *Seven Ways of Knowing* by David Lazear)

a Write an outline about your hobby with four subpoints.
b. Compare a computer with a typewriter in two paragraphs.
c. Analyze the benefits of an island that doesn't exist.
d. Make a batch of brownies following the recipe in a cookbook and/or write down the instructions for using a new piece of equipment or software
e. Write down a twelve digit number and memorize it. Write down the numbers from memory.
f. Write down a twenty digit number that is a series of dates that are well known like 1492 1776, only run them together as 14,921,776 and so forth. Memorize them and write them from memory. Which list is easier to write down from memory?
g. Create an inductive reasoning exercise where the students put clues together to figure out a solution (the car is carrying items one would take to the beach, etc.).
h. Create a deductive reasoning exercise where students start with a rule and figure out a solution (only teachers come to school on staff development days; here is the attendance report for each day last semester; when was the staff development day?).

The following activities were adapted from *Science and Society* by Rita W. Peterson.

i. Talk to senior citizens to see how an environment has changed. Apply the following:

• concept: environments change with new development
• learning process: gather and organize information

- psychomotor skills: use equipment available
- attitudes and values: find disagreements

j. Go to a museum to see equipment from another time and how it worked. Apply the following:

  - concept: environments change with new development
  - learning process: gather and organize information
  - psychomotor skills: use equipment available
  - attitudes and values: find disagreements

k. Read an old magazine or newspaper to see how viewpoints change. Apply the following:

  - concept: environments change with new development
  - learning process: gather and organize information
  - psychomotor skills: use equipment available
  - attitudes and values: find disagreements

l. Visit an office to gather information about one of the things they do. Apply the following:

  - concept: environments change with new development
  - learning process: gather and organize information
  - psychomotor skills: use equipment available
  - attitudes and values: find disagreements

m. Study wildlife. Apply the following:

  - concept: environments change with new development
  - learning process: gather and organize information
  - psychomotor skills: use equipment available
  - attitudes and values: find disagreements between old and new times

3. I enjoy drawing and making maps.

never (0)
sometimes (1)
frequently (2)

very frequently (3)
always (4)

Suggested Activities

a. Use a colored marker to express an idea.
b. Write a description of vacation spot you can imagine even though you have never seen it.
c. Write down a conversation you might have had with President Kennedy.
d. Create a poster for an assembly at your school.

4. How often do you like to play sports?

never (0)
sometimes (1)
frequently (2)
very frequently (3)
always (4)

Suggested Activities (several adapted from *Multiple Intelligences in the Classroom* by Thomas Armstrong)

a. Role play two of your friends on the playground.
b. Demonstrate a gorilla like you were playing charades.
c. Show how you walk when you are: happy; tired; and afraid.
d. Pretend to walk on a high wire between two buildings.
e. Act out (mime) new words and the content of a story.
f. Make new words into pictures (hang on word tree).
g. Sculpt new words using clay.
h. Draw pictures about the content of a book.
i. Jog in place slowly; after a while move your head back and forth from left to right.
j. Keep jogging and move your head and arms in opposite directions from each other.
k. Keep jogging and snap your fingers; snap your fingers in rhythm with your head movement.
l. Sit in a chair and think about the phases of getting up.

m. Now get up and see if you remembered all the phases correctly.

n. Walk briskly around the room; now focus on your feet. How do they feel?

o. What do your hips do when you walk?

p. As you walk think about smells, about your feelings.

q. Create a facial expression that indicates happiness; anger; curiosity.

r. Place your hands on a table. Rap on the table with each finger with one hand; with both hands.

s. Think of a skill you would like to improve like a tennis serve. Go through all the movements and pay attention to what happens in each part of your body.

Now go through the movements mentally, concentrating carefully. Continue until the set of movements are almost the same.

t. Apply the imagining approach to another part of your life like an interview.

u. Apply the concept to one of your goals that is being blocked. Act out breaking through the block, first mentally and then physically.

v. Apply the concept to other blocked goals as you have the energy. Pretend you are actually doing these things.

w. Try walking different ways to express your feelings like meeting your boss or going to a test. What did you learn?

x. Attach a physical movement or gesture to something you are trying to learn like a math activity. Act it out so it is encoded with both the body and the mind.

y. Breathe in and out through your nose and think of the earth below. Imagine you are drawing the earth's life-giving energy up through your body. Continue breathing this way as you walk. You will walk with new determination.

5. I like to sing and listen to music.

never (0)
sometimes (1)
frequently (2)
very frequently (3)
always (4)

Suggested Activities (several adapted from *Multiple Intelligences in the Classroom* by Thomas Armstrong)

a. Bring a tape to class that you would play at the opening ceremony for a new school.
b. Make up a (rap) song about one of your teachers that you like.
c. Hum a note that makes your head vibrate a lot.
d. Make a tape of some sound from nature.
e. Make up a song using new words.
f. Read the words to songs from a song book.
g. Teach a younger child a song you know.
h. Have different students hum, sing, and whistle the same tune.
i. Have students bring as many kinds of recorded music as they can find and play them so each student can learn to name the type as they hear it.
j. Play live music with as many instruments and players as you can find.
k. Have groups of students sing different types of songs to each other.
l. Use background music with different activities and talk about its effect.
m. Link old tunes with the concepts they call to mind (I've been working on the railroad).
n. Have students create new melodies. See if they can create words to go with the melodies.
o. Listen to tunes that help you think of images (storm).
p. Have students make up sounds for punctuation marks and voice them in unison while a student is reading aloud.
q. Use a tape recorder in many ways: send oral letters; share experiences; get feedback on how they are doing in an activity; collecting interviews; and talking books.
r. Use a percussion instrument to help set a rhythm for learning things like spelling words and times tables.
s. Try the same thing with rap songs; then with chants.
t. Get an encyclopedia on CD and go through the many musical options it offers.
u. Find phrases from songs that help you remember concepts you are working on.
v. Try supermemory music like baroque music used as a background as you read the students information they need to remember.

w. Create a story and find music to illustrate key parts such as conflict.

x. Find music to go with certain emotional states such as contemplation and excitement.

y. Listen to classical music and identify the emotions that you think of.

6. How often do you like to work in a group?

never (0)
sometimes (1)
frequently (2)
very frequently (3)
always (4)

Suggested Activities (several adapted from *Seven Ways of Knowing* by David Lazear)

> We learn 10% of what we read 20% of what we hear 30% of what we see 40% of what we both see and hear 50% of what is discussed with others 70% of what we experience personally 95% of what we teach to someone else. William Glasser

a. Choose three classmates and do a job for your teacher so that each member has different things to do.

b. Have one person in the previous activity write down only the important things that are said to get the job done and leave out all the other things.

c. Have the same person write down something one person indicated without saying it, like making a face about a suggestion.

d. Have the person who makes the best faces give a report to the class on what you did using lots of different faces and gestures.

e. Discuss effective communication criteria such as "can accurately paraphrase what was just said," and "understood nonverbal message."

f. Have groups keep track of effective communication based on approved criteria.

g. Have each student write to two friends and then score their communication according to criteria that you set with the students.

h. Have the class brainstorm ways to improve communication.

i. Let them practice using their brainstorming ideas on a task of interest.

j. Have partners read a short piece to each other and sense their feelings about it.

k. Tell your partner what you thought they expressed and what clues you used.

l. Use the exercise above for music and get the response.

m. Use the same exercise for a physical object and get the response.

n. Have a group build a Lego type construction and put it behind a screen. Then have another group build one with the same pieces with only one person being able to see it. This person can only give answers to questions from the group.

o. Have two students who are articulate and who disagree on a topic of interest debate it for five minutes. The class then cites examples of the extent to which the debaters seemed to understand what the opponent said or merely planned what they were going to say while the opponent was speaking.

p. Then have each student analyze a recent conversation they had where they both listened carefully and did not. Have them write down an example of each behavior.

q. Ask the class to find examples of such careful listening and identification that the person was "inside the other person's point of view or perspective."

r. Ask each student to identify the characteristics of two people who really can identify with each other.

s. Now ask them to find a fellow student they do not identify with and tell them of a recent event of interest. They should set a couple of areas for improvement. Now have them see if they can improve their identification in telling of another event.

t. Have each student think of a group they belong to and ask them to evaluate the effectiveness of the communication according to criteria you set with the class.

u. For effective aspects of communication in each student's group have the student identify why the communication is successful. Have them do the same for aspects that are not effective. (How about analyzing your class?)

v. Have each student list the people they interact with where interpersonal skills are important. Ask them to rank which people and groups are most important to them.

w. Have the students look at their list and see if they can list ideas for improving their interpersonal skills by thinking of why they succeed with certain people and groups.

x. Introduce the concept of exchange between people. When two people each offer something to each other the exchange is in balance. When one offers too much the exchange goes out of balance, and eventually the relationship ceases to exist. Have the students list the people where they have the most balanced exchange and the least balanced exchange.

y. Have the students list strategies for getting relationships they care about back into balance.

7. Do you like to sit and think about who you are?

never (0)
sometimes (1)
frequently (2)
very frequently (3)
always (4)

Suggested Activities

a. Have a quiet team member from the activity in number 6d above tell what they were thinking while the face maker gave the report to the class.

b. Have one of the team members tell what the team was doing as if they were watching from a distance.

c. Tell who on the team really figured out what to do when the teacher told your team what the job was.

d. Write a paragraph telling "who am I, really?"

e. Have your students describe someone they know who seems to be comfortable with who they are.

f. What are some of the characteristics of such a person? List them on the board as the class thinks of them.

g. The research tells us that some of the following characteristics lead one to have a strong intrapersonal intelligence. For example, awareness of the greatness of human life leads us to be comfortable with who we are. Have the students name someone they know who exhibits such awareness.

h. Have them name someone who has a sense of interdependence with nature.

i. Have the students list several states of consciousness such as thinking of your own situation, thinking of another person's situation, thinking of solving a problem, thinking of having fun, thinking of being in another location, and so forth. Have them name someone who seems to be able to shift from one focus or state of consciousness to another when they need to.

j. Have the students name someone who is good at transferring things they have learned from one arena to another.

k. Have the students name someone who is good at problem solving. What are the advantages of learning to be a better problem solver?

l. Ask the students if they know of anyone who can reduce their heart rate when they want to. Have them list other things about the body that one can learn to control? (blood pressure, body temperature) How is this done? (learning to concentrate)

m. Howard Gardner's research indicates people can learn to be more creative through use of inward directed intelligence such as we are working on here. Often the improved creativity comes from examination of our own preferences and feelings and a resultant willingness to try new things that we have been afraid to try previously. Ask your students to think quietly about something they would like to be able to do and the feeling that has kept them from doing it.

n. Have the students talk to each other in pairs about their feelings and the possibility of trying something they would like to do.

o. In order to get better at intrapersonal intelligence we need to learn to "get outside ourselves" and be objective about what we can and cannot do. Have the students practice this by listing something about themselves where they have not been very objective. Have them list an example of what happened to improve a situation they were in, where they did discipline themselves, take an objective view of what they were doing that was not working, and change what they were doing so they become successful.

p. Now ask them to "be a witness" to their partner's life and help them find another area where an objective look can lead to a change of behavior and success.

q. Have the students think of a more significant area where they need to think objectively and plan a change.

r. Now have them do the same thing again following this model:

- What was I expected to do?
- If I had this to do over, what would I do differently?
- What help do I need?
- Where can I get that help?
- How will I know if I am improving?

s. Have the students partner and list what type of situation makes them ready for each of the following: looking at art; reading a poem; singing; dancing; running; and being alone to think and plan.

t. We are working toward expressing our feelings better here. Do the students think they can consciously "turn their heads around" and get ready to do the various activities listed in s. above?

u. Have the students list the moods they were in yesterday. Now have them draw a chart and use color if it is available to show the moods. They can tell what color should be used if none is available.

v. One of the activities that is key in developing intrapersonal intelligence is thinking. We will work on three levels of thinking. Level one is recalling memorized information. Have the students give an example of this.

w. The second level of thinking is comparing and analyzing. Have the students give an example of this.

x. The third level is higher order thinking which includes synthesis and evaluation. Have the students give an example of each.

y. Predicting is also a third level of thinking. Have the students partner and predict several things that will happen in (a) your classroom; (b) your school; and (c) your community this year.

z. Have the students indicate in what ways they can use the skills of intrapersonal intelligence to contribute to the changes that are happening in your class.

BIBLIOGRAPHY ON MULTIPLE INTELLIGENCES

Armstrong, Thomas, *Multiple Intelligences in the Classroom*, Association for Supervision and Curriculum Development, Alexandria, VA, 1994.

Case, Robbie, *The Mind's Staircase: Exploring the Conceptual Underpinnings of Children's Thought and Knowledge*, Lawrence Erlbaum Associates, Publishers, Hillsdale, NJ, 1992.

Gardner, Howard, *Art, Mind & Brain: A Cognitive Approach to Creativity*, Basic Books, New York, 1982.

Gardner, Howard, *Frames of Mind*, Basic Books, New York, 1983.

Gardner, Howard, *Multiple Intelligences: The Theory in Practice*, Basic Books, New York, 1993.

Gardner, Howard, *The Unschooled Mind: How Children Think & How Schools Should Teach*, Basic Books, New York, 1991.

Goleman, Daniel, *Emotional Intelligence: Why It Can Matter More Than IQ*, Bantam Books, New York, 1995.

Goodlad, John, and T. C. Lovitt, Eds., *Integrating General and Special Education*, Merrill/Macmillan Publishing Co., First edition, New York, 1993. This text examines the systems or processes associated with the administration of special and general education programs.

Lazear, David, *Seven Ways of Knowing: Teaching for Multiple Intelligences*, Skylight Publishing, Palatine, IL, 1991.

Levine, Mel, *All Kinds of Minds: A Young Student's Book about Learning Abilities and Learning Disorders*, Educator's Publishing Service, Inc., Cambridge, MA, 1993.

Levine, Mel, *Getting a Head in School*, Educator's Publishing Service, Inc., Cambridge, MA, 1993.

Lewis, R. B., and D. H. Doorlag, *Teaching Special Students in the Mainstream*, Merrill/Macmillan Publishing Co., Third edition, New York, 1991. This text offers strategies for teaching students who have various kinds of handicapping conditions.

Peterson, Rita W., et al., *Science and Society*, Merrill Publishing Co., Columbus, OH, 1984.

Appendix B

All Kinds of Minds

THEIR PERSPECTIVE AND MISSION

All Kinds of Minds provides programs, tools, and a common language for parents, educators, and clinicians to help students with differences in learning achieve success in the classroom and in life. Founded in 1995, All Kinds of Minds is a private nonprofit institute, affiliated with the University of North Carolina at Chapel Hill, that offers a powerful system of programs for helping kids succeed.

Our primary goal is to educate teachers, parents, educational specialists, psychologists, pediatricians, and students about differences in learning, so that children who are struggling in school because of the way their brains are "wired" are no longer misunderstood. Our programs have been developed by Dr. Mel Levine and his colleagues based on scientific research and over twenty-five years of clinical experience. They provide a comprehensive framework for understanding how all kids learn.

All Kinds of Minds enables a student (K–12), his parents, and his teachers to understand why he is having difficulty in school. As we see it, the key to helping a child is to identify his or her learning profile, a "map" which pinpoints the child's strengths and weaknesses in learning. Once this profile is created, All Kinds of Minds provides the language and tools for parents, educators, and clinicians to develop a concrete, practical action plan to help the child succeed.

This has been the lifework of the professionals at All Kinds of Minds. As we've grown and expanded our capabilities, we've learned that our approach increases the likelihood that every child will be able to learn in a way that reduces frustration right away and ensures greater success in life. The institute's programs facilitate greater success in school, build greater self-confidence and self-esteem, and restore hope to the student and his or her family.

THE NEED

Too many kids struggle and fail needlessly simply because the way in which they learn is incompatible with the way they're being taught. Schools are filled with kids who give up on themselves, are convinced they're "losers," and conclude they're just dumb. It's tragic. It's also painful—painful for the student, teacher, and parent who may be unaware that the "wiring" of that child's brain simply is not in synch with the demands and expectations of the situations at hand.

Telling a student "you can do better" doesn't help, particularly when he's doing his best or has done his best to no avail. Punishing him for an inability to complete a particular task in a particular way, similarly, is ineffective—not to mention inappropriate. And publicly humiliating him for circumstances beyond his control is simply hurtful and unnecessary. Yet these types of responses to those highly vulnerable kids are common.

These are kids with good minds, real and obvious intellectual strengths. Yet they suffer from what are often subtle dysfunctions—patterns of brain wiring that make certain aspects of learning exceedingly difficult—and they're slipping between the cracks.

In general, kids have very little tolerance for humiliation or failure. These kids with differences in learning, however, are at risk of growing up deprived of any success whatsoever. Naturally, they compare themselves to their peers. While some may see themselves as "different," many will feel inferior. Unfortunately, these feelings often endure and develop serious complications including plummeting self-esteem, a wide range of behavior problems, excessive dependence on friends, alienation from the family, deep anxiety, and a loss of motivation.

The sad reality is that a difference in learning, not addressed as just that, can, in the long run lead to antisocial behavior, substance abuse, dropout, and other serious forms of maladjustment.

Success is a vitamin that every kid must take in order to thrive during the school years. We, as teachers and parents, must make sure that this critical learning "supplement"—access to mastery—is available to all students. All Kinds of Minds believes that our odds of succeeding at this essential task will be increased by embracing the unique and logical set of ideas and practices described below.

BEING SPECIFIC

Simple labels such as "LD" and "ADD" may help to secure funding or some types of services for the diagnosed kid, but, unfortunately, they are inadequate in helping to pinpoint exactly where a student is experiencing a breakdown in learning. Knowing that a child is "ADD," does not address what's going on when he tries to write a report, decode written words, solve a math problem, or attend to the details in a teacher's presentation.

Having insight into the specific nature of the breakdown is critical to creating the appropriate set of solutions to remedy or work around the particular situation. Does this kid have a memory problem? And what about his memory seems to be causing the problem? Is there something about her language abilities? Is it a processing problem—the way she takes information in or a production problem—the way she puts information back out? Is there some type of motor deficiency? Does this child struggle when following directions, breaking things down into steps, or otherwise getting things or herself organized?

We must look carefully at each of the functions of the brain that affects the ways a student learns as well as performs in school—functions such as memory, language, and attention, the ability to organize information, neuromotor functions such as fine and gross motor skills or physical coordination, social cognition—the ability to understand as well as have appropriate and successful social interactions, and higher order cognition—being able to solve problems, think critically, or otherwise reason about oneself and the world.

Finding precisely where the breakdown is occurring when a student is falling behind begins with the teacher, parents, clinicians, and the student himself working together to create a neurodevelopmental profile—a kind of balance sheet that accounts for the student's strengths and weaknesses. Once a weakness is clearly identified, a highly individualized plan can be developed.

Every plan starts with "demystification," a process that teaches the student all about his or her strengths and weaknesses using understandable language. This empowering and respectful process makes kids part of the solution team, helps them to feel better about themselves as well as recognize and appreciate individual differences in general. It also sets the stage for introducing bypass strategies or direct interventions.

Bypass strategies are methods designed to help a child work around a particular problem. Imagine asking a student with average to strong organizational and creative skills but poor handwriting skills to draft an essay by hand. The result, more than likely, will be frustrating and disappointing for both student and teacher. Allowing that student to use a keyboard, in effect "bypassing" the motor problem will, more than likely, lead to success.

Now imagine giving the same assignment to a student who has perfect motor skills but trouble organizing his thoughts. In this case, direct intervention or addressing the area of weakness makes the most sense. Rather than simply having that student work at the computer, helping him to learn a particular brainstorming strategy, break the task into steps, or work with a writer's checklist, for example, increases the odds that the student will succeed.

RECOGNIZING CHANGE OVER TIME: A DEVELOPMENTAL PERSPECTIVE

Kids change over time. The kinds of dysfunctions that affect a six-year old are profoundly different from those that impair the progress of an eighth grader. Just think about how differently an inability to summarize a chapter, take notes, or manage one's time would impact a high school student versus a second grader, for example. Academic and social demands keep changing and so do kids' brains. Essentially, this means that it's quite possible to experience a learning problem during one period of your academic career while succeeding earlier or later on. It also means that sooner or later most kids will encounter a learning situation for which they are not optimally wired.

Most of us can probably name someone who had a tough time during the school years but went on to become an incredibly successful adult. Similarly, we can also point to those we considered "most likely to succeed" who simply didn't. We have an intuitive understanding that those kids who are not especially adapted to excelling in school can, nevertheless, become highly accomplished adults in their chosen niches.

We also know that as adults we're allowed, if not encouraged, to practice our brain's specialties. Yet we expect school-aged kids to be rather good at everything. Some kids are. Most kids aren't. This expectation can have traumatic effects on students. It is critical, therefore, in an effort to preserve and protect these kids' minds, that we adopt a developmental perspective when evaluating a student's strengths and weaknesses.

STRENGTHENING STRENGTHS

Helping kids get better and better at what they are good at makes a lot of sense. After all, in the adult world it's the strength of your strengths not the weakness of your weaknesses that really counts.

Similarly, taking advantage of a student's special interests or content orientation—her "affinities"—can both motivate as well as help her to work through or around a learning impasse. For example, reading about something that excites you can help enhance reading skills. The same can be said for writing, remembering information, and for concentrating.

Unfortunately, however, strengthening strengths and accommodating a student's content interests are rarely traveled instructional paths. We must not only recognize these strategies as practical, but apply them widely in an effort to help kids achieve their potential.

TAKING A COLLABORATIVE APPROACH

Given the complexity of both learning processes and individual differences in learning, no single discipline or profession could or should be expected to have all the answers. Taking a multidisciplinary and multiperspective approach to interpreting and working with children has a far greater likelihood of achieving positive results.

Toward that end, we've developed a range of evaluation and management tools appropriate for clinicians from various backgrounds as well as for teachers, parents, and kids themselves. We facilitate collaboration by providing a common language. We create ways to foster communication and meaningful alliances between physicians, psychologists, educators, language specialists, social workers, and others concerned with optimizing kids' learning potential.

These joint efforts can promote a way of understanding and helping kids with differences in learning without stigmatizing them and without treating them as "diseased," simply by creating a richer, more dimensional, more specific, and ultimately, truer profile of each learner.

CULTIVATING OPTIMISM

Pessimism is one of the worst complications of a disappointing school performance. Far too many kids have been told or come to feel that because of their learning difficulties, they "will never amount to anything."

Unfortunately, these prophecies can come true. Aggressive counteraction is warranted. We believe that parents, teachers, and clinicians must devote considerable time and effort to helping kids see the possibilities for themselves in the future.

Interestingly, when we asked a group of parents and students to name what they felt was the key benefit to our approach, the overwhelming majority echoed "it gave us hope." Optimism is central to our mission. All kids need to gaze ahead with excitement and a positive outlook. All kids should forge and sustain lofty aspirations. All kids deserve a hopeful vision of the future.

HELPING EVERY CHILD SUCCEED

Every mind is uniquely endowed. As a result, our emphasis on the different ways individual kids learn and find success in their lives has relevance for all kids. Every student—not just those who are struggling—can benefit from having a greater understanding of his own strengths and weaknesses—a picture of how his mind works—along with insight and a plan for optimizing learning and performance.

Helping parents, teachers, and students to acknowledge and appreciate these differences is the first step. Helping them to celebrate the differences is the goal. If achieved, the long-term benefits are bound to include a very large group of people who feel good about themselves, feel good about their careers, and in general, feel good about life.

Copyright by All Kinds of Minds, www.allkindsofminds.org, used by permission.

Appendix C

Abstract of Proposal for Sea View Elementary Charter School

Sea View Elementary Charter School is a charter school in its first year and we are working to see that it will become a trendsetter and a model for replication of an effective school within public education. The grant will provide opportunities for educators, parents, pupils, university faculty, the business sector and community members to fully implement an effective educational program that operates independently from the existing school district structure. This independence will allow the school to:

- Improve pupil learning.
- Increase learning opportunities for all pupils, with special emphasis on expanded learning opportunities for pupils who are identified as academically low achievers.
- Utilize multiple and innovative teaching methods, including Multiple Intelligences and Differentiated Teaching.
- Create new professional opportunities for teachers, including the opportunity to be responsible for the learning program and access to the diverse resources of a university.
- Provide parents and pupils with an expanded choice in the type of educational opportunity within the public school system.
- Establish and maintain a performance-based accountability system.

In this application the charter school founders strive to illustrate:

- The program needs for this charter school.
- The charter school's educational vision, mission, goals, specific objectives, philosophy and the unique characteristics that will distinguish

the Sea View Elementary Charter School from the existing public schools.

• The business and organizational management capacity of the school.
• A description of the grant project goals and activities for the approval of our charter proposal
• A self-assessment and procedures for monitoring our progress toward the completion of the grant proposal

The Sea View Elementary Charter School is in the initial phase of operation. Our vision and plans are unique and represent a new and important dimension to the charter school movement. Our funding will allow the founders and developers to take the final steps necessary for making this dream of a charter school a reality in Adobe.

APPLICATION NARRATIVE

The Sea View Elementary Charter School is a premier learning community of excellence in elementary education.

Baseline Information about the School: Demographic Characteristics and Performance Levels of the Students

Sea View Elementary Charter School is a new start-up charter school located in the Adobe community. Eighty students in grades K–3 will comprise Sea View's student body during the first year of operation. Additional students will be added yearly to bring the total to 120 students in K–6. The student body will reflect the community's diverse ethnic, cultural, and socioeconomic diversity.

Historically, there has existed education performance level disparity between ethnic groups, and this trend continues. A significant majority of white and Asian students score at or above Adobe Unified School District's and California's standard level of performance in the areas of reading, language, and mathematics. Unfortunately, the majority of Hispanic and African American students score below district and state standards for performance in reading, language, and mathematics. There also exists some similar educational disparity among certain Asian cultures. Sea

View has been structured to minimize and/or eliminate this educational performance disparity.

Characteristics of the Community(ies) in Which These Students Live

The Sea View campus will be located in the Adobe community. It will be a school of choice within the Adobe Unified School District. Sea View anticipates that the majority of its students will live within a twenty-mile radius of the school campus. The profile of the surrounding communities reflects Adobe's socioeconomic diversity. The majority of the residents are homeowners. The most impressive characteristic of these communities is that they want their children to attend the best school and receive the best education.

EDUCATIONAL VISION: OVERALL PROGRAM GOALS

Sea View Elementary Charter School will:

- Provide a child-centered learning environment that focuses on critical thinking and learning and producing lifelong learners.
- Share accountability for the success of each individual between Sea View staff, university/college faculty, future educators, educational partners, parents, and students.
- Maintain a staff dedicated to providing a program that values the development of the whole child and pays attention to each child's timetable for learning.
- Promote a classroom environment that emphasizes time for children to explore, question, and learn without being fearful of making mistakes or taking risks.
- Have graduates equipped with the skills necessary for their success.

PHILOSOPHICAL, THEORY, AND RESEARCH BASE

Developmental approaches to schooling have a long and reputable history. Jean Piaget, in his numerous works, demonstrates that we must understand

and address students' developmental readiness if academic success, and hence, high self-esteem are to occur. John Goodlad, one of America's most highly regarded educational researchers, urged us from as far back as the 1960s to consider thoughtful creation of nongraded (multiage) schools where the focus would be on students' developmental readiness and not on artificially segmented grade levels.

A significant portion of the basis for our educational structure is based on our cumulative years of successful work with children in a variety of educational settings. Further, one of the most unique and important values of having a charter school with university associations is that the school will directly benefit from the ongoing scholarly and action research conducted both at the school and in the wider field by the university education department faculty at the University of California at Irvine.

SPECIFIC EDUCATIONAL OBJECTIVES

- to provide a strong academic environment aligned with statewide standards of excellence that will improve student thinking and learning and that is responsive to the needs of children.
- to create classroom environments that facilitate learning as an interactive process.
- to build a learning community that is dedicated to academic excellence.
- to design a technology component that is central to the educational program.
- to expand student learning beyond the classroom.
- to implement a written school-wide social curriculum.

SUMMARY OF PROJECTED ACHIEVEMENTS

The vision statement of the Sea View Elementary Charter School illustrates the manner in which the educational goals and objectives are blended with the philosophical and theoretical basis of the school to provide an excellent educational experience for students and the entire learning community.

VISION STATEMENT

We are committed to providing a child-centered learning environment that focuses on critical thinking. School staff and university faculty, along with future educators, parents, and elementary students, share joint accountability for the success of each individual.

The varied experiences and knowledge children bring to school, combined with their natural curiosity and sense of wonder, are the foundation for learning. The school respects and values the different interests, abilities, learning styles, ethnic diversity, and cultural backgrounds of each child.

The staff is dedicated to providing a child-centered program that values the development of the whole child and pays attention to each child's timetable for learning. It is designed to teach children with dignity. The safe, nurturing environment promotes the physical, social, emotional, and cognitive development of children. The program is developmentally appropriate for the age span of the children within the class and is implemented according to the developmental levels of each child. The program reflects the belief that how children learn is just as important as what children learn. The children are equipped with skills necessary for their future success. Skills such as critical thinking, teamwork, problem solving, communication, decision making, and the uses of technology are integrated throughout the curriculum. Critical to the program is teaching children the skills that will enable them to take charge of their own thinking, thus, empowering them to become self-motivated learners.

The learning environment is planned to meet the academic needs of each child so that individual learning is maximized. The mastery of basic skills is a primary goal. The learning experiences encourage children to develop prosocial behaviors by interacting with others cooperatively and collaboratively. This is critical since the criteria for admission of students is that they are predicted to drop out of school at a future time. There is time for children to explore, question, and learn without being fearful of making mistakes or taking risks. Children are challenged to reach their potential and to do their best thinking in each learning situation. The educational experiences ensure growth in competence and confidence, as well as in academic and thinking skills. Teachers endeavor to enhance children's internal motivation and positive attitudes toward learning through a thought-provoking curriculum.

The assessment and evaluation procedures focus on each individual child's progressive development. It is a daily, ongoing, integral component of the teaching-learning process. The assessment procedures are used to inform instruction by assisting the teacher in making appropriate educational decisions. The assessments are performance-based, multidimensional, include communication skills in all disciplines, and they are in alignment with the educational program. They will include the dropout prediction instrument developed by Dr. William Callison and his colleagues that has been used successfully in Irvine Unified School District, Irvine, California and many other school districts nationally.

Each individual associated with the Sea View Elementary Charter School is a lifelong learner and a teacher. There is an environment of honesty, trust, and collaboration that generates enthusiasm and fosters creativity. People of all ages assemble in a safe and nurturing atmosphere to teach and learn together each day. An ongoing relationship is formed through the collaborative efforts of the faculty, the students, the university, and the community to fulfill the vision of the school.

Unique Charter School Features

An association between the charter school and a large elementary school next door allows research-based and innovative approaches to instruction, learning, and assessments that promote academic excellence. The school will operate on a year-round calendar. Before- and after-school enrichment programs will be offered as will student support services.

Support services available to students and teachers will include a psychologist, a speech therapist, and a reading instructional assistant and a special education teacher to work with children who are assigned to a regular classroom but qualify for additional assistance. Also available are credentialed teachers who travel from classroom to classroom teach physical education and music programs and an instructional aide who will assist those children who are limited or non-English speaking.

Charter school teachers and university personnel work together to ensure that research is well informed by the real life issues that occur every day in the learning process.

The school has an organizational classroom model that is a heterogeneous multiage grouping in a developmental setting that accommodates individual learning abilities and styles. The focus is on critical thinking in all academic, social, and personal learning experiences.

The implementation of a Multiple Intelligences curriculum includes the eight intelligences: linguistic, logical-mathematical, spatial, bodily-kinesthetic, musical, interpersonal, intrapersonal, and naturalist. The Multiple Intelligences curriculum will be linked to Differentiated Teaching, the approach used in teacher education at Nearby. Dr. Joan Brown is on the Nearby faculty and is a national expert in making this connection. She will provide training and consultation to our staff. She will be assisted by a doctoral student at Nearby, and a teacher at Clinton Elementary School.

Differentiated Teaching uses many models to improve instruction. To understand the approach used by Dr. Jones, the reader should read information on Dr. Mel Levine's work at the University of North Carolina. Dr. Levine is a pediatrician who directs the Schools Attuned national program. It can be summarized as follows:

Our primary goal is to educate teachers, parents, educational specialists, psychologists, pediatricians, and students about differences in learning, so that children who are struggling in school because of the way their brains are "wired" are no longer misunderstood. Our programs have been developed by Dr. Mel Levine and his colleagues based on scientific research and over twenty-five years of clinical experience. They provide a comprehensive framework for understanding how all kids learn.

The school encourages a project oriented approach that provides meaningful opportunities for students to make connections with the world around them.

Multiple-measures are used to assess learning which will provide a comprehensive profile of student achievement.

Technology design within the school facilitates learning, provides access to information, and produces proficient technology users.

The school includes a parent/community education center that provides ongoing, structured support for building effective parenting skills and enables community members to be active participants in students' education.

THE ORGANIZATIONAL STRUCTURE
OF EFFECTIVE CHARTER SCHOOLS

The educational theory of Sea View is best described as child-centered with a critical thinking approach. Sea View will provide a high-quality education that will nurture the social, physical, emotional, intellectual, aesthetic, and artistic needs of the children. The theoretical underpinnings of our approach will be largely drawn from the works of the following educators:

Howard Gardner's Multiple Intelligences will serve as an important basis for designing the School's learning experiences linked to real life. "MI" theory calls for performance-based assessment and will guide instruction.
Jean Piaget's stages of cognitive development will be utilized so that children's intellectual growth proceeds in a developmental sequence.
John Dewey's concepts of educating the whole child and interactive learning will help provide coherence to the curriculum.

Additionally, Sea View will draw on the works of various other educators for theory and instructional practices that will enhance the educational program in areas such as critical thinking, instructional strategies, social development, and cooperative learning.

The program will maintain a child-centered and content-centered curriculum in which a balance will be maintained among children's abilities and interests, learning styles, and the curriculum standards. A love of learning will be fostered which will enable students to become self-motivated, competent, and lifelong learners.

The School will reflect the National Association for the Education of Young Children's (NAEYC) definition of developmentally appropriate programs:

Developmentally appropriate programs are both 1) age appropriate and 2) individually appropriate; that is, the program is designed for the age group served and implemented with attention to the needs and differences of the individual children enrolled.

These two concepts of developmental appropriateness are grounded in human development research. The research speaks to the predictable and universal sequences of growth and change that occur in children, and to each child's developing abilities that emerge at different ages. A major premise of developmentally appropriate practice is that each child is unique and has an individual pattern and timing of growth, as well as an individual personality, learning style, and family background. Sea View will provide a learning environment that is responsive to this research.

CLEAR AND MEASURABLE
OUTCOMES FOR STUDENT PERFORMANCE

Students attending the Sea View Elementary Charter School will meet statewide standards in the areas of literacy, mathematics, science, history-social science, applied learning, music, art, health, and physical education. Pupil outcomes will be aligned closely to the state standards and designed by Sea View staff to ensure, among other things, the following:

- Students demonstrate the ability to use critical thinking skills.
- Students demonstrate the intellectual skills and knowledge necessary to meet the challenges of a changing world.
- Students demonstrate mastery of the basic skills.
- Students demonstrate the ability to appropriately apply knowledge in a variety of ways.
- Students demonstrate the ability to be effective communicators through speaking, listening, reading, and writing.
- Students demonstrate quality work by making wise choices and being responsible learners.
- Students demonstrate the ability to effectively use technology to support learning.
- Students develop a positive self-concept and attitude toward learning.
- Students become creative and critical thinkers and problem solvers.
- Students demonstrate a support of one another socially and academically.
- Students understand the importance of and pursue a healthy lifestyle.
- Students exhibit positive work habits that reflect honesty and personal integrity.
- Students demonstrate an understanding and acceptance of diverse cultures.

• Students become responsible citizens of the community through their participation in a variety of service projects.
• Students demonstrate a realization of their own continuous progress and growing competence.

Additionally, there will be benchmarks set at appropriate levels to measure student progress towards achieving the outcomes. There will also be entry and exit assessments to determine the progress of those students not completing a full course of study at Sea View.

The Sea View faculty, under the direction of the administration, will have the primary responsibility for determining and writing specific pupil outcomes and determining benchmarks based on the statewide standards. The school will maintain high expectations for all students and will pledge to give the support necessary to achieve academic success.

Sea View is committed to building a community of motivated, responsible students who are curious, caring, and competent lifelong learners. Achieving student outcomes will be a natural outgrowth of learning in the academically challenging environment.

STUDENT ASSESSMENT PROGRAM

You can't assess kids' performance unless you give them the tasks, and you can't assess their degree of achievement unless they actually perform the tasks. But first you must be clear about what you want kids to know and be able to do. Those standards become the target for creating the assessment.

Marc Tucker, Co-director of the New Standard Project, 1992

The above quote exemplifies what Sea View believes necessary to align standards and performance tasks. The school will adhere to the statewide standards and conduct student assessments that include performance-based assessment.

Many changes have occurred in the field of student assessment. Finding ways of assessing student learning that gives a true picture of the student's accomplishments is a challenging and complex task. Sea View recognizes the need for finding alternative ways in which to measure learning. The school will work collaboratively with a university/college to be a research site to develop a balanced assessment system.

The goal of assessment will be to provide information for:

- curriculum planning and determining and improving instructional practices.
- special needs and interests of students.
- feedback to students regarding their individual progress.
- program evaluation and accountability.
- students to be self-assessors of their own work.
- communication with parents and the larger community.

Multiple measures of assessments will be used to maintain a balanced assessment system. The assessments will be linked to the standards for literacy, mathematics, science, history-social science, applied learning, art, music, health, and physical education. The assessment procedures will be a part of the school's comprehensive and ongoing evaluation process.

Performance-Based Assessment

The school will implement performance-based assessments in ways that will enable children to demonstrate what they know and are able to do in meeting the statewide standards. Performance-based assessments may include, but not be limited to the following items:

- Exhibits, Demonstrations, and Presentations. These projects will represent a cumulative show of the student's learning, and may be either written or oral.
- Portfolios. This includes a systematic collection of student work over a period of time that exhibits a student's work and progress. Portfolios will be used for measuring student progress toward mastery of statewide standards. Portfolio assessment will also be used to document mastery of the standards and determine student progress in developing critical thinking skills. It will provide the students with the unique opportunity to be self-assessors of their own learning. They will be able to reflect critically and thoughtfully on their work, set goals for improvement, and celebrate their accomplishments. It will provide the staff and parents with an authentic picture of the student's progress over time while at the same time giving information for future instruction and student needs.

- Standardized Tests. The school will administer nationally norm-referenced tests required by his/her state. The school may also administer supplemental standardized tests as appropriate.
- Teacher-Prepared Assessment Instruments. Teachers will be responsible for designing appropriate tasks that will measure understandings and mastery of classroom work.
- Teacher Observation and Documentation. The work children do and how they do it will be a basis of educational decisions. Student work and work habits will be documented. Skills that are mastered and those requiring more instruction will be noted. An ongoing educational assessment for each student will be developed from a variety of measurements.
- Student Journals. These will be used to reflect the student's own performance in academic areas and the use of critical thinking skills.
- Conferences. A variety of conferences will be conducted throughout the year and may include:
  (1) Parent/teacher conferences will be scheduled two times during the school year. At these conferences, the parents will share their expectations and views of the developing educational program and help set goals for their child. The teacher will report the child's academic accomplishments and social achievements. Such things as the child's portfolio and project work will also be shared at this time.
  (2) Child/teacher conferences and informal meetings addressing the child's academic work, study habits, and social interactions will be scheduled.
  (3) Student-led teacher/parent conferences will be implemented as appropriate.
  (4) Other conferences may be scheduled as needed to ensure that the program is meeting the student's needs.
- Attitudes and Behaviors. These actions will be assessed and documented through teacher observations and other related assessment tools.

PROFESSIONAL DEVELOPMENT

To ensure the highest level of teaching, learning, and school operations standards, and to obtain the recognition as educational reform and restructuring trailblazers, Sea View will operate a summer institute. This institute will provide professional development tailored to ensure that all of the staff confidently functions at the highest level of competency within their respective discipline and scope of responsibility and accountability. The staff will receive instruction and coaching by individuals defined as experts in their disciplines. In addition, the staff will be eligible to receive compensation for preapproved external professional growth and development credits obtained by accredited colleges or universities.

The Sea View Board of Directors (Board) may initiate and carry on any program, activity, or may otherwise act in any manner which is not in conflict with or inconsistent with, or preempted by, any law and which is not in conflict with the purposes for which charter schools are established.

The Board of Directors may execute any powers delegated by law to it and shall discharge any duty imposed by law upon it and may delegate to an officer or employee of Sea View any of those duties. The board, however, retains ultimate responsibility over the performance of those powers or duties so delegated.

Prior to the formation of the board, the developer group will make decisions affecting the school, such as the hiring of the administration, faculty and staff. They will also be responsible for selecting initial members of the board. The Board of Directors will be comprised of five to seven members who have the responsibility for, among other things, the following:

- monitoring and updating mission, vision, and operational business plan that focus on student learning.
- maintaining fiscal responsibility for the charter school.
- establishing, approving, and monitoring the annual budget.
- establishing Bylaws (to be established not more than 60 days after the Board of Directors is in place).
- selecting a president, vice president, secretary, treasurer, and historian.
- establishing a foundation to raise money for the school.
- employing the principal of the school.
- approving personnel policies and monitoring their implementation.
- monitoring and assessing the school's compliance with the requirements and intent of state legislation.
- contracting with outside sources for operations oversight and audit in conjunction with the principal of the school.

All other duties as allowed for or required by the California Corporations Code and the Bylaws.

An insurance policy will cover board members. Meetings of the board will be held monthly, and as needed, and will be open to the public in accordance with law.

The principal of the school will serve as secretary to the board. The principal will attend board meetings and contribute to discussions, provide input, and advise the board on issues relevant to the daily operation of the school.

The administration of the school will be comprised of the principal and assistant principal. The primary responsibility of the administration is to establish and maintain an environment that is consistent with the mission and vision of the school and to ensure the academic and social success of the students. The administration will be responsible for management of the day-to-day operations, staff development, supervision, and evaluation of teachers and staff members, and parent/community relations, among other things.

SCHOOL FACILITIES

Sea View Charter School is located in the community of Adobe. The developers and business consultant group is currently negotiating a facilities agreement. Sixty-three thousand dollars has been allotted in the general budget for facility leasing. A grant writer/resource developer has been retained and will assist Sea View in securing and maintaining school facilities. Fifteen thousand dollars has been allotted in the general budget for contracted custodial and gardening services.

EXPERIENCE AND KNOWLEDGE
OF THE BUSINESS SERVICES STAFF

Sea View Elementary Charter School has retained Norman & Norman, Inc. to manage its business services while in planning and implementation phase. Norman & Norman has over twenty-five years of successful school business services operations, risk management, resource development, and school construction project management experience. Norman & Norman, Inc. is recognized throughout the state of California as a leading expert in the field of school business services.

COLLABORATION AND NETWORKING STRATEGIES

Involvement of Parents and Community Members

Sea View is founded on the premise that positive student outcomes are a direct result of a highly qualified, highly committed, and highly active learning community working together. Sea View's learning community is comprised of parents, college/university faculty and students, social and civic organizations, community-based organizations, private sector businesses, and policy makers along with the sponsoring school district. Parents and the community have the opportunity to be involved in the following areas: school governance, curriculum development, before and after school program development, implementation and evaluation, staff development, student assessment/evaluation, and resource development. In addition to the above mentioned areas for involvement, university/college faculty and students have the following opportunities for involvement:

- observational experiences for undergraduate students.
- field experience for pre-service teachers enrolled in a teacher credential program.
- pre-student teaching observational hours for pre-service teachers.
- student teaching experiences for credential students.
- faculty who will serve as guest lecturers for education courses and as adjunct professors for content area courses.
- community service hours for undergraduate students
- research site for doctoral and masters students interested in curriculum development, leadership, technology, second-language acquisition, etc.

Collective Knowledge and Experience of Partnerships

Sea View intentionally aligned itself with postsecondary educational institutions to ensure that the staff, parents, and students have direct access to the highest level of theoretical knowledge and experience Adobe has to offer. In addition, the developers had the foresight to establish a school in the midst of Adobe's primary location for high-tech and bio-medical companies. The groundwork has been laid for the staff to develop partnerships with the business sector. High-tech business partnerships will give the Sea View learning community the highest level of practical knowledge and experience to enhance its theoretical base, thus setting the foundation for phenomenal student outcomes.

External Means of Technical Support

Experts in the fields of educational reform, curriculum development, assessment and evaluation, technology, school operations, diversity, parent involvement, classroom management, and business services will provide instruction and coaching tailored to meet the needs of the staff and the entire learning community. In addition, Sea View will retain the services of qualified consultants to manage its business services division and resources will be developed to contract with other professionals for technical assistance. Furthermore, Adobe Unified School District provides excellent technical assistance for schools serving their students. Finally Sea View will participate in California State Department of Education sponsored technical support programs.

COMPREHENSIVE ASSESSMENT PROGRAM AND MEASUREMENTS TO EVALUATE SUCCESS

In addition to the multiple measures of assessments previously mentioned that will be used for measuring student progress toward meeting and exceeding statewide standards, overall program evaluation will be a collaborative effort. Sea View will participate in a variety of formative and summative evaluation procedures to monitor the overall progress of the school. Formative evaluation will be used to monitor progress toward the mission and vision. It will be ongoing and provide information as to success as well as areas in need of refinement. Summative evaluations will be applied at completion points of various events such as the end of the year or the completion of a major project or program. Comparisons will be made on the basis of what was accomplished and recommendations will be provided to determine what worked and what needs to be changed.

Sea View will also utilize committees comprised of teachers, staff, administrators, parents, students, university/college representatives, community members, and business people to assist with overall program evaluation. The committees may cover a variety of program areas such as leadership, curriculum and instruction, community relations, and health and safety and will explore opportunities to design and implement evaluation procedures that will advance the mission and vision of the School.

Additionally, Sea View will participate in ongoing workshops, conferences, state- and federal-sponsored programs, and other professional development opportunities in order to ensure that the most forward-thinking evaluation and assessment procedures are practiced.

DESCRIPTION OF GRANT PROJECT GOALS AND ACTIVITIES

Involvement of Learning Community

During the planning phase of Sea View, focus groups were held throughout the Adobe communities. Participants of these focus groups were parents, students, teachers, administrators, policy makers, public and private business representatives, and concerned citizens. One of the major outcomes of the focus groups was the identification of the school's implementation needs.

Program Needs Alignment

The focus group participants (Sea View's learning community) identified the following implementation needs:

- resources for facility improvements and/or re-locatable units
- a mechanism for the learning community's participation in curriculum development
- classroom furniture and equipment
- technology in every classroom
- library
- playground equipment

The implementation needs identified were directly aligned with the effective organizational variables of Sea View Elementary Charter School.

The process of evaluation will be an integral part to the overall administration of this grant. We will be accountable for and focus all our efforts on achieving the goals and objectives so that we may create the foundation for making the Sea View Elementary Charter School a reality. Regularly scheduled meetings of the learning community will include a self-evaluation component focusing on progress being made in implementing the plan, as well as the effectiveness of the plan in achieving the target goals and objectives.

Appendix D

Evaluation Competencies

The purpose of evaluation is to provide timely, useful information for decision making. Evaluation studies, therefore, tend to be one year or less in length and to allow for program alteration during the evaluation. Evaluation that tests a tentative hypothesis that results in positive findings may in turn lead to research studies that are designed to create new knowledge. These studies are frequently one or more years in length, and they often test hypotheses that are part of a theoretical framework. Evaluation utilizes measurement and statistical concepts and may be divided into four types of activity: context or environmental evaluation; input or design evaluation; process or feedback evaluation; and product or outcome evaluation.

CONCEPT 1.1

The process of measurement is secondary to that of defining objectives. The ends to be achieved must be stated clearly, and then measurement techniques may be utilized.

Performance Statement 1.1.1

The administrator recognizes the need for clearly stated objectives as the basis for evaluation. In order to improve the quality of our students' communication of mathematical relationships, it was necessary for the staff to decide on a few key actions that would provide students with opportunities to communicate their mathematical ideas. With this over-riding goal in mind, staff members agreed to implement math journals and cooperative groupings to allow students the opportunity to com-municate their knowledge of mathematical relationships. After decid-ing on the goal and key strategies that would be needed to implement the goal, an objective could be written that would help determine if the goal was accomplished.

Measurable Indicator 1.1.1.1

From your reading and experience, list two specific examples that support the performance statement above.

The purpose of evaluation is to provide timely, useful information for decision making. Evaluation studies, therefore, tend to be one year or less in length and to allow for program alteration during the evaluation. Eval-uation that tests a tentative hypothesis that results in positive findings may in turn lead to research studies that are designed to create new knowledge. These studies are frequently one or more years in length, and they often test hypotheses that are part of a theoretical framework. Evaluation uti-lizes measurement and statistical concepts and may be divided into four types of activity: context or environmental evaluation; input or design evaluation; process or feedback evaluation; and product or outcome eval-uation.

(1)

(2)

From the above example, teachers wrote clear objectives. If the teachers were interested in the overall achievement of the class, they might write an objective, such as "By June, 70% of the fifth grade students will score a three or above on the CLAS rubric on journal entries." This objective is measuring the achievement of the entire class. With this information, the administrator and the teachers can reflect on the overall achievement of the fifth grade class and make needed changes to the instructional pro-gram.

The administrator at my school clearly recognizes this need by encour-aging the staff to commit to an anecdotal program evaluation of their grade-level program each year.

Measurable Indicator 1.1.1.2

The administrator also encourages teachers to reflect on the growth of their own students by including teacher research evaluation strategies in each teacher's evaluation. A teacher might indicate that to encourage communication of mathematical ideas, he or she will give the students opportunities to work on mathematical units twice a week in cooperative groups and, though these experiences, 90 percent of his or her students will be able to verbally explain how the group completed a mathematical project.

CONCEPT 1.2

Satisfactory use of measurement techniques requires comprehension of the basic concepts in measurement.

Performance Statement 1.2.1

The administrator can accurately interpret standardized test results. The administrator can use general summaries of standardized tests to give him or her an idea of the overall achievement of the entire school, grade-level, or classroom of students. It is important to know what skills were tested and in what context. With this information and information collected from the teachers, the administrator can make informed decisions about strengths and weaknesses of the instructional program.

Measurable Indicator 1.2.1.1

List two examples of the misuse or misinterpretation of standardized or normative test scores.

(1)

(2)

1.2.1.1.1   Because a student scores the grade-level equivalency of an eight grader on a CTBS test, the teacher tells the parent the student is capable of entering an eight grade math class.

1.2.1.1.2 Printing the average score of a school's CAP test in the newspaper does not give a true picture of the achievement level of the school. Disaggregated data give a better picture. For example, a GATE cluster school may have very high average scores as compared to a non-GATE cluster school. But when data are disaggregated, the non-GATE cluster school's GATE students may score higher then the GATE cluster school's GATE students, and the non-GATE cluster school's other students may score higher as a group as well.

CONCEPT 1.3

Measurement activities provide results such as classification, rankings, and scores. Statistics give us tools for analyzing measurement results for groups of individuals. Competencies in measurement and statistics are needed for many evaluation activities.

Performance Statement 1.3.1

The administrator can learn to perform many useful statistical exercises, by referring to Carol Taylor Fitz-Gibbon's book *How to Analyze Data*, which is part of the Program Evaluation Kit from Sage Publications.

CONCEPT 1.4

Context evaluation helps us to determine objectives by focusing attention upon the relevant environment, special needs, and opportunities to improve the situation. Input on changes we needed to make to our math program came from the context of our community as well as from the results of testing and staff observations.

Performance Statement 1.4.1

The administrator can distinguish goals and objectives and generate data to write appropriate goals and objectives through a needs assessment. Through a community survey, the administrator and the teaching community determined that our community wanted our students to understand and accurately calculate basic number operations. Data from standardized tests also reflected this need.

Measurable Indicator 1.4.1.1

Given a common problem (specified by the student) seen in schools, differentiate goals, objectives, and behavioral objectives that focus upon the problem.

Students at Los Naranjos cannot calculate basic number operations quickly and accurately.

Goal: Students will improve their understanding of basic number operations, and students will improve their accuracy in the calculation of basic number operations.

Objective: By June, 90% of the fifth grade students will complete the fifth grade computation test with 100% accuracy.

By June, 90% of the fifth grade students will be able to write a word problem for a given computational problem in their journal that would generate that computational problem, and then the student will solve it correctly.

Objective: Computational homework will be given twice a week, limited to ten problems. Quality or accuracy will be the focus.

Objective: Understanding of computational processes will be the focus of class journal writing once a week.

Measurable Indicator 1.4.1.2

Describe two procedures, one for a school and one for a classroom, for gathering needs assessment data that will allow one to write appropriate objectives.

(1)

(2)

We surveyed teachers, students, and the community on the strengths and weaknesses of our math program. Teachers gathered input from parents at back-to-school night and at conference time. These comments were shared with staff and the school site council. This year, teachers are tracking individual student groups within each class with a teacher portfolio to see how different student groups are progressing. These data will be combined with data we've used in the past to make decisions about what program changes we need to make so that every student can succeed.

CONCEPT 1.5

Input evaluation is the design aspect of the evaluation outline. It focuses upon the capabilities of the program being evaluated, strategies for achieving program goals, and the specific objectives to be accomplished.

Input evaluation would be the evaluation of our school plan, which is our SB 1274 grant proposal.

Performance Statement 1.5.1

The administrator can assess program needs, select program alternatives in a systematic fashion, and prepare measurable objectives.

The administrator, in conjunction with the teaching staff, reviews data from student, staff, and parent surveys, standardized test scores, and teacher assessments along with input from staff and parent meetings, and the administrator's input from his or her own individual conversations with teachers at their evaluation conferences to determine areas of strength and need. Using the state frameworks and district guidelines, new goal areas are decided on by staff through a shared decision-making model.

Measurable Indicator 1.5.1.1

Four sources of information that could be used to determine whether a proposed program would need outside assistance to meet its objectives are listed:

1. Staff survey
2. Parent survey
3. Grade-level teacher research
4. Standardized test scores

Measurable Indicator 1.5.1.2

The following are criteria that an administrator might consider in deciding which of several possible program alternatives is most appropriate in achieving program goals.

1. Time required
2. Broadly applicable for all students
3. Cost
4. Proven track record
5. Backed by current research
6. Meets frameworks

Measurable Indicator 1.5.1.3

Describe the administrator's function with respect to the use of written objective in an evaluation: To help obtain the goal by working with the staff to choose the appropriate strategies needed to reach the goal. To monitor the progress of the school as a whole and the individual members of the school community toward achievement of the goal.

Measurable Indicator 1.5.1.4

The following are characteristics of a well-formed objective:

1. Relates to the goal (validity)
2. Is achieveable
3. Is measurable

Then prepare a sample objective including each characteristic.

CONCEPT 1.6

Process evaluation provides feedback to decision makers about whether the program design is being implemented according to plan and how well the plan is working.

Performance Statement 1.6.1

The administrator demonstrates a variety of competencies including research design, evaluation strategies, and data gathering procedures.

Measurable Indicator 1.6.1.1

Describe an evaluation design or approach for each of the following:

1.6.1.1.1 Teacher retention
1.6.1.1.2 New science program
1.6.1.1.3 Competency-based business course

Measurable Indicator 1.6.1.2

List the primary elements of the following three research designs, and give an example of an appropriate situation where each might be used:

1.6.1.2.1 Nonequivalent control group design
1.6.1.2.2 Pretest-post-test control group design
1.6.1.2.3 Post-test-only control group design

Measurable Indicator 1.6.1.3

List two situations when it would be appropriate for an evaluator to collect subjective data.
   (1)
   (2)

Measurable Indicator 1.6.1.4

List three means often utilized for gathering subjective data.
   (1)
   (2)
   (3)

Measurable Indicator 1.6.1.5

List two situations when it would be appropriate for an evaluator to collect objective data.
(1)
(2)

Measurable Indicator 1.6.1.6

Give an example from a classroom setting where it would be appropriate for the teacher to

1.6.1.6.1 Use a criterion referenced test

1 1.6.1.6.2 Use a norm referenced test

Measurable Indicator 1.6.1.7

Not all data are useful in decision making. List a minimum of five characteristics that would help to assure decision makers that data they receive are believable and useful.
(1)
(2)
(3)
(4)
(5)

Measurable Indicator 1.6.1.8

In order to acquire valid data, evaluators place restrictions on how a program will be run. Define the following concepts, and give an example of when each might be a restriction:

1.6.1.8.1 History
1.6.1.8.2 Maturation
1.6.1.8.3 Testing procedure
1.6.1.8.4 Instrumentation
1.6.1.8.5 Regression

1.6.1.8.6 Selection
1.6.1.8.7 Mortality
1.6.1.8.8 Interaction

CONCEPT 1.7

Product evaluation is designed to provide go-no go information at the end of an evaluation cycle and may also include activities carried out during the cycle. Typically, the results of measurable objectives are the key element in such a final evaluation. These results are compared with a pre-determined standard or criterion and interpreted with other final data, such as test results, in mind.

Performance Statement 1.7.1

The administrator demonstrates his or her ability to put the entire project in perspective as he or she considers data from the complete evaluation cycle, including context, input, process, and product evaluation findings.

Measurable Indicator 1.7.1.1

State an evaluation problem, and describe a sequence of events that will allow orderly consideration of data from each of the four phases in an evaluation cycle.
- (1)
- (2)
- (3)
- (4)

Measurable Indicator 1.7.1.2

Describe the steps you as a decision maker would take when the hard data results from a product evaluation are in conflict with the attitudes of those involved as staff and students.
- (1)
- (2)
- (3)

Measurable Indicator 1.7.1.3

List two evaluation situations where you would want to have a research design (for example, post-test only control group design) as part of the evaluation plan.

(1)

(2)

Measurable Indicator 1.7.1.4

Describe the steps you might take to integrate ongoing evaluation with a budgeting process.

(1)

(2)

(3)

Appendix E

Supervision Strategies

INTRODUCTION

The role of the school administrator has never been more complex or more complicated than it is today. With more demands placed on administrators and fewer human resources available to meet the needs, it has become critical that school administrators maximize their effectiveness. This is particularly true when it comes to evaluating staff members' job performance.

One area where it is critical for administrators to be effective is in the supervision and evaluation of staff members. Too often, an administrator does not take the necessary time or energy to monitor the behavior of staff members. Too often, staff members behave in an unprofessional manner. Very often, this behavior is an indicator of an overall unsatisfactory job performance. Because of this, these employees gain legal rights to continued employment simply because their evaluator did not follow district procedures for proper classroom observations and evaluation.

In order to effectively monitor staff performance and conduct, administrators must learn what to look for. They must also be familiar with employee contracts, applicable state laws, and the State Education Code. Evaluating and documenting employee performance is a difficult, time consuming, and, often, unrewarding task. While the primary goal of documentation is to improve employee performance, this is not always the end result. Therefore, it is critical to have thorough, accurate documentation to support appropriate disciplinary actions that might have to be taken.

The purpose of this manual is to provide school administrators with information and models to assist in the ongoing processes of evaluation and documentation. Each school district has its own unique criteria for evaluation as agreed upon by both district and employees. The documentation process, however, can be applied to a variety of situations and districts. Because of this, the emphasis of this manual will be placed on developing effective documentation.

PROGRESSIVE DISCIPLINE OPTIONS

As former classroom teachers, we are familiar with the importance and value of using progressive discipline with students. This technique can be equally effective when supervising staff members. Keeping in mind that the primary goal is to improve staff performance, it is important to use the most appropriate form of discipline when an employee has performed unsatisfactorily. Listed below are the steps available to administrators when disciplining a staff member:

- Oral Conference: This should be used at the first indication of misconduct or poor job performance. It is important to clearly state what the problem is and offer suggestions on how to remedy the situation. A written summary of the oral warning should be provided within two days of the conference.
- Written Warning: If a staff member who has received an oral conference has shown no improvement in the inappropriate conduct or job performance initially identified, the next step would be a written warning.
- Letter of Reprimand: Oftentimes a particular action might require some form of discipline that is "stronger" than a warning. This would be the appropriate time to use a letter of reprimand. If a letter of reprimand is written, your district personnel director should be notified and kept abreast of any further disciplinary measures taken with that employee.
- Suspension without Pay: Once an employee reaches this level, it is imperative that district personnel be involved. Without their support and services, it is very difficult to make this happen.
- Dismissal: This is the decision and responsibility of district personnel and your school board. Sometimes it happens because of one particular

incident and sometimes because of a history of misconduct and failure to improve.

EFFECTIVE DOCUMENTATION CRITERIA

Rarely is an employee dismissed because of a single incident. If there is a history of inappropriate behavior on the part of a staff member, it is the district's/administrator's responsibility to prove so. For this to happen, there has to be consistent and accurate documentation that addresses the problem area(s). This documentation should include the following:

- Report the Facts: It is critical that in stating the facts that you specifically identify the behavior or performance that was unsatisfactory. This should include what happened, when, who was involved, and what was wrong. If it is more than one thing, then identify each one separately and completely. Leave no room for confusion or misunderstanding.
- Cite the Source that Was Violated: It is important to specifically cite the rule, Education Code provision, directive, contract provision, law, or standard of authority that was violated. If this is a repeated violation, it is critical that this be stated in the documentation.
- State the Impact Action Caused: It is very important that the documentation state the effect that this action caused. Included in this is who was affected, how were they affected, and the seriousness of the incident.
- Provide Suggestions for Improvement: Keeping in mind that the primary goal of documenting inappropriate staff behavior is to correct that behavior, it is very important that realistic suggestions be provided in the documentation. This is particularly true when documenting Oral Warnings, Letters of Reprimand, and Unsatisfactory Evaluations.
- Document Any Further Course of Action: If the memo is to be placed in an employee's personnel file it must state so. Failure to do so will disqualify its value in the future. Employees must be given the opportunity to respond to the memo. Be sure to state when that response must be made by. If the employee responds in writing, it should be attached to your documentation before being placed in the personnel file at the district office.

THINGS TO CONSIDER

When creating a file for disciplinary reasons, it is important to ask yourself these questions:

- Has the employee's specific conduct been identified and factually reported?
- Has each unsatisfactory performance been separately and explicitly described?
- Have specific examples been given to supplement generic statements?
- Has proper language been used in the report, thus avoiding technical terminology?
- Can an outsider understand the conduct documented without having to consult other sources of information?
- Is there visual evidence available to substantiate the report? Is it included in the documentation?
- Have all objective facts (dates, names, titles, document descriptions, references, etc.) been carefully and accurately cited?

Answering "no" to any of these questions could weaken your case or have it dismissed. Be as thorough, neat, and complete as possible. If you have any questions, consult district personnel.

Reproduced with permission from Yolanda Finley, Lisa A. Hinshaw, and Janet Olsavsky, Improving the Job Performance of Staff Members through Effective Evaluation and Documentation Procedures *(Fullerton, Calif.: Department of Educational Administration, California State University, 1980).*

Appendix F

An Evaluation Case Study at Los Naranjos Elementary School

STATING THE PROBLEM

In order to improve the quality of our students' communication of mathematical relationships, it was necessary for the staff to decide on a few key actions that would provide students with opportunities to communicate their mathematical ideas. With this overriding goal in mind, staff members agreed to implement math journals and cooperative groupings to allow students the opportunity to communicate their knowledge of mathematical relationships. After deciding on the goal and key strategies that would be needed to implement the goal, objectives could be written that would help determine if the goal was accomplished.

TEACHERS WROTE CLEAR OBJECTIVES

If the teachers were interested in the overall achievement of the class, they might write an objective, such as "By June, 70% of the fifth grade students will score a three or above on the achievement rubric on journal entries." This objective is measuring the achievement of the entire class. With this information, the administrator and the teachers can reflect on the overall achievement of the fifth grade class and make needed changes to the instructional program.

The administrator encouraged the staff to commit to an anecdotal program evaluation of their grade-level program each year.

The administrator also encouraged teachers to reflect on the growth of their own students by including teacher research evaluation strategies in each teacher's evaluation. A teacher might indicate that to encourage communication of mathematical ideas, he or she will give the students opportunities to work on mathematical units twice a week in cooperative groups and, through these experiences, 90 percent of her students will be able to verbally explain how the group completed a mathematical project.

INTERPRET STANDARDIZED TEST RESULTS

The administrator was able to accurately interpret standardized test results. The administrator used general summaries of standardized tests to give him an idea of the overall achievement of the entire school, grade-level, or classroom of students. It is important to know what skills were tested and in what context. With this information and information collected from the teachers, the administrator was able to make informed decisions about strengths and weaknesses of the instructional program.

CONTEXT EVALUATION

Context evaluation helps us to determine objectives by focusing attention upon the relevant environment, special needs, and opportunities to improve the situation. Input on changes we needed to make to our math program came from the context of our community as well as from the results of testing and staff observations.

Through a community survey, the administrator and the teaching staff determined that our community wanted our students to understand and accurately calculate basic number operations. Data from standardized tests also reflected this need.

IDENTIFYING GOALS, OBJECTIVES, AND BEHAVIORAL OBJECTIVES

We identified goals, objectives, and behavioral objectives that focused upon the problem.

Students at Los Naranjos cannot calculate basic number operations quickly and accurately.

Goal: Students will improve their understanding of basic number operations. Students will improve their accuracy in the calculation of basic number operations.

Objective: By June 90% of the fifth grade students will complete the fifth grade computation test with 100% accuracy.

By June, 90% of the fifth grade students will be able to write a word problem for a given computational problem in their journal that would generate that computational problem, and then the student will solve it correctly.

Objective: Computational homework will be given twice a week, limited to ten problems. Quality or accuracy will be the focus.

Objective: Understanding of computational processes will be the focus of class journal writing once a week.

SURVEYING TEACHERS, STUDENTS, AND THE COMMUNITY

We surveyed teachers, students, and the community on the strengths and weaknesses of our math program. Teachers gathered input from parents at back-to-school night and at conference time. These comments were shared with staff and the school site council. This year, teachers are tracking individual student groups within each class with a teacher portfolio to see how different student groups are progressing. These data will be combined with data we've used in the past to make decisions about what program changes we need to make so that every student can succeed.

This appendix is authored by Jane Holm, Irvine Unified School District, Irvine, California.

Appendix G

A Tutoring Program for At-Risk Students that Works

Many educators are becoming increasingly frustrated because they teach in isolation and do not always have the resources and time to deal with the wide range of abilities of their student population. More specifically, teachers are unable to meet the needs of all the students who fall into the "at-risk" category. These students can be helped through your version of the tutoring program described here. Key concepts include the following:

- case for need
- limits on learning
- development of vision
- after-school tutorial program
- target populations
- tutors
- program aims
- program objectives
- conclusion

CASE FOR NEED

Recently, at a national conference attended by more than 600 school administrators, state legislators, teachers, governors, and higher education officials, calls were repeatedly made for dealing with at-risk students. Some attendees concluded that a failure to respond to this most compelling agenda would threaten America's position as a world economic power. The challenge of the at-risk student is one we cannot afford to refuse. In some measure, the response of today's citizens and educators will be felt by everyone in the years ahead.

LIMITS ON LEARNING

The purpose of schools is to maximize learning for all students. An obvious way to do this is through direct instruction in curriculum areas. Another way is to control or limit those factors that limit the learning and potential of children. Some of the following factors that place limits on learning are ones that educators must understand.

The first concern is the question of equity in access to education. There are many laws and policies implemented to educate the disabled student, the bilingual student, and gifted student. It can be argued that "the disaffected students, the majority of whom have normal intelligence, require specialized programs to truly benefit from their educational experience" (Ogden et al., 1988). The second concern is that a variety of social problems are, in part, a result of inadequate education. Society can avoid more costly problems in the future by investing in the development of all youth. A third reason for concern are the changing societal expectations of schools in dealing with issues that were addressed within the family. Parents are increasingly looking to schools for help in teaching their children essential life skills. Lastly, at-risk students have the potential to negatively affect the behaviors, attitudes, and achievements of other students.

The entire elementary school experience of a child should be viewed as contributing to maximizing learning and reducing risk. Research consistently show that children who exhibit certain behaviors are at particular risk:

1. One major attribute of at-risk students is poor academic achievement. Everything a school does to reduce failure or perceived failure can be a part of a prevention program. (This chapter is authored by Heather D. Phillips, Springbrook School, Irvine Unified School District, Irvine, CA 92714.)
2. At-risk children frequently come from homes with inconsistent expectations and discipline. Consistency is important when dealing with all students.
3. Many at-risk students have trouble with peer relationships. Educators need to take the opportunity to assist students in developing positive relationships.

4. Students who fall into the at-risk category frequently do not like school and feel like they don't belong. Educators need to create an environment of inclusion and minimize alienation.

Many educators are becoming increasingly frustrated because they teach in isolation and do not always have the resources and time to deal with the wide range of abilities of their student population. More specifically, teachers are unable to meet the needs of all the students who fall into the at-risk category as outlined above. These students have the potential of "falling through the cracks" because their test scores do not mandate that they receive extra assistance. In allowing this to happen, the system is only perpetuating the problem of at-risk students and contributing to the major attributes that qualify them as at-risk.

DEVELOPMENT OF VISION

Researchers indicate that, with enough time, we can teach almost anyone just about anything. The implications for all students, especially those at risk, are quite clear. This raises the question, "How can we find time to provide students the powerful one-to-one instruction that is so effective?"

One significant source of help for this dilemma is, of course, the students at any school site. Cohen, Kulick, and Kulick (1982) completed a meta-analysis of sixty-five peer tutoring programs, noting significant academic and social benefits for tutees and tutors, especially if the program was consistent, well-structured, and supervised.

Tutoring is one of the oldest forms of instruction known to society. According to Bloom and his associates at the University of Chicago (Bloom et al., 1984), one-to-one tutoring is also far and away the most powerful form of teaching (producing gains up to two standard deviations above comparison groups).

AFTER-SCHOOL TUTORIAL PROGRAM

With these facts in mind, I decided to develop an after-school tutorial program for high-risk elementary school children who did not qualify for special education services. This intervention involves high school honor students as the tutors. This program was developed with the assistance of a special education teacher, a parent, and two high school teachers. This intervention plan requires no budget due to the fact the all participants are involved on a voluntary basis, school supplies are donated, and school facilities are utilized. Furthermore, the program is provided to at-risk students at no cost to the student's family.

The tutoring program began in October of 1995, after teachers had an opportunity to identify at-risk students and to meet with parents to set goals for the year. This timeline afforded the high school students time to acclimate to their workload, attend a tutoring training session, and schedule time for tutoring. The once-a-week tutoring sessions take place on Tuesdays, from 3:15 to 4:15, in the third grade classrooms of Springbrook Elementary. This program ran for the entire length of the 1995–96 academic year and continues to run in subsequent years. By involving other staff members in the development of the tutoring program, I am ensuring that there is at least one other person on-site who understands how to pull the program together. My ultimate vision is one where the program manager changes every one to two years, thereby not overloading one staff member year after year.

The elementary students are provided with one-on-one support for math, reading, and writing skills. This program affords elementary students a chance for extra support in areas of the curriculum that are difficult for them. The classroom teacher supplies the weekly lessons for the tutors, so the program supplements what is being taught in the specific classroom. As the students' skills develop, they are able to participate more successfully in classroom activities. The students are also able to complete their homework assignments, which gives them the extra practice they need on a regular basis. The program offers an appropriate means of helping at-risk individuals, as well as supporting educators and offering high school students credit for community service.

TARGET POPULATIONS

High-risk students were identified by their classroom teachers by the middle of October. Teachers used a form (Attachment A) and made their recommendations taking the following into consideration: classroom participation, attendance, attitude toward school, self-esteem, performance and test scores, homework completion, and parental support with school assignments. Students already receiving special education services were not eligible for the tutoring program. Teachers turned in lists of high-risk students, prioritizing children by ranking those who were at the highest risk first and those who did not need as much support last.

After recommendations were made by each classroom teacher, lists were shown to on-site support staff. The resource specialist, speech and language specialist, and psychologist made further recommendations based on their own experiences with and knowledge of the at-risk population at Springbrook Elementary.

The last step in identifying students to participate in the tutoring program was obtaining parental approval. Classroom teachers who made the initial referral were obligated to contact the parents and obtain support. When parental approval was not obtained, the next high-risk student was a candidate for the program.

TUTORS

An essential part of this program is the aspect that involves high school honor students as the tutors. Honor students were selected based on interest in the tutoring program. In addition to the support they give the elementary students and their teachers, the high school students will receive community service credit toward high school graduation. These community service hours are required for high school graduation in the Irvine Unified School District.

There are twenty-seven high school tutors who service part of the at-risk population at Springbrook Elementary, therefore allowing the program to service twenty-seven at-risk elementary students who would otherwise go without extra support. Tutors were asked to indicate gender and grade-level preference regarding their tutees. Attempts were made to honor all requests, although many students indicated that they had no preference. Tutors attended a one-hour training session where techniques were outlined and resources were provided. Most importantly, program aims were presented, and the tutors' roles regarding those aims were emphasized.

PROGRAM AIMS

Students in various circumstances need more individual attention than most teachers can offer. Some students tend to misunderstand assignments, allow their attention to wander, disrupt the work of others, and miss opportunities to learn. Other students may have no confidence in their own abilities, may be frequently absent from or late to class, or may not speak English as his or her first language and have difficulty understanding what is required. One solution to the need for individual attention is to provide such students with tutors. When students know that someone cares and that individual attention is being provided, their academic performance often improves. Our high school tutors are directly supporting the classroom curriculum and assisting the students with individual assignments. Classroom teachers supply tutors and tutees with materials and lessons. The valuable one-to-one experience supports instruction.

Students receiving tutoring help are not the only ones who profit. Classmates benefit as an otherwise distracted student begins to focus on learning. Teachers gain as the student becomes a successful learner. Parents see their children happy and successful instead of sad and frustrated. The total school population generally benefits from seeing a tutoring program as a helping program in which learning is important. The tutoring program helps to promote a productive work climate, as outlined above. All individuals involved profit.

In many cases, the person who profits most from the tutoring experience is the tutor. You really learn the material when you teach it. Tutors learn to be responsible for someone else's needs and must master the skills that they are to impart. Hence, a program might be designed to use average or even some below-average students as tutors. As they develop a caring relationship for another person, tutors learn that such a relationship is a very positive one.

Because tutoring programs are inexpensive to operate, they greatly increase the teaching potential of the staff at minimal cost. Our program has no expense whatsoever, yet it brings resources to the school that are otherwise not available.

In light of the possible benefits tutoring programs provide for all involved, our program has two main goals: the development of skills and the enhancement of self-concept. Our program focuses on the development of academic skills such as reading, writing, and mathematics. In addition to skill development, an overall aim of our tutoring program is to help students feel good about themselves and about learning in general.

PROGRAM OBJECTIVES

The main purpose of the tutoring program is to promote student learning. To achieve this purpose, the program must have and deliver a well-defined and appropriate curriculum. In addition, the program must strive to develop an environment that maximizes learning and minimizes conditions that interfere with learning. This particular program has five objectives that support the main purpose. Each objective is specific and measurable. They are as follows:

1. The tutees will show an increase in completion of homework assignments. Classroom teachers will be responsible for keeping track of number of assignments turned in prior to the tutoring program and during the tutoring program (Attachment B).
2. The tutees will show a decline in unexcused and excused absences and tardies. Attendance records from throughout the year will be used to measure decline.
3. Tutees will show an increased knowledge of specific study skills. A survey will be given to tutees prior to starting the tutoring program and again after completing the program. Results will be tallied and compared. Tutors will be trained regarding specific study skills (Attachment C).
4. Tutees will show an increase in self-esteem and a more positive attitude toward school. Again, a survey will be used to establish attitudes before and after program participation.
5. High school tutors will show an increased knowledge of teaching and tutoring skills. Tutors will be given an assessment prior to training and after program participation.

Not only do we plan to evaluate the above objectives, but we also plan on having each participant journal about their activities at the end of each tutoring session. Furthermore, the high school students will be required to write about their experiences as an assignment for their honors class.

We hope to show positive benefits for both the high school and elementary students. By providing the at-risk students with one-on-one support for math, reading, and writing skills and encouraging the students to develop personal relationships with their tutors, we hope to see a marked improvement in their attitudes toward school and their attitudes toward themselves. Many of these students are second language speakers who cannot get home support for their studies and, through this program, are able to complete and understand homework assignments. Some of the younger students are at the emerging level in literacy and lack confidence in their developing skills; for them, the program offers a "friend" who listens and provides guidance on a personal level.

We also hope to see the high school students gain confidence in their own skills and enjoy the role shift from student to teacher. Many of them recognize the need for additional student support and believe they are offering something extremely positive to their tutees that is unavailable from other sources. One of the students has already improved her own attendance at high school through her participation in the tutoring program, seeing herself as a role model for the first time. Another benefit we hope to achieve will be a rise in the level of self-esteem in all participating students.

CONCLUSION

Tutoring programs differ in many ways depending on the needs of participating students. However, there are several components that make a tutoring program successful, no matter what the target audience. The components that we have attempted to integrate into Springbrook's program are as follows:

- *Tutor training*: Tutors need to be explicitly trained how to tutor (give clear directions, provide encouragement, correct in a non-punitive way, study strategies, etc.). Tutor training needs to be ongoing. Successful programs have an explicit tutor training curriculum.
- *Active supervision and positive class climate*: Respect and mutual concern must be hallmarks of the tutoring center. The program manager

must maintain high standards for both the tutor and tutee as well as interact with each dyad, at least briefly, each tutoring session. In all cases, the teacher/supervisors actively support the tutors by teaching, modeling, encouraging, and ensuring that all tutees are getting what they need.

- *Structured lesson formats*: Structured lessons allow the tutors to function much more independently and the teacher to serve as a monitor and guide.

- *Clarify the content of instruction*: The content is tied directly to the curriculum being taught in the regular classroom program. Tutoring provides the opportunity for extra instruction, practice, repetition, clarification, and elaboration. The program manager must work closely with the faculty to ensure that the tutoring corresponds to the demands of the classes in question. Couple this with generalized study skills (e.g., keeping a notebook and calendar) and you have an appropriate curriculum.

- *Staff and administrative support*: It is important to have principal support, teaching staff support, elective course credit for tutors, and a teacher (program manager) as an advocate of the tutors and tutees.

- *Focus on mastery*: Tutors need to continually check with the tutees to ensure they are mastering the lesson. This focus allows both the tutor and tutee to know what the goal/purpose of each lesson is and if the session is working. It provides immediate feedback, a powerful intrinsic reinforcer for both.

- *Effective program organization*: Program managers serve on a rotating basis, and there is viable scheduling for tutors and tutees.

- *Measurement of progress*: Several types of records can be kept to help monitor progress, for example, attendance, homework completion, test scores, etc.

- *Selecting and pairing tutors with tutees*: The most crucial factors in tutor selection relate to personal characteristics. For example, is the tutor dependable, caring, approachable, patient, etc.?

This program should meet the needs of many of the at-risk students at Springbrook. It specifically targets the problem areas outlined earlier in the proposal.

1. Academic achievement should improve. Everything a school does to reduce failure or perceived failure can be a part of a prevention program.

2. Consistency is important when dealing with all students. This program provides consistency by requiring students to meet with their tutors every week. Many at-risk students do not get consistency at home.
3. Many at-risk students have trouble with peer relationships. This tutoring program provides students with the opportunity to develop a positive relationship with their tutors.
4. Students who fall into the at-risk category frequently do not like school and feel like they don't belong. By providing students with extra support, their attitudes toward school may become more positive.

The tutoring movement has become an important aspect of schooling. Once we realize the importance of the one-to-one relationship that tutoring can offer, we need to search for ways to implement tutoring programs.

ATTACHMENT A
September 26, 1995
Dear Springbrook Staff Members,

We've been on the phone with the teachers from Woodbridge, and the honors students are anxiously awaiting the beginning of tutoring! Please start thinking about your high-risk students. Whom would you recommend to have a high school tutor one afternoon a week to help with reading, math, writing, homework, etc.? Get a list to us by October 1. Your list should be ranked by priority (those who would benefit most from the program should be ranked highest) and should not include students who already receive special education services.

We are not sure how many tutors we will have. We may not be able to service all the recommended students in the beginning, but we plan to switch at the semester if we have enough tutees and tutors.

We are planning on the sessions taking place Tuesday afternoons from 3:15 to 4:15 in our rooms and plan on starting the end of October.

Please return the bottom of this form with your recommended list. Thanks!

Teacher Name:
Recommended students for tutoring program:
1.
2.
3.

4.

5.

ATTACHMENT B
CLASSROOM TEACHER QUESTIONNAIRE
Pre and Post Evaluation
Teacher's Name:
Student's Name:
   Use the following scale to answer each question to the best of your knowledge:

1. Never 2. Seldom 3. Occasionally 4. Frequently 5. Always

1. The student turns in homework assignments.
    1 2 3 4 5
2. The student does quality work on homework assignments.
    1 2 3 4 5
3. The student completes classroom assignments.
    1 2 3 4 5
4. The student does quality work on classroom assignments.
    1 2 3 4 5
5. The student performs well on assessments.
    1 2 3 4 5
6. The student has a positive attitude toward school.
    1 2 3 4 5
7. The student gets along well with others.
    1 2 3 4 5
8. The student attends class.
    1 2 3 4 5
9. The student is on time to class.
    1 2 3 4 5

ATTACHMENT C
TUTEE QUESTIONNAIRE
STUDY SKILLS
Pre and Post Evaluation
Student's Name:

Use the following scale to answer each question:

1. Never 2. Seldom 3. Occasionally 4. Frequently 5. Always

1. I am able to organize school and homework time effectively in order to get the best grades possible. 1 2 3 4 5
2. I keep my desk, backpack, folder, and other school materials organized in a way that helps me to be successful. 1 2 3 4 5
3. I am able to listen effectively in class so that I hear all the information and don't waste time by needing to have it repeated. 1 2 3 4 5
4. All my school work is neat and clean. 1 2 3 4 5
5. I have a study area set up at home that allows me to have a productive work station. 1 2 3 4 5
6. When I have a question in class, I ask. 1 2 3 4 5
7. I know how to manage my time so I am able to fit everything in. 1 2 3 4 5

Selected Bibliography

Allen, Jeanne. "What the Research Reveals About Charter Schools." www.edreform.com (accessed January 18, 2002).

Brownstein, Ronald. "2 Gloomy Education Reports Should Serve as Guideposts for Reform Effort." *Los Angeles Times*, April 16, 2001.

California Department of Education. www.cde.ca.gov/fc/family/board. html (accessed April 18, 2001).

Gardner, H. *Multiple Intelligences: The Theory in Practice.* New York: Basic Books, 1993.

Henderson, Anne T., and Nancy Berla. "New Generation of Evidence: The Family Is Critical to Student Achievement." ERIC Identifier ED375968, 1994.

McCarney, Stephen B., Kathy Wunderlich, and Angela Bauer. *The Pre-Intervention Manual.* Columbia, Mo.: Hawthorne Educational Services, 1993.

National School Board Association. "Reinventing School-Based Management: A School Board Guide to School-Based Improvement." www.nsba.org/na/achievement/reinvent_execsum.htm (accessed January 10, 2002).

Novak, J., and B. Dougherty. *Staying in . . . a Dropout Prevention Handbook K–12.* Madison: University of Wisconsin Press, 1986.

Sarason, Seymour. *The Creation of Settings and the Future Societies.* Cambridge, Mass.: Brookline Books, 1998 [1972].

Index

About the Author

William Callison is a professor of educational leadership at California State University at Fullerton and holds a Ph.D. from Stanford. He has been deeply involved in the creation of a new charter school in Orange County, California. He has also been involved as the western regional director in the creation of alternative programs such as Project Upward Bound, a national program for potential dropouts, started in 1965; as the director of Head Start Supplementary Training, an alternative staff training effort involving scores of small staff and parent groups in every state; and in supervising dozens of school administrators for the past twenty-seven years as they sought to create new programs and schools, including a number of alternative schools.